Prayers
for all seasons

A comprehensive resource for public worship

NICK FAWCETT

Kevin Mayhew

First published in 1998 by
KEVIN MAYHEW LTD
Buxhall
Stowmarket
Suffolk IP14 3 BW

2 3 4 5 6 7 8 9

ISBN 1 84003 201 4
Catalogue No 1500210

Cover design by Angela Palfrey
Printed in Finland

CONTENTS

LENT

HOLY WEEK

EASTER

WEEK OF PRAYER FOR CHRISTIAN UNITY

LEPROSY SUNDAY

EDUCATION SUNDAY

MOTHERING SUNDAY

CHRISTIAN AID WEEK

FATHER'S DAY

HARVEST FESTIVAL

ONE WORLD WEEK

THE LORD'S SUPPER

BLESSINGS

This book is dedicated to Allan and Maureen Cox of
Belle Vue Baptist Church, Southend-on-Sea – simply two of the best
people you could ever hope to meet.

ABOUT THE AUTHOR

Nick Fawcett was born in 1957. He studied Theology at Bristol University and Regent's Park College, Oxford. His early years of ministry were spent in Somerset and Lancashire, and from 1989 to 1996 he was Minister of Gas Green Baptist Church, Cheltenham. Since 1996 he has been Toc H's Chaplain and Development Officer for Wales and the West of England. He is married to Deborah and they have a young son, Samuel.

He is the author of *No Ordinary Man* (Kevin Mayhew, 1997).

INTRODUCTION

When I started out in ministry as a raw recruit some fourteen years ago, I never imagined I would one day make use of a prayer book, still less that I would end up writing one. Blessed with all the assurance of youth, if someone had offered me such a book, I would probably have looked at them as if to say, 'What need could I have of that?' And why not? As a student I had led worship in numerous churches and had always been more than happy to pray 'as the spirit led', confident that God would give me the words I needed when I needed them.

For a time that was sufficient. Leading prayer on the whole came naturally and easily – and a good thing too, for, inexperienced as I was, I needed all my study time to prepare the sermons, family talks, Bible studies and magazine articles expected of me, as well as other pastoral responsibilities. But slowly I began to realise that I was repeating Sunday by Sunday the same old ideas, even the same words, week in and week out. Worse still, all too often my prayers were ill thought-out, jumping from one idea to another or simply petering out in mid-flow. In personal devotion that may not matter too much, but in the context of public worship it was a different story – to my mind little short of a dereliction of duty. Entrusted with the responsibility of leading prayer on behalf of the gathered congregation, I was selling both them and myself short.

So it was that I finally took to preparing in advance the prayers I would use each Sunday – a time-consuming process but, I felt, a worthwhile one – and the result is this collection of prayers. The book is divided into three sections. *The Christian Year* offers prayers for the principal days of the Christian Calendar from Advent through to All Saints' Day. *Life and Faith* focuses on the passage of life from birth through to death, and on significant events in the life of the Church and the individual believer. *Ordinary Sundays* offers a range of prayers for use in worship generally and in the Lord's Supper.

Responses and prompts within the prayers have been kept simple so that they can be memorised by the congregation and repeated without each member needing the words before them. Responses can be left out if preferred, without in any way altering the prayer's meaning. Flexibility and sensitivity in the use of these prayers is essential, there being times – such as at weddings and funerals – when some words are inappropriate or others need to be added. Similarly, prayers covering both Infant Baptism and the Dedication of Infants, or Believers' Baptism and Confirmation, are necessarily broad, and the user may well feel some additional words of their own are needed to bring out the theological significance of the event in question.

There is, of course, no right way to pray. Sometimes words are appropriate, sometimes not. Sometimes a degree of formality seems fitting, at other times quite the opposite. Much depends on the person and situation in question. This book does not pretend to be an example of how we should pray for I am still, and always will be, a learner myself. It is offered simply as a resource to those leading worship, each prayer within it having been prepared and used in the context of my own ministry in Lancashire and Cheltenham. It is my hope that the collection offered here may prove useful to those who lead worship, and all on whose behalf they pray.

NICK FAWCETT

PART ONE

THE CHRISTIAN YEAR

PART ONE

THE CHRISTIAN YEAR

ADVENT

ADVENT

1

ADVENT PRAISE AND CONFESSION

Loving God,
    we praise you again for this season of Advent,
        this time of preparation, thanksgiving, challenge and reflection.
    Open our hearts to all you would say now,
        and help us to listen.

We praise you that in fulfilment of your eternal purpose
        you came to our world in Christ,
        revealing the extent of your love,
        showing us the way to life,
        allowing us to know you for ourselves.
    Open our hearts to all you would say now,
        and help us to listen.

We praise you that you came again in Christ
        to his disciples after his resurrection,
        bringing joy where there had been sorrow,
        hope where there had been despair,
        and faith where there had been doubt.
    Open our hearts to all you would say now,
        and help us to listen.

We praise you that through your Holy Spirit
        you make Christ real to us each day,
        filling us with his power,
        his peace,
        and his love.
    Open our hearts to all you would say now,
        and help us to listen.

And we praise you for the promise that Christ will come again
        to establish his kingdom,
        to begin a new era,
        to bring us and all your people life everlasting.
    Open our hearts to all you would say now,
        and help us to listen.

Loving God,
  forgive us that so easily we lose sight of that message of Advent,
    allowing its wonder to be swamped
    by our busy preparations for Christmas,
    by concerns which are so often unimportant,
    by our carelessness and disobedience in discipleship.
  Open our hearts to all you would say now,
    and help us to listen.

Forgive us that we forget your promises,
  we frustrate your Spirit,
  we lose sight of your love.
Open our hearts to all you would say now,
  and help us to listen.

Meet with us, we pray, through this time of worship,
  through your living Word,
  through the fellowship we share,
  and through the risen Christ.
Open our hearts to all you would say now,
  and help us to listen.

So may we truly celebrate the Advent of your Son,
  and be equipped to serve him better,
  to the glory of your name.
  Amen.

2

ADVENT THANKSGIVING

Loving God,
    we thank you for this glad time of year,
        this Advent season which reminds us of so much,
        and which reveals so wonderfully the extent of your love.
    For your coming and coming again in Christ,
        we thank you.

This is a time for looking back
    and remembering the birth of your Son,
    light into our darkness;
    a time for looking forward and anticipating his coming again,
    as he returns to establish your kingdom and rule in your name;
    but above all a time for the present moment,
    for examining our lives, searching our hearts,
    exploring your word, and renewing our faith;
    a time for recognising more fully
    that Jesus is with us each moment of every day, now and always.
For your coming and coming again in Christ,
    we thank you.

Loving God,
    you came to our world in humility,
        born of Mary in a stable.
    You will come once more in glory,
        through the risen and ascended Christ.
    You are with us now even as we speak,
        here through your Holy Spirit making Jesus real!
    We praise you the great truth of Advent.
    For your coming and coming again in Christ,
        we thank you,
        in his name.
        Amen.

3

ADVENT PETITION

Father God,
  we praise you once more for this season of Advent,
    for its mood of expectation,
    its message of hope,
    its call to prepare ourselves,
    its spirit of confidence and trust.
God made flesh,
  hear our prayer.

We praise you for the way you have spoken,
    in the fulfilment of ancient prophecies,
    in promises yet to be realised,
    and in the living presence of Christ
    made known through his Holy Spirit.
God made flesh,
  hear our prayer.

Touch our lives again at this time,
    as we remember the coming of Jesus,
    as we anticipate his coming again,
    and as we strive to serve him better here and now.
God made flesh,
  hear our prayer.

Grant that through this season
    we shall be renewed in hope and strengthened in faith,
    trusting more completely in the future you hold.
May our confidence be deepened
    in your eternal love and purpose,
    despite all that seems to work against it.
And may we be ready to welcome Christ,
    in the assurance that as he came so he shall come again.
God made flesh,
  hear our prayer,
  for we ask it in the name of Christ.
  Amen.

4

ADVENT INTERCESSION

Lord Jesus Christ,
   at this time supposedly of goodwill among all,
     we pray for peace in our world –
     an end to division and discord,
     hatred and hostility,
     death and destruction.
   Prince of Peace,
     hear our prayer.

Lord Jesus,
   we speak of peace
     but in our hearts we do not believe it possible.
   When we look at our world
     we see little hope of an end to its troubles.
   We are sceptical,
     uncertain,
     filled with doubts,
     cautious about expressing any optimism.
   Even where there are signs of hope,
     moves towards reconciliation,
     we know it will take many years
     before we dare believe it is really possible.
   But, we pray in this Advent season,
     renew our ability to look forward,
     rekindle our belief in the future,
     and restore our capacity to hope for better things.
   Prince of Peace,
     hear our prayer.

Help us –
  as we remember your coming,
  as we serve you now,
  and as we look forward to your coming again –
  to anticipate your kingdom
  through the service we offer and the lives we live.
Prince of Peace,
  hear our prayer.

Teach us to work for that day
  when your throne shall be established,
  your justice prevail,
  and the earth be filled with the knowledge of you
  as the waters cover the sea.
Prince of Peace,
  hear our prayer.
  for your name's sake.
  Amen.

5

ADVENT EXPECTATION

Loving God,
  you have told us to look forward to a time
      when your kingdom will come and your will be done –
      a time when there will be an end to sin and evil,
      suffering and sorrow;
      when all your people will live together in peace and harmony;
      when Christ will come again in glory.
  Come to us now, we pray.

Loving God,
  forgive us that so often we have lost our sense of expectation,
      content simply to get by,
      settling for the way things are,
      failing to believe you can change our lives or transform the world.
  Come to us now, we pray.

Forgive us that we have been too full of our own expectations,
      believing we know all there is to know,
      pushing you into little boxes we have made for you,
      presuming your thoughts and your ways are the same as ours.
  Come to us now, we pray.

Forgive us that our expectations have been small and limited,
      tied down by our own limited vision,
      restricted to our own narrow horizons,
      shaped by looking at life from an immediate
      rather than an eternal perspective.
  Come to us now, we pray.

Loving God,
>help us through all this season of Advent has to say to us,
>>to gain a new sense of expectation
>>and new confidence in the future;
>Help us to be open to all you would do among us,
>>and to gladly respond.
>Help us to catch sight of the wonder of your coming in Christ,
>>and so may we be ready to greet him when he comes again.
>**Come to us now, we pray,**
>>**in his name.**
>>**Amen.**

6

ADVENT WAITING
(based on Habakkuk 2)

Eternal God,
   Ruler over space and time,
      Lord of history,
      before all, in all, and beyond all,
      we worship and acknowledge you,
      recognising afresh that your ways are not our ways,
      nor your thoughts our thoughts.
   Lord, in your mercy,
      hear our prayer.

Forgive us for sometimes losing sight of that fact,
      presuming we know better than you,
      even expecting you to do our bidding
      rather than we do yours.
   Lord, in your mercy,
      hear our prayer.

Teach us that you are beyond our greatest imagining,
      higher than our loftiest dreams;
      and that you do things in your own way and time,
      expecting us to wait patiently,
      trusting in your wisdom and purpose.
   Lord, in your mercy,
      hear our prayer.

When our prayers do not seem to be answered,
      our ambitions remain unfulfilled,
      and our faith appears to be in vain,
      save us from premature judgements.
   Lord, in your mercy,
      hear our prayer.

Teach us that it is often at such times as these –
    especially at such times as these –
    that we need to believe in you and your timing.
Give us grace to accept our part in your scheme of things,
    and leave the rest to you.
Lord, in your mercy,
    hear our prayer,
    through Jesus Christ our Lord.
    Amen.

7

THE WAY OF CHRIST

Lord Jesus Christ,
    you came to our world, sharing our humanity,
        identifying yourself with us,
        expressing through actions and self-sacrifice your love for all.
Teach us to follow in your footsteps.

Yours was the way of service, compassion and reconciliation.
Despite the rejection of so many,
    you saw the best in people,
    the good,
    the worth that others overlooked.
Teach us to follow in your footsteps.

You loved all,
    without prejudice,
    without passing judgement,
    without any strings attached.
Teach us to follow in your footsteps.

Lord Jesus Christ,
    you come to our world still each day,
        but to do that fully you need our co-operation,
        our willingness to be used for your purpose.
Teach us to follow in your footsteps.

You need us to speak for you,
    to act for you,
    to show your love and share your life.
Teach us to follow in your footsteps.

You need us to take that way of service,
    to break down barriers,
    to bring people together.
Teach us to follow in your footsteps.

You need us to take the Way of the Cross –
    valuing people for what they are,
    offering them trust and encouragement,
    helping them to believe in themselves.
Teach us to follow in your footsteps.

Lord Jesus Christ,
    you came to our world to establish a new kingdom,
        a new era,
        a new dimension to life.
    Help us through who we are
        and all we do to bring that kingdom nearer.
Teach us to follow in your footsteps,
    for in your name we ask it.
Amen.

8

GOD'S NEED OF US

Living God,
    you promised to come to your people of old
        through the Advent of the Messiah.
    You promise to come to each of us
        in the triumphant and glorious return of your Son.
    Open our hearts to his coming.

Loving God,
    you came into our world through Mary,
        entering our world of space and time.
    You want to come afresh through each of us,
        Christ made real in our day to day lives.
    Open our hearts to his presence.

Gracious God,
    you needed Mary's assent
        before you could work through her.
    You need our willingness
        to let you work through us.
    Open our hearts to your Spirit.

Sovereign God,
    you called Mary to believe that with you
        nothing is impossible.
    You need us to show that same faith
        if your kingdom is to come.
    Open our minds to all that you can do.

Mighty God,
    you brought a new beginning to Mary,
        to Joseph,
        to your people Israel,
        to all the world.
    You offer a new beginning to each of us,
        this and every day.
    Open our lives to your renewing, transforming love,
        through Christ our Lord.
        Amen.

9

A VOICE IN THE WILDERNESS

Living God,
    we thank you today for those who have the courage
        to stand up and speak out against evil and injustice;
        those who are ready, if necessary,
        to stand alone for their convictions,
        enduring mockery and rejection,
        sacrificing status and security,
        willing to risk everything for what they believe to be right.
    We thank you for their vision,
        their determination,
        their willingness to be a voice in the wilderness.
    May your glory be revealed,
        and all people see it together.

Living God,
    we thank you for those who have the compassion
        and concern for others to reach out and bring help –
        ministering to the sick,
        comforting the bereaved,
        visiting the lonely,
        providing for the poor,
        giving hope to the oppressed,
        bringing laughter to the sorrowful.
    We thank you for their dedication,
        their understanding,
        their goodness,
        their willingness to speak your word in the wilderness.
    May your glory be revealed,
        and all people see it together.

Living God,
    you call us to reach out to your broken world –
        to those walking in darkness,
        wrestling with despair,
        craving affection,
        thirsting to find purpose in their lives.
    Give us faith,
        wisdom,
        tenderness,
        and love to meet that challenge.
    Help us to venture into the wilderness ourselves,
        and there, gently but confidently,
        to speak your word of life.
    May your glory be revealed,
        and all people see it together,
        in the name of Christ.
        Amen.

10

THE CHRIST WHO WILL COME AGAIN

Gracious God,
  we praise you that you came to our world in Christ,
    fulfilling your promise of old,
    vindicating the long-held expectations of your people.
  We praise you that you came again to the Apostles in the risen Christ,
    appearing when you were least expected
    bringing new hope and immeasurable joy.
  We praise you for the promise that you will come again in Christ
     to establish your kingdom
    and to give life to all your people.
  Come, Lord Jesus, come!

Yet we recognise there were many
    who were not ready for the coming of Jesus –
    many who were not as prepared as they thought they were,
    whose lives were not what they could have been
    and whose response was not what it should have been.
  Help *us* to be prepared –
    to live such lives that at any moment we would be happy
    to be confronted by the returning Christ.
  Help us to examine ourselves –
    our words and deeds, thoughts and attitudes;
    living each day and moment
    as though Jesus were visibly by our side –
    and so may we commit ourselves wholeheartedly to his service.
  Come, Lord Jesus, come!

Gracious God,
  we pray not only for ourselves but our world,
    and those many people who have no thought
    of Christ or his coming –
    those who live only for themselves,
    who seek fulfilment solely in material satisfaction,
    or who have no spiritual dimension to their lives.
  Come, Lord Jesus, come!

We pray for those who profess to love
  but who have drifted away from your side –
  their faith shallow and empty,
  their hearts full of bitterness, pride, envy,
  or their minds troubled by doubts and disillusionment.
Come, Lord Jesus, come!

We pray for those who work against your kingdom –
  who knowingly cheat and deceive,
  who serve self at the cost of others,
  who spread hatred and incite violence in pursuit of their aims.
Come, Lord Jesus, come!

We pray for those who long for your kingdom –
  who hunger for a new beginning,
  who pray for a fresh chance,
  or who simply see no hope for themselves in this world.
Come, Lord Jesus, come!

And finally we pray for those who work towards your kingdom,
  who strive for peace and harmony,
  who campaign for freedom and justice,
  who demonstrate love and compassion in action.
Come, Lord Jesus, come!

Gracious God,
  we thank you for the assurance
    that your kingdom shall come and your will be done –
    the knowledge that we do not hope or wait in vain.
  Teach all your people to live always
    as those ready for Christ's coming,
    so that those who have no faith may hear and respond
    to your word of challenge.
  Grant to those who despair
    the knowledge that you are with them,
    and to all who work to bring your kingdom nearer
    the assurance that in your own time it will come.
  In that faith we pray:
    Come, Lord Jesus, come!
    Amen.

11

ADVENT FULFILMENT

Living God,
we remember this day how you prepared the way for your coming.
To your servant Abraham you promised blessing
for all the world through his offspring.
To your prophets you spoke your word,
promising the Messiah would come,
bringing peace, justice and deliverance for all your people.
To Elizabeth and Zechariah you promised a son
who would prepare the way of the Lord,
making his way straight in the wilderness.
To Mary you promised a child
who would be called Emmanuel, God with us,
born to save his people from their sins.
And through John the Baptist
you announced the fulfilment of those prophecies
in the person of Jesus,
the light of the world shining in the darkness.
You promise us that Christ will come again:
prepare our hearts for his coming.

Living God,
you spoke your word to so many,
yet when the time came and Jesus was born
so few were ready to receive him.
He was the word made flesh, but was accused of blasphemy,
he offered life to the world, but was put to death on the cross,
he came to his own people, and they would not receive him.
You promise us that Christ will come again:
prepare our hearts for his coming.

Living God,
help us as we remember his birth, life, death and resurrection,
to be ready to receive him,
not just when he comes again,
but each day into every part of our lives.
Help us to read your word with new insight,

to offer you our living worship,
and to turn from all that is wrong and faithless in our lives.
Help us to focus on what is central to this season
and not on the trappings with which we surround it.
Help us to open our hearts and minds
to the guidance of your Holy Spirit,
and respond to his prompting.
Help us to follow in the way of Christ,
loving him as he has loved us.
You promise us that Christ will come again:
prepare our hearts for his coming.
In his name we pray.
Amen.

12

GOD WHO USES THE SMALL THINGS OF THIS WORLD

Eternal God,
> you came to our world not in a blaze of publicity,
>> surrounded by pomp and show,
>> nor to the frenzied acclaim of crowds
>> gathered to greet your coming,
>> but quietly,
>> unassumingly,
>> almost unnoticed,
>> in the quiet of the night in the little town of Bethlehem –
>> born in a manger,
>> to the Virgin Mary,
>> your coming first witnessed by shepherds
>> out working in the fields.

As the heavens are higher than the earth,
> **so our ways are not your ways,**
> **nor our thoughts your thoughts.**

Time and again you have chosen the small,
> the humble,
> the insignificant,
> and worked out your purposes through them.

You have shown your strength in what the world counts weakness,
> you have made the last first, and the least the greatest.

As the heavens are higher than the earth,
> **so our ways are not your ways,**
> **nor our thoughts your thoughts.**

Teach us what that means today –
    that you can use us beyond our imagining,
    that you can take what seems unimportant
    and turn it into something wonderful,
    that you can work among us in ways
    that exceed our wildest expectations.
Teach us to see life not merely from our own perspective
    but from yours,
    and so may your strength be made perfect in our weakness.
As the heavens are higher than the earth,
    so our ways are not your ways,
    nor our thoughts your thoughts.
Thanks be to God, through Jesus Christ our Lord.
    Amen.

CHRISTMAS

13

CAROL SERVICE
REMEMBERING AND RELIVING

Almighty and loving God,
    we come together on this day
        to celebrate the birth of your Son,
        the child laid in a manger,
        our Lord and Saviour Jesus Christ.
    You have done great things for us,
        and we are glad.

We come recalling that first Christmas centuries ago;
        the message proclaimed by the angels –
        news of great joy!
    You have done great things for us,
        and we are glad.

We come remembering the faith of Mary,
        the thanksgiving of the shepherds,
        and the worship of the wise men.
    You have done great things for us,
        and we are glad.

We come reminding ourselves of your great love
        shown to us and all people
        through your coming and sharing our humanity,
        through your living and dying amongst us.
    You have done great things for us,
        and we are glad.

Loving God,
    we thank you for this time of year –
        its mood of joy and celebration,
        its spirit of goodwill and desire to work for peace,
        the renewing of old friendships
        and the coming together of families,
        the lessons and carols which we know and love so well.
    You have done great things for us,
        and we are glad.

Save us, O Lord, from becoming over-familiar with this season,
from ever imagining we know all there is to know about it,
or presuming we have understood all there is to understand.
You have done great things for us,
and we are glad.

Teach us to listen for your voice and look for your presence,
to hear your call and respond to your guidance.
You have done great things for us,
and we are glad.

May we, like Mary, have the faith to believe
that with you nothing is impossible;
like the shepherds to go in heart and mind even to Bethlehem
to see what you have done;
like the wise men to offer you our worship
and present to you our gifts;
like the great company of angels
to sing glad and joyful songs of praise.
You have done great things for us,
and we are glad.

And so may we, when the festivities are over and Christmas is past,
return to our daily lives glorifying and praising you
for all we have seen and heard,
the wonder of your love revealed in Christ!
You have done great things for us,
and we are glad.
Praise be to you, now and for ever!
Amen.

14

CAROL SERVICE
COMING TO SEE

Father God,
  we thank you for this day of praise and celebration -
      this day on which we set aside time
      to relive that first Christmas long ago,
      on which we remind ourselves
      of the wonder of the birth of Christ,
      on which we remember once more the glad tidings
      proclaimed to the shepherds,
      witnessed by the wise men,
      made possible through Mary.

Loving Father,
  we come to give thanks for this season –
      to rejoice at your great love in sending your Son,
      to see for ourselves the truth discovered by the shepherds,
      to worship Christ and offer our gifts
      as wise men came before us.

  We come asking you to use us,
      just as you used your servant Mary to enter our world.
  Take our faith, small though it is,
      take our gifts, few though they are,
      take our love, poor though this seems,
      take our lives, weak though we may be.

Loving Father,
  speak to us through this service.
  May all we hear draw us closer to you,
      may all we share remind us of your love,
      and so may the message of Christmas
      come alive in our hearts,
      to the glory of your name.
      Amen.

15

Carol service
In the footsteps of faith

Almighty God,
  we have heard once more the wonderful message
    of your coming to us in Christ –
    tidings of great joy,
    Good News for all people.
  As you have come to us,
    so may we go for you.

We thank you for that message,
    the well-loved words we have heard and sung again today –
    so familiar,
    so often repeated,
    yet still so special and meaningful.
  As you have come to us,
    so may we go for you.

We thank you for the faith and trust of Mary –
    her willingness to accept your will;
    for the pilgrimage and gifts of the wise men –
    their determination to seek and respond;
    for the simple actions of the shepherds –
    who hearing the message and seeing its truth for themselves,
    shared with others what they had experienced!
  As you have come to us,
    so may we go for you.

Teach us, we pray, as we celebrate this Christmas-time,
    to learn from their example,
    to follow in their footsteps,
    to share their faith.
  As you have come to us,
    so may we go for you.

Teach us to know the reality of Christ born for *us*,
    and in our turn to pass on
    what we have discovered through him to those around us!
  As you have come to us,
    so may we go for you,
    in the name of Christ.
    Amen.

16

CHRISTMAS EVE INTERCESSION

God of love,
  we pray for all those many people
    who will be celebrating Christmas this year,
    enjoying presents, parties, food and fun,
    yet not having heard or accepted or understood
    what Christmas is all about.
  Speak to them now,
    and help them to respond.

We pray for those who have never heard the Gospel,
    or received a distorted picture of its message,
    or failed to recognise it is good news for them.
  Speak to them now,
    and help them to respond.

We pray for those who have closed their hearts and minds to Christ,
    refusing to listen or consider further,
    rejecting your Son as so many rejected him at his coming.
  Speak to them now,
    and help them to respond.

We pray for those who have come to faith
    but barely realised what that means,
    seeing perhaps just a small part of all you have done,
    or seeking to know more but troubled by doubts and questions.
  Speak to them now,
    and help them to respond.

God of love,
  come again to our world this Christmas,
    breaking through our cosy traditions,
    our narrow horizons,
    our neatly packaged celebrations.
  Speak to *us* now,
    and help *us* to respond.

Help us and all people
     to glimpse the wonder of your awesome love –
     a love revealed in the Christ who came and lived among us,
     who suffered and died on the Cross,
     who rose and reigns with you,
     and who shall come again to draw all things to himself.
Speak to *us* now,
     and help *us* to respond,
     for in his name we pray.
     Amen.

17

CHRISTMAS EVE FINAL PRAYER

Loving God,
    we thank you for the message
        we have been reminded of once more this evening.
We praise you for the glad tidings
        of your coming to us in Christ.
We rejoice in the fulfilment of your word,
        the ancient promises of Scripture.
We celebrate with wise men and shepherds long ago
        the birth of your Son, our Saviour.
Speak to us afresh through all we have heard and shared,
        so that we, with them,
        may go on our way rejoicing,
        knowing the reality of your love for ourselves,
        and offering our service to Christ
        in grateful praise and heartfelt worship,
        for his name's sake.
        Amen.

18

CHRISTMAS PRAISE AND THANKSGIVING

Loving God,
    we thank you for this day and all it speaks of –
        your promise of old to send a Messiah to your people,
        the fulfilment of that promise through the sending of your Son,
        the realisation of those long years of expectation,
        the glad tidings proclaimed by the angels,
        the wonder and mystery of that first Christmas.
For all this time means and will always mean,
    we praise you.

We thank you for this season's power to move, inspire and challenge,
        to gladden the hardest of hearts and most broken of spirits,
        to stir our minds and capture our imagination.
For all this time means and will always mean,
    we praise you.

We thank you for the special things we associate with Christmas –
        the spreading of goodwill,
        the sharing of friendship,
        the longing for peace,
        and the expressing of love.
For all this time means and will always mean,
    we praise you.

But above all we thank you for the truth behind this day –
        the message that you have come to us,
        that you love us,
        that you have shared our humanity,
        and that you want us to share in your everlasting life,
For all this time means and will always mean,
    we praise you.

Loving God,
  accept our praise,
      receive our thanksgiving,
      bless our celebrations,
      and may the wonder of the Gospel
      come alive in our hearts this day,
      through Jesus Christ our Lord.
      Amen.

19

SOMETHING TO CELEBRATE

Loving God,
　　we praise you for all we have to rejoice in at Christmas,
　　　　this special reminder year by year of your coming to us
　　　　in Christ.
　　Come to us now,
　　　　and help us to keep you at the centre of our celebrations.
　　Lord, in your mercy,
　　　　hear our prayer.

Come to our loved ones,
　　　　our families,
　　　　our friends,
　　　　all those we hold dear
　　　　and whom we shall share with or think of
　　　　over these coming days.
Help us as we celebrate and make merry
　　　　to think also of Christ,
　　　　and through drawing closer to him
　　　　to grow closer together.
Lord, in your mercy,
　　　　hear our prayer.

Come to those in special need –
　　　　the poor, the sick, the lonely and sad,
　　　　the homeless, the helpless,
　　　　the oppressed and persecuted;
　　　　all those for whom life is hard and the future seems bleak.
Reach out to them in love,
　　　　and give them something to celebrate.
Lord, in your mercy,
　　　　hear our prayer.

ing God,
        may the light of Christ break into the lives of people everywhere,
            bringing your joy,
            your peace,
            your hope,
            and your love,
            a song of praise on their lips,
            and celebration in their hearts.
    Lord, in your mercy,
        hear our prayer.

    Come to them,
        come to us,
        come to all,
        and send us on our way,
        rejoicing in the Gospel,
        and praising you for the wonder of your grace.
    Lord, in your mercy,
        hear our prayer,
        through Jesus Christ our Lord.
        Amen.

20

THE TRUE MEANING OF CHRISTMAS

Loving God,
    we thank you for this season of Christmas –
        for all it has meant to so many over the years,
        all it continues to mean to us,
        and all it will mean in generations to come.
    You have given us so much:
        receive our praise.

We thank you for carols old and new,
        for familiar and much-loved words of Scripture,
        for all that speaks of your coming among us in Christ.
    You have given us so much:
        receive our praise.

We thank you for reunions with family and friends,
        for the spirit of giving and receiving,
        for the mood of goodwill and celebration.
    You have given us so much:
        receive our praise.

We thank you for all the good things we will enjoy –
        good food,
        good company,
        good fun.
    You have given us so much,
        receive our praise.

Loving God,
    help us in all of this to keep sight of the heart of Christmas,
        what it all really means –
        to celebrate the birth of the infant Christ,
        to worship him as joyfully and reverently
        as shepherds and wise men long ago,
        to welcome and follow him as faithfully
        as those who left everything to be his disciples.
    You have given us so much:
        receive our praise.

Loving God,
    forgive us if we have lost sight of what this season truly means.
    Forgive us if we have become over-familiar
        with its simple yet wonderful message.
    Forgive us if we have failed to make room for Christ
        in our Christmas celebrations.
    You have given us so much:
        receive our praise.

Speak to us now
    through all that we shall do and share,
    all we shall sing and hear,
    so that our lives may be touched by the wonder of his presence.
    You have given us so much,
        receive our praise
        through Jesus Christ.
        Amen.

21

CHRISTMAS PETITION 1

Almighty and loving God,
    in the name of your Son Jesus,
        we join together to worship you.

Through his coming you have blessed us
    with the light of your love,
    you have filled our world of darkness with your light,
    you have illuminated our hearts with Good News,
    you have made your glory shine upon us,
    so that nothing shall ever overcome it.

So now we come,
    with glad thanksgiving,
    with eager expectation,
    with heartfelt praise.

Help us, as we sing your praise and hear your word,
    to kneel before the manger in our hearts,
    to offer our gifts,
    to bring our worship,
    to recognise you are with us now.

And so help us to go on our way this and every day,
    glorifying and praising you
    for all that we have seen and heard.
    In the name of Christ.
    Amen.

22

CHRISTMAS PETITION 2

Lord of all,
    we pray for all who worship you today,
        all across the world who rejoice
        in the good news of the birth of Jesus Christ.
Speak your word of life,
    and be born in our hearts today.

May the reading of Scripture,
    the singing of carols,
    the offering of prayers,
    and the sharing of fellowship,
    convey something of the wonder of your love.
Speak your word of life,
    and be born in our hearts today.

May the faith of all your people be enriched,
    and the life of the Church renewed
    by the presence of the living Christ,
    so that the Gospel may be proclaimed
    through its joyful witness,
    and the glad tidings of your coming in Christ
    bring new hope, joy, meaning and purpose
    to the lives of all.
Speak your word of life,
    and be born in our hearts today.

Lord of all,
    reach out to your Church and to people everywhere
        at this glad time of year,
        touching our lives with the living presence of Christ.
Speak your word of life,
    and be born in our hearts today,
    to the glory of Jesus Christ our Lord.
    Amen.

23

CHRISTMAS INTERCESSION FOR THOSE IN NEED

Lord Jesus Christ,
    born an outcast and refugee,
      in weakness and frailty,
      as we rejoice today hear our prayers
      for all those who have no cause for celebration.
    Lord, in your mercy,
      hear our prayer.

We pray for the hungry and the homeless,
    the poor and the unemployed,
    the oppressed and the exploited,
    the lonely and the downhearted.
Lord, in your mercy,
    hear our prayer.

We pray for the sick and the dying,
    the sorrowful and the bereaved,
    victims of violence and war,
    all whose lives have been shattered
    by tragedy and disaster.
Lord, in your mercy,
    hear our prayer.

Lord Jesus Christ,
    born to set your people free,
      come again to our world,
      bringing reconciliation where there is division,
      and comfort where there is sorrow,
      hope where there is despair,
      and confidence where there is confusion.
    Lord, in your mercy,
      hear our prayer.

Come and bring light where there is darkness,
   and love where there is hatred,
   faith where there is doubt,
   and life where there is death.
Lord, in your mercy,
   hear our prayer.

Lord Jesus Christ,
   come again to our world,
      and bring that day nearer when your kingdom will come,
      and your will be done.
   Lord, in your mercy,
      hear our prayer,
      for we ask it in your name.
      Amen.

24

CHRISTMAS INTERCESSION
FOR OUTCASTS AND REFUGEES

Lord Jesus Christ,
 you came to our world,
  but there was no place for you.
 You came to your own people,
  but they were not ready to receive you.
 You were born in Bethlehem,
  but there was no room for you in the inn.
 You walked among us, sharing our humanity,
  but had no place to rest your head.
 You returned to your home town,
  but were without honour in your own country.
 You came to bring life to all,
  but you were put to death on a cross.
 You know what it is to be homeless,
  hungry, abandoned, rejected,
  and so we bring you our prayers
  for all those who endure such need today.
Friend of the friendless,
 hear our prayer.

We pray for those who have no roof over their head
 or no place to call their own –
 waiting perhaps on council housing lists,
 or evicted because they cannot pay the rent,
 homes destroyed by natural disaster,
 or left behind as they flee from persecution or the threat of war.
Friend of the friendless,
 hear our prayer.

We pray for those who live
    in poor and overcrowded conditions,
    in shanty towns, or refugee camps,
    hostels, or bed-and-breakfast accommodation,
    tenement blocks, or run-down slums;
    for those who sleep rough on the streets.
Friend of the friendless,
    hear our prayer.

And we pray too for those
    who feel they have no place in society –
    the unemployed,
    the poor,
    the lonely,
    the oppressed,
    the persecuted,
    the terminally ill.
Friend of the friendless,
    hear our prayer.

Lord Jesus Christ,
    reach out to all who face such situations.
    Grant the assurance that you care,
        courage to believe in the future,
        and strength to meet the present.
Friend of the friendless,
    hear our prayer.

Grant your help to those who offer help,
    your support to those who campaign for justice,
    your blessing to all who seek to bring hope
    where there is only hopelessness.
Friend of the friendless,
    hear our prayer.

May we, with them, make real your love,
    and show your compassion,
    working together for your kingdom.
Friend of the friendless,
    hear our prayer,
    for in your name we ask it.
    Amen.

25

SHARING THE GOOD NEWS

Living God,
we thank you for the great message of the Gospel,
the glad tidings of your love,
the good news of your coming to our world
through your Son Jesus Christ.
May that message inspire us again this Christmas-time
and in the days to come.
Speak your word of love,
and move in the hearts of all who hear it.

We thank you that the Good News of Christ
has challenged people across the ages,
and that though it has been proclaimed countless times,
though we have heard it ourselves so many times before,
it continues to be news for us and news for all –
able still to speak to individuals across the world
and change their lives.
Speak your word of love,
and move in the hearts of all who hear it.

So now we pray for those you have specially called
to proclaim the Good News –
ministers,
preachers,
evangelists,
teachers –
all those with the special gift and responsibility
of communicating your word.
Grant them wisdom,
dedication,
inspiration,
and courage,
that they may faithfully witness to you
in the power of the Holy Spirit.
Speak your word of love,
and move in the hearts of all who hear it.

We pray also for those who hear the Good News,
responding in different ways –
those who have closed their minds
to what you would say to them –
may your love break through the barriers they erect;
those who have heard but failed to understand –
may their hearts be opened to the truth;
those who have yet to grasp
that the Gospel is good news for them –
may the experience of meeting Christ transform their lives;
those who have responded and come to faith –
may their knowledge of you continue to grow.
Speak your word of love,
and move in the hearts of all who hear it.

Finally we pray for those who long for good news,
who cry out for glad tidings –
the poor, starving, sick and lonely,
the oppressed, persecuted, unloved, bereaved –
so many people across the world
who despair of ever seeing hope rekindled.
May the message of the Gospel mean good news for them.
Speak your word of love,
and move in the hearts of all who hear it.

Living God,
come again to your world this Christmas-time,
through your word, your Spirit, your people,
and the living presence of Christ,
and so may the message of the Gospel
truly be good news for all people.
Speak your word of love,
and move in the hearts of all who hear it,
through Jesus Christ our Lord.
Amen.

EPIPHANY

EPIPHANY

26

EPIPHANY PRAISE

Loving God,
    we remember today that from the beginning
        the Good News of Jesus Christ was not just for a few,
        but for all.
Receive our praise.

You made it known to shepherds
        tending their flocks by night,
        ordinary, everyday people
        pursuing their daily life and work,
        unlikely yet special representatives
        of your chosen nation.
Receive our praise.

But you made it known also to wise men from the East,
        strangers living far away,
        with no knowledge of you,
        and regarded by many at the time
        as having no part in your promises.
Receive our praise.

Loving God,
    for the truth this symbolises –
        that there is no one outside your love,
        that the message of the Gospel transcends all barriers,
        that you want to bring light to all corners of the world –
Receive our praise.

For the fact that we are part of your great purpose –
        heirs of the promise made to Abraham,
        members of the great company of your people,
        called to proclaim the gospel to those around us –
Receive our praise.

For the knowledge that your light continues to shine –
    despite opposition,
    persecution,
    and rejection by so many –
Receive our praise.

For the way so many have followed the example of Jesus
    and responded to your call –
    through the waters of baptism,
    through commitment to your Church,
    through a life of faith and witness –
Receive our praise.

Loving God,
    you have made your light shine in our hearts.
    Help us to show our gratitude
      by walking in the path it illuminates,
      and shedding that light on those around us,
      to the glory of your name.
Receive our praise,
    through Jesus Christ our Lord.
    Amen.

27

EPIPHANY CONFESSION

Loving God,
  you guided the wise men to Bethlehem,
    offering a light for their path,
    and in faith they responded.
  Forgive us that all too often we fall short of their example.
  Gracious Lord,
    have mercy.

You offer us guidance in innumerable ways –
    through the light of your word,
    the illumination of your Holy Spirit,
    the fellowship of your Church,
    and the encounter of prayer,
    yet so often we either fail to hear or refuse to see.
  Gracious Lord,
    have mercy.

We are too preoccupied with our own small affairs,
    eyes only for the immediate moment,
    our vision impeded by trivial concerns,
    so we fail to recognise where you are leading us.
  Gracious Lord,
    have mercy.

We believe we know just where we are going,
    just what we want from life,
    and exactly how we can get it,
    and we resist any suggestion that we need to think again.
  Gracious Lord,
    have mercy.

Loving God,
  forgive us our foolishness,
    our stubbornness,
    our weakness.
  Gracious Lord,
    have mercy.

Forgive our pride,
    our lack of faith,
    our closed minds.
Gracious Lord,
    have mercy.

Forgive us for ignoring your guidance,
    for resisting your will,
    and as a result so often walking in darkness.
Gracious Lord,
    have mercy.

Meet with us again we ask,
    and may the light of your love shine in our hearts,
    so that we cannot but see it or fail to respond
    in grateful praise and joyful service.
Gracious Lord,
    have mercy,
    in the name of Christ.
    Amen.

28

Epiphany petition

God of love,
  we remember today, on this Epiphany Sunday,
    how wise men from the East came seeking the new born king,
    how finally they reached the end of their journey,
    and how they knelt in worship before the infant Jesus.
  Help us to learn from their example.
  Guide our footsteps,
    and lead us closer to Christ.

Teach us to continue faithfully on the path you set before us,
    remembering that true faith involves a journey of discovery
    as well as arrival at a destination.
  Guide our footsteps,
    and lead us closer to Christ.

Teach us to seek your will resolutely,
    even when the way ahead is not clear.
  Guide our footsteps,
    and lead us closer to Christ.

Teach us to look at the world around us,
    and to recognise the signs
    through which you might be speaking to us.
  Guide our footsteps,
    and lead us closer to Christ.

Teach us to keep on trusting in your purpose,
    even when the response of others
    may give us cause for doubt.
  Guide our footsteps,
    and lead us closer to Christ.

Teach us to offer to Jesus our wholehearted devotion –
    not simply our gifts but our whole lives,
    given to him in joyful worship and grateful praise.
  Guide our footsteps,
    and lead us closer to Christ,
    for in his name we ask it.
    Amen.

29

EPIPHANY INTERCESSION

Lord of Light,
    we have remembered today the journey of the wise men –
        how, inspired by what they took to be a sign,
        they set off in search of a new-born king,
        a king who would change not simply their lives,
        nor merely the life of his people,
        but the life of the world.
Come again now,
    and may light shine in the darkness.

We remember how they persevered in their quest,
        travelling in faith
        even though they had no clear idea of where they were heading,
        or any certainty of what they would find
        when they reached their destination.
Come again now,
    and may light shine in the darkness.

We remember how they refused to be discouraged,
        despite their reception in Jerusalem,
        despite the fact that no one seemed to have any idea
        that a new king had been born.
Come again now,
    and may light shine in the darkness.

We remember how they kept going,
        single-minded in pursuit of their goal,
        until at last their determination was rewarded
        and they came face to face with the infant Jesus.
Come again now,
    and may light shine in the darkness.

Living God,
we pray for all who seek today,
all those who are looking for a sense of purpose in their lives,
all who are searching for spiritual fulfilment,
all who long to find you for themselves.
Come again now,
and may light shine in the darkness.

Help them to keep looking,
even when the journey is demanding
and no end seems in sight;
to keep believing,
even when others seem oblivious to their quest
or scornful of it;
to keep on trusting,
even when those they look to for guidance
seem as confused and as lost as they are.
Come again now,
and may light shine in the darkness.

Living God,
you have promised through Jesus Christ
that those who seek shall find.
May the experience of the wise men
inspire all who seek for truth to keep on searching,
in the assurance that they too, come what may,
will one day complete their quest,
and discover you for themselves.
Come again now,
and may light shine in the darkness,
in Jesus' name.
Amen.

LENT

30

SHROVE TUESDAY

Living God,
  we thank you for this day you have given us,
    a day that reminds us of your mercy,
    your forgiveness,
    your offer of a new beginning for all who truly seek it.
  Search us, O God,
    and lead us in the way of life eternal.

We thank you for this time you have given us,
    this season of Lent which reminds us
    of the need for prayer and reflection,
    discipline and self-examination.
  Search us, O God,
    and lead us in the way of life eternal.

We thank you for all this season leads towards,
    the days of Holy Week and Easter
    which remind us of your great love shown in Christ,
    and your great victory won through him.
  Search us, O God,
    and lead us in the way of life eternal.

Living God,
  help us to use this day wisely and this season fully,
    so that our faith may be deepened,
    our horizons stretched,
    and our love for you increased.
  Search us, O God,
    and lead us in the way of life eternal.

Cleanse us of all that is wrong,
    put a new heart and a right spirit within us,
    and so prepare us to rejoice again at the wonder of your love
    revealed in Christ crucified and risen.
  Search us, O God,
    and lead us in the way of life eternal,
    for in his name we pray.
    Amen.

31

ASH WEDNESDAY

Living God,
   on this first day of Lent we come together
      seeking your presence,
      offering our worship,
      and asking for guidance.
   Lord, hear our prayer.

We come, remembering once more
      the temptation of Jesus in the wilderness,
      and his refusal to give way.
   Lord, hear our prayer.

We come remembering those forty days and nights of trial,
      that time of prayer and meditation,
      preparation for the future.
   Lord, hear our prayer.

We come remembering the life,
      the death,
      the resurrection and exaltation that followed.
   Lord, hear our prayer.

Living God,
   help us, learning from his example,
      to use this season wisely,
      making time to hear your voice
      and reflect on your word.
   Lord, hear our prayer.

Help us to honestly examine ourselves,
      carefully and prayerfully searching our hearts.
   Lord, hear our prayer.

Help us to see ourselves as we really are,
    and as you would have us be,
    ready to follow you and do your will,
    no matter what the cost.
Lord, hear our prayer.

Help us to know where we are faithful to you
    and where we fail,
    recognising our strengths and also our weaknesses.
Lord, hear our prayer.

Living God,
    give us courage to stand before your searching gaze
    and accept your verdict,
      humility to accept your correction and receive forgiveness,
      wisdom to hear your word and feed on it through faith.
So in the days ahead may we grow closer to you
    in the likeness of Christ.
Lord, hear our prayer.
    for we ask it in his name.
    Amen.

32

FIRST SUNDAY IN LENT

Gracious and merciful God,
  on this first Sunday of Lent we come together to worship you,
    to praise and thank you,
    to seek your forgiveness and to ask for renewal.
  Create in us a clean heart, O Lord,
    and put a right spirit within us.

We come in the name of Christ,
    remembering his lonely days in the wilderness,
    his time wrestling with temptation,
    and the ministry that followed,
    restoring and transforming so many lives.
  Create in us a clean heart, O Lord,
    and put a right spirit within us.

Help us to learn from his example –
    to search our hearts as he did,
    to consider our calling,
    to reflect on our faith,
    to resist temptation,
    and to commit ourselves more wholly to you.
  Create in us a clean heart, O Lord,
    and put a right spirit within us.

Help us to recognise all Jesus has done for us
    through his life, death and resurrection;
    and so may we come gladly to you,
    confessing our sins,
    acknowledging our faults,
    accepting our weaknesses,
    and receiving your forgiveness.
  Create in us a clean heart, O Lord,
    and put a right spirit within us.

Gracious and merciful God,
  we come together on this first Sunday of Lent.
  Speak to us today and in the days ahead,
    so that we may know you and love you better.
  Create in us a clean heart, O Lord,
    and put a right spirit within us,
    through Jesus Christ our Lord.
    Amen.

33

LENT CONFESSION

Loving God,
we remember in this season of Lent
the temptation of Jesus in the wilderness,
the pressures he faced,
the choices he had to make,
the evil he had to resist,
the path he chose.

We remember that though he was tempted as we are
he did not give way,
though he could have used his powers for his own ends
he used them instead for us,
though he could have taken the easy way
he took the hard.

Loving God,
forgive us that our testimony is all too often so different.
We have failed you in so much,
refusing to take up our cross
and follow in the footsteps of Jesus.
We have not obeyed your commandments,
or loved as you have loved us,
or in any way lived faithfully as your people.
We have been narrow in our vision,
weak in our commitment,
careless in our worship,
self-centred in our attitudes,
repeatedly preferring our way to yours
and wandering far from you.

Loving God,
have mercy upon us.
Renew us in heart and mind and spirit,
strengthen our wills and deepen our faith,
and send us out once more as your people,
forgiven and restored,
to live and work for you, in the name of Christ.
Amen.

34

LENT PETITION

Loving God,
  we remember today how much Christ loved us,
    how much he was willing to sacrifice
    and endure for our sakes.
  Teach us to follow.

You set before him the need to choose –
    between the way of self and the way of the cross,
    the way of the world and the way of love,
    the way of life that leads to death
    and the way of death that leads to life.
  Teach us to follow.

We thank you for the choice he made,
    and all that lay behind it –
    the faith that gave him the inner strength
    to resist temptation and accept your will,
    the courage to take the path of suffering and death,
    the love which guided all.
  Teach us to follow.

Forgive us that having received so much from him
    we give so little in return.
  We are self-centred,
    putting ourselves before others and before you,
    shying away from sacrifice and self-denial.
  Teach us to follow.

We are narrow in our vision,
    more concerned with earthly satisfaction
    than spiritual fulfilment,
    taking the easy, comfortable way
    rather than the way of Christ.
  Teach us to follow.

Loving God,
    once more, we pray, assure us of your constant mercy,
        once more cleanse and renew our hearts,
        once more give us strength, faith and courage
        to follow where you would lead us.
Teach us to follow.

Teach us to hunger and thirst for righteousness,
    knowing that you are able to fill us;
    to trust in you always, come what may,
    knowing your love will never fail us;
    to offer you our worship
    through all we are and all we do,
    knowing you alone are God.
Teach us to follow.

Loving God,
    lead us when our time of trial comes,
        when we are faced by the need to choose,
        and deliver us then from evil.
Teach us to follow,
    in the name of Christ.
    Amen.

35

Time and space for God

Lord of all,
  we come to you at the close of another day,
    in the quiet of this evening,
      to make a space in the busy routine of our lives,
      to be still and know that you are God,
      to listen in the peace and calm of these moments
      to your still, small voice.

Lord of all,
  forgive us that we make time like this all too rarely,
    believing ourselves sometimes to be too busy even for you!
  Forgive us that we fill our lives with noise and activity –
    rushing around doing this and that,
    yet neglecting the most important part.
  Forgive us that we ask you to speak,
    but fail to hear your voice because we fail to listen.
  Forgive us that we deny ourselves the peace of your presence
    through misplaced independence or wilful disobedience.

Lord of all,
  accept us now, as we are, despite our many failings.
  Forgive us for forgetting you,
    and renew us through your Holy Spirit.
  Help us to recognise that Christ is with us now
    as we meet together in his name,
    and teach us that through him you are with us always,
    speaking, guiding, encouraging, enriching,
    wanting and waiting to touch our lives with your grace.

  Open now our hearts to you,
    and fill us with the peace that only you can give,
    through Jesus Christ our Lord.
    Amen.

36

FOLLOWING JESUS

Gracious God,
>once more we meet together during this season of Lent.
>**We come in the name of Christ**
>>**remembering again those lonely and testing days**
>>**he endured in the wilderness.**
>We come recalling how deliberately he spent time there alone,
>>reflecting on who he was and what you wanted of him.
>**We come reminded of the courage, the faith,**
>>**and the commitment he showed during that time –**
>>**qualities that were to characterise the rest of his ministry.**

Gracious God,
>help us to use this time given to us.
>**May we draw closer to you through it,**
>>**understanding more of your nature and our own.**
>May it deepen our faith,
>>strengthen our commitment,
>>and confirm our sense of calling.
>**May we learn what it means to follow Christ**
>>**and what it means to serve you.**
>May we recognise more clearly the true cost of discipleship
>>but equally the rewards.
>**May we understand more fully**
>>**why you have put us here,**
>>**what you would have us do,**
>>**who you would have us be,**
>>**how you would have us live,**
>>**and where you would have us go.**

Gracious God,
>prepare us through this time of worship,
>>this day, and this season,
>>to understand and celebrate more fully
>>all you have done for us in Christ.
>**And so may we love you more truly**
>>**and serve you more faithfully,**
>>**to the glory of your name.**
>>**Amen.**

37

Examining ourselves

Almighty and all-seeing God,
 we thank you for this season of Lent –
  a time to reflect upon our discipleship,
  to consider our calling,
  to test ourselves and see whether we are in the faith.

Almighty God,
 help us for once to be honest with ourselves,
  to see ourselves as we really are,
  with all our weaknesses,
  all our ugliness and sinfulness.

Help us to face all those things
 which we usually prefer to push aside –
  the unpleasant truths we sweep under the carpet,
  pretending they are not there.

All-seeing God,
 we can fool ourselves
  but we cannot fool you.
 We can pretend all is well
  but cannot conceal our inner pain.
 We can deny our need of you
  but cannot disguise our emptiness without you.
 We can seek fulfilment in this world
  but will never find real peace outside your love.

Almighty and all-seeing God,
>we claim to be in the faith
>>but sometimes that faith is skin-deep.
>**We claim to love you**
>>**but often that love is flawed.**
>We claim to serve you
>>but all too frequently we serve self first.
>**Search us and help us to search ourselves,**
>>control us, and help us to control ourselves,
>>**and give us grace to grow strong in faith**
>>**and whole in Christ,**
>>**for in his name we ask it.**
>>**Amen.**

38

FACING TRUTH
(inspired by Micah 2 v.6)

God of truth,
    you know us better than we know ourselves.
    You search our hearts and minds,
        seeing us as we really are,
        and confronting us with our true selves.
    Teach us to face the truth,
    for the truth will set us free.

Forgive us that all too often
    we shy away from what is hard to accept,
    refusing to countenance anything
    which contradicts the image we have of ourselves.
We find it so hard to be honest,
    closing our ears to truths we would rather not hear.
We avoid those who challenge and disturb us,
    preferring instead those who soothe and flatter our egos.
Teach us to face the truth,
    for the truth will set us free.

God of truth,
    we thank you today for all those
        with the rare gift of speaking the truth in love –
        not spitefully, vindictively, or harshly,
        nor from any ulterior motives,
        but because they genuinely care.
Teach us to face the truth,
    for the truth will set us free.

We thank you for those who are willing
    to risk our resentment,
    our misunderstanding or anger,
    our retaliation or rejection,
    to help us grow as individuals.
Teach us to face the truth,
    for the truth will set us free.

God of all,
  give us true humility and meekness of spirit,
    so that we may be ready to listen and examine ourselves,
    ready to ask searching questions about who we are
    and to change where necessary.
  Teach us to face the truth,
    for the truth will set us free.
    In the name of Christ we pray.
    Amen.

39

LENT INTERCESSION

Lord Jesus Christ,
   we are reminded today, in this season of Lent,
      of the time you spent in the wilderness –
      facing choices,
      wrestling with temptation,
      experiencing a period of testing
      that would shape the course of your ministry;
      a time which reminds us of your humanity,
      which tells us you were one with us,
      tempted just as we are.
   In the wilderness of life today
      be present, O Lord.

Lord Jesus Christ,
   we thank you that you came through that time the stronger –
      more sure of the path you must take,
      and more confident of your ability to take it.
   So now we pray for those experiencing similar times of testing.
   In the wilderness of life today
      be present, O Lord.

We pray for those facing difficult and demanding choices –
      choices which entail pain and self-sacrifice,
      which mean letting go of cherished dreams,
      which involve facing awkward facts about themselves and others.
   In the wilderness of life today
      be present, O Lord.

We pray for those wrestling with temptation –
      torn between conflicting desires,
      unsure of where they stand,
      uncertain about their ability to stand firm.
   In the wilderness of life today
      be present, O Lord.

We pray for those experiencing a period of testing in their lives –
  problems they fear they cannot cope with,
  challenges they feel unable to rise to,
  questions they would rather not face.
In the wilderness of life today
  be present, O Lord.

Lord Jesus Christ,
  give strength to all facing such times –
  a sureness of purpose and clearness of mind.
Give the knowledge of your will –
  then courage to make right decisions
  and resolve to see them through.
May each emerge the stronger for all they experience,
  and better equipped to face the future.
In the wilderness of life today,
  be present, O Lord,
  for in your name we pray.
  Amen.

HOLY WEEK

40

PALM SUNDAY PRAISE

Loving God,
  we join this day in glad and joyful praise.
  We welcome Christ once more
      as our King, Lord, and Saviour –
      we promise him our loyalty,
      we bring him our love,
      we bow to him in worship,
      we greet him with wonder.
  Hosanna to the Son of David,
    glory in the highest heaven.

Loving God,
  come to us again through Christ this day.
  Speak to us as we read familiar words,
      as we sing familiar songs,
      as we recall his triumphal entry into Jerusalem long ago,
      as we remember all it meant and all it cost.
  Hosanna to the Son of David,
    glory in the highest heaven.

Help us to see that it was not only in the welcome of Palm Sunday,
      but in the rejection which followed
      that Jesus revealed your glory,
      and so help us to offer him our service in the days ahead,
      through the good times and the bad.
  Hosanna to the Son of David,
    glory in the highest heaven,
    now and for evermore.
    Amen.

41

PALM SUNDAY
WELCOMING THE KING

Gracious God,
  as we remember this day
    how Jesus entered Jerusalem to cries of celebration,
    help us to welcome him afresh
    into our own hearts and lives.
  Accept the praise and worship we bring you,
    and give us a real sense of expectation
    as we look towards his coming kingdom.
  Hosanna to the Son of David,
    glory in the highest heaven.

Gracious God,
  like your people long ago we do not always see clearly,
    our faith shallow and self-centred;
    we do not understand as we should,
    our praise short-lived and superficial.
  But, we ask, take the faith we offer,
    weak though it may be,
    and deepen it through this day,
    so that we may truly welcome Christ as our King,
    and worship him with joyful praises,
    now and always.
  Hosanna to the Son of David,
    glory in the highest heaven,
    now and always.
    Amen.

42

PALM SUNDAY CONFESSION 1

Lord Jesus Christ,
>we welcome and praise you this day.
>We lift up our voices in glad hosannas.
>We joyfully acknowledge you as King of kings
>>and Lord of lords.
>Yet we know in our hearts, even as we greet you,
>>sincere though we may be,
>>>that our worship and commitment is sometimes
>>>as weak and shallow as that which greeted you
>>>as you entered Jerusalem long ago.
>Son of David,
>>**have mercy upon us.**

Lord Jesus Christ,
>forgive us that we go on making
>>the same mistakes made on that first Palm Sunday.
>We profess to follow you
>>but in our hearts follow our own inclinations.
>We are self-centred in our discipleship,
>>looking as much for what we can receive as give.
>We are preoccupied with appearances,
>>our external show disguising an inner poverty
>>which only you can see.
>We are ready to serve when life is good,
>>but reluctant when it involves the way of sacrifice.
>Son of David,
>>**have mercy upon us.**

Lord Jesus Christ,
>you knew, as you entered Jerusalem,
>>that the welcome of the crowd would turn to rejection,
>>yet still you came and still you died for them.
>We praise you for that truth,
>>and we thank you that still you come to us,
>>inviting us to respond and share in your kingdom.
>Son of David,
>>**have mercy upon us.**

Come again now into our hearts,
>cleansing us of all that is evil,
>all that is impure and unworthy,
>all that keeps us from you.
Son of David,
>**have mercy upon us.**

Come to your Church,
>filling it with love,
>harmony,
>humility,
>and faith.
Son of David,
>**have mercy upon us.**

Come to your world,
>blessing it with peace,
>justice,
>freedom,
>and hope.
Son of David,
>**have mercy upon us.**

Lord Jesus Christ,
>we welcome you today as the Prince of Peace,
>>the King of kings,
>>the Servant of all,
>>the Lord of all,
>>all in all!
>Son of David,
>>**have mercy upon us,**
>>**for your name's sake.**
>>**Amen.**

43

PALM SUNDAY CONFESSION 2

Lord Jesus Christ,
 you came to Jerusalem and were greeted by shouts of joy,
  welcomed as God's promised deliverer,
  the one he had chosen to rescue his people.
 But when the nature of your kingdom became clear,
  the sort of freedom you offered fully apparent,
  so the response changed.
 The shouts of 'Hosanna!'
  turned to cries of 'Crucify!'
 The hands outstretched in friendship
  became fists curled up in hate.
 The declarations of loyalty
  became voices raised in mockery and rejection.
 Lord Jesus,
  have mercy.

You come to *our* lives
  and *we* welcome you with gladness.
 We have accepted you as our Saviour,
  the one who sets *us* free.
 But we too can so quickly change our tune
  when you overturn our expectations,
  when you do not act as we hope,
  when you turn out to have different ideas from our own.
 We, too, even while professing faith
  and going through the motions of commitment,
  can push you aside,
  preferring our own way to yours.
 Lord Jesus,
  have mercy.

Lord Jesus Christ,
 on this day we are reminded of how easy it is
  to welcome you as King of kings,
  but how hard to follow in the Way of the Cross.
 Lord Jesus,
  have mercy,
  for in your name we ask it.
  Amen.

44

PALM SUNDAY PETITION

Father God,
    we thank you for this day –
        for all it recalls,
        all it means,
        all it says to us.
Speak to us now as we worship you.

Teach us, through our reading and reflection on your word,
        through our hymns and prayers,
        through our meeting with one another and with you,
        to understand more
        of what Palm Sunday signified and signifies.
Speak to us now as we worship you.

Help us to picture Jesus riding into Jerusalem,
        in triumph yet humility,
        to a welcome yet also rejection,
        to a crown but also a Cross.
Speak to us now as we worship you.

Father God,
    may this day lead us
        to a deeper understanding of your kingdom,
        a greater awareness of your love,
        and a clearer sense of your purpose,
        yesterday, today and tomorrow.
Speak to us now as we worship you,
    through Jesus Christ our Lord.
    Amen.

45

PALM SUNDAY INTERCESSION

Lord Jesus Christ,
　　you entered Jerusalem in quiet humility,
　　　　taking the form of a servant,
　　　　even to the point of death on a cross,
　　　　emptying yourself so that we might be filled.
　　Come again now
　　　　and establish your kingdom.

Come afresh to our troubled world,
　　　　with all its needs,
　　　　its tensions,
　　　　its problems,
　　　　and its evil.
　　Come again now
　　　　and establish your kingdom.

Bring healing where there is division,
　　　　love where there is hatred,
　　　　hope where there is despair,
　　　　joy where there is sorrow,
　　　　confidence where there is fear,
　　　　strength where there is weakness,
　　　　healing where there is sickness,
　　　　life where there is death.
　　Come again now
　　　　and establish your kingdom.

Lord Jesus Christ,
　　reach out to your Church and world,
　　　　despite the weakness of our faith,
　　　　and the rejection of so many.
　　May your will be done on earth
　　　　even as it is in heaven.
　　Come again now
　　　　and establish your kingdom,
　　　　for in your name we pray.
　　　　Amen.

46

HOLY WEEK APPROACH 1

Loving God,
> Father of Jesus Christ, the Word made flesh,
>> friend and guide to your people across the ages,
>> with joy and gladness we praise you.
> Draw near to us,
>> **as we draw near to you.**

> You have shown your mercy,
>> revealed your love,
>> and spoken through your prophets.
> You have lived amongst us,
>> you have shared our life and death,
>> and you offer to all who truly seek you
>> the assurance of everlasting life!
> Draw near to us,
>> **as we draw near to you.**

Loving God,
> we thank you for all you have done through Christ,
>> and we ask you now to help us glimpse more fully
>> the wonder of his love.
> Draw near to us,
>> **as we draw near to you.**

> As we seek your word, speak to us.
> As we confess our faults, have mercy upon us.
> As we acknowledge the weakness of our discipleship,
>> cleanse and renew us
>> through the saving love of Christ.
> As we recognise our lack of vision and courage,
>> inspire and challenge us
>> through your Holy Spirit.
> Draw near to us,
>> **as we draw near to you.**

Loving God,
    we have come together in this time of Holy Week.
    Confront us with the Christ who gave his life for us,
        and help us to offer our lives to him.
    Draw near to us,
        as we draw near to you,
        through Jesus Christ our Lord.
        Amen.

47

HOLY WEEK APPROACH 2

Loving God,
    we come before you,
        in worship, praise, thanksgiving and remembrance.
    Open our hearts to the presence of Christ,
        and lead us in his way.

We come recalling that last week in the life of Jesus
        and all it teaches us of him –
        his faithfulness to the last,
        his willingness to take the Way of the Cross,
        his courage in the face of opposition, suffering and death.
Open our hearts to the presence of Christ,
        and lead us in his way.

We come consecrating our lives to his service,
        committing ourselves to his cause.
Open our hearts to the presence of Christ,
        and lead us in his way.

We come thankful for all he has done
        and continues to do,
        celebrating his great love.
Open our hearts to the presence of Christ,
        and lead us in his way.

We come acknowledging him as our Lord and Saviour,
        and desiring to be his true disciples.
Open our hearts to the presence of Christ,
        and lead us in his way.

Receive now this time of worship that we offer to you,
        and speak through it so that we may grow in faith
        and be strengthened in your service.
Open our hearts to the presence of Christ,
        and lead us in his way,
        for in his name we ask it.
        Amen.

48

THE WAY OF THE CROSS

Lord Jesus Christ,
    we find it hard to walk the Way of the Cross,
        hard to face persecution,
        hard even to risk opposition.
    We want to be popular,
        accepted,
        one of the crowd,
        not different from all the rest.
    Teach us to follow your way.

Lord Jesus Christ,
    forgive us all the times
        we have shied away from our responsibilities,
        taking the easy path,
        the way of least resistance.
    Teach us to follow your way.

Forgive us that whenever possible
    we have avoided the cost of discipleship,
    serving ourselves instead of others.
Teach us to follow your way.

We thank you for those who have the courage
    to stand up for their convictions,
    and stand out against everything they believe to be wrong.
Teach us to follow your way.

We thank you that there are some ready to accept censure,
    even hostility,
    for the sake of what they know to be right.
Give us something of their faith and their courage,
    so that when the moment of challenge comes
    we shall not be found wanting.
Teach us to follow your way,
    for in your name we pray.
    Amen.

49

REMEMBERING AND UNDERSTANDING

Loving God,
  we have come together in this Holy Week to remember –
    to remember that last week in the life of Jesus
    before his death;
    to remember the events from Palm Sunday
    through to Good Friday and on to Easter;
    to remember the faithfulness
    that went all the way to the Cross,
    even as the crowds and his closest friends deserted him.
Open our eyes to the wonder of your love.

We have come to remember.
But more than that we have come
    so that we might understand the extent of your grace,
    the cost of our redemption,
    the pain of body, mind and soul endured by Jesus,
    everything he means for us and all people.
Open our eyes to the wonder of your love.

Loving God,
    help us both to remember and to understand,
    so that we may live in the light of Christ,
    and follow faithfully in his way.
Open our eyes to the wonder of your love,
  for his name's sake.
  Amen.

50

THE FAITHFULNESS OF CHRIST

Loving God,
  we praise you for the ministry of Christ,
    his faithfulness to his calling,
    his denial of self,
    his willingness to face even death itself
    that we might find the true meaning of life.
  Help us to be faithful to him,
    even as he has been faithful to us.

Forgive us that our commitment to him is so poor,
    our faith in him often skin-deep,
    our lives a denial of everything we profess to believe.
  Help us to be faithful to him,
    even as he has been faithful to us.

Help us to understand what it means to follow Christ,
    what is involved in confessing him as Lord,
    what is entailed in being his Church.
  Help us to be faithful to him,
    even as he has been faithful to us.

Help us to live as his people,
    recognising the cost but also the reward of discipleship.
  Help us to be faithful to him,
    even as he has been faithful to us,
    for in his name we pray.
    Amen.

51

HOLY MONDAY

Loving God,
>   we look back today to Jesus in the wilderness,
>>   faced with the temptation to compromise,
>>   forced to choose between the easy and the demanding path,
>>   the way of the world or the way of costly sacrifice.
>   Speak through the example Christ has given,
>>   **and help us to listen.**

>   We remember today Jesus in Jerusalem,
>>   the shouts of the crowd still ringing in his ears,
>>   their welcome still fresh in his memory –
>>   once more faced with the temptation to compromise,
>>   forced to choose between the easy and the demanding path,
>>   and we remember how he chose the costly way,
>>   the way of suffering, humiliation and death.
>   Speak through the example Christ has given,
>>   **and help us to listen.**

Loving God,
>   forgive us that we lack the same courage,
>>   the same faith,
>>   the same commitment,
>>   the same love.
>   Speak through the example Christ has given,
>>   **and help us to listen.**

>   Forgive us that so often we choose the easy option –
>>   conforming to this world's expectations
>>   rather than risk rejection or confrontation,
>>   more concerned with present happiness and earthly success
>>   than the things which bring eternal fulfilment.
>   Speak through the example Christ has given,
>>   **and help us to listen.**

Loving God,
we thank you that through the love of Christ
we are assured of your mercy,
accepted as we are with all our faults and failings,
daily renewed by his Spirit.
Inspire us then, by his example,
to serve you more faithfully and love you more deeply,
even as you have loved us.
Speak through the example Christ has given,
and help us to listen,
for in his name we ask it.
Amen.

52

HOLY TUESDAY

Lord Jesus Christ,
    You continued on your way,
        fulfilling the purpose for which you came,
        despite hostility, opposition, rejection, persecution.

You walked the Way of the Cross,
    standing up for what you knew to be right,
    despite the cost.

You refused to take the easy way,
    the way of least resistance,
        preferring instead to offer your life for the life of the world.

You gave your all, holding nothing back,
    no sacrifice too great,
    willingly enduring the agony of the cross to set us free.

Lord Jesus Christ,
    we praise you for your courage and faithfulness,
        your compassion and immeasurable love.

Help us, as we meet now,
    to recognise more clearly all we owe to you,
    and so commit ourselves more fully to your service,
    for your name's sake.
    Amen.

53

Holy Wednesday

Lord Jesus Christ,
 once more we remember that last week
  before you faced the cross –
  your pain and hurt as you faced betrayal,
  denial, rejection and abandonment,
  and we confess that we have added to your pain.
Lord Jesus Christ, have mercy upon us.

Through our thoughts, words and actions,
 so often we have deserted you when you needed us most.
Lord Jesus Christ, have mercy upon us.

Through our lack of thought, our failure to speak,
  and our reluctance to act,
  so many times we have denied
  the faith and love we declare.
Lord Jesus Christ, have mercy upon us.

We have cared too much for the good opinion of others.
We have been fearful to contemplate the true cost of discipleship.
Like lost sheep we have gone astray.
Lord Jesus Christ, have mercy upon us.

Yet you have called us to be your Church.
You have forgiven us, cleansed and restored us,
  giving your own life for our sakes.
Receive our thanks.
Receive our praise.
And help us to follow you more faithfully,
  for in your name we pray.
  Amen.

54

Maundy Communion
Prayer of Approach

Lord Jesus Christ,
  you invited all who love you,
    all who sincerely desire to be your disciples,
    to share together in this Supper.
  So now we come around this table,
    in fellowship with you,
    with one another,
    and with all your people in every place and time.
  Lord Jesus, as we come to you,
    so come to us.

We come to remember your sharing bread and wine
    with your disciples in the upper room;
    a simple expression of fellowship
    with one who would soon betray you,
    one who would deny you,
    and others who would abandon you.
  Lord Jesus, as we come to you,
    so come to us.

We come to remember your anguish in Gethsemane
    as you faced the awful, awesome cost of your calling, alone.
  Lord Jesus, as we come to you,
    so come to us.

We come to remember your arrest and brutal interrogation,
    your sorrow and humiliation,
    your suffering and death.
  Lord Jesus, as we come to you,
    so come to us.

We come to remember your quiet acceptance
of human evil and hatred directed against you,
you who had done no evil and knew no hate.
Lord Jesus, as we come to you,
so come to us.

Lord Jesus Christ,
we remember your great love,
and we marvel at how much you were willing to bear
for our sakes!
So now we praise, thank and worship you,
with all our hearts and minds and souls.
Lord Jesus, as we come to you,
so come to us,
for your name's sake.
Amen.

55

MAUNDY COMMUNION – THE BROKEN CHRIST

Lord God, almighty and omnipotent,
    for your love that goes on creating,
        your power that goes on strengthening,
        your mercy that goes on forgiving,
        your purpose that goes on working,
        and your goodness that goes on giving:
Receive our praise.

Lord Jesus Christ,
    revealer of the Father's love,
        proof of his power,
        instrument of his forgiveness,
        fulfiller of his purpose,
        agent of his goodness:
Receive our praise.

Loving God,
    in the name of Christ we worship you,
        we welcome you,
        we acknowledge your greatness,
        we celebrate your goodness.
Receive our praise.

Lord Jesus Christ,
    once despised and rejected,
        broken and beaten,
        condemned and crucified,
        we welcome you as our risen Lord;
        the King of love,
        the Prince of Peace,
        the Lord of lords,
        the bringer of life.
Receive our praise.

Loving God,
    you showed us through Christ
        that what seemed to be weakness was strength,
        what appeared to be defeat was victory.
        what appeared to be the end was a new beginning.
Receive our praise.

Forgive us for so easily being deceived by appearances,
    for measuring success by our own flawed standards.
Teach us to recognise that it is
    not only in the risen Christ but the broken Christ,
    not only in the victorious Christ but the crucified Christ,
    not only in the living Christ but the dying Christ,
    that we see your purposes fulfilled
    and your will being done.
Receive our praise,
    in his name.
    Amen.

56

MAUNDY THURSDAY INTERCESSION

Lord Jesus Christ,
    We are reminded today that you were broken for us,
        that you gladly endured sorrow, suffering and death
        for our sakes.
    You identified yourself with humanity,
        standing alongside the broken-hearted,
        accepting the limitations of life and death.
    So now we pray for all who are broken in body, mind or spirit.
    Lord, in your mercy,
        hear our prayer.

We pray for those who are in pain,
    racked by illness and disease,
    physically disabled,
    maimed or injured through war, terrorism,
    disaster or accident.
Lord, in your mercy,
    hear our prayer.

We pray for those who mourn loved ones
    or who face death themselves,
    those tormented by fear or anxiety,
    the mentally ill or handicapped,
    and all who are confused or overwhelmed
    by the complexities of daily life.
Lord, in your mercy,
    hear our prayer.

We pray for those whose spirit
    has been broken in the storms of life –
    overwhelmed by sorrow,
    overcome by disappointment,
    crushed by tragedy.
Lord, in your mercy,
    hear our prayer.

We pray for those whose faith has been battered
by the harsh realities of this world –
their confidence shaken,
their trust destroyed,
their love grown cold.
Lord, in your mercy,
hear our prayer.

Lord Jesus Christ,
who endured such turmoil of mind in Gethsemane,
whose body was broken on the cross,
who surrendered your spirit to the Father,
reach out now in love and compassion
to all in any such need,
bringing the assurance of your presence,
the comfort of your peace,
and the joy of your love.
Lord, in your mercy,
hear our prayer,
for we ask it in your name.
Amen.

57

GOOD FRIDAY THANKSGIVING

Gracious God,
    you have done so much for us,
        giving us a world rich in wonder
        and filling our lives with so much that is special.
    Receive our thanks.

    But above all today we come to thank you
        for your most precious gift of all –
        the great love you have shown to us in Christ.
    Receive our thanks.

In him you came and lived amongst us,
    fully part of our world.
Through him you revealed your grace, your mercy,
    your will, your kingdom.
By him you identified yourself
    with the sin and suffering of our world,
        opening the way through his death and resurrection
        to forgiveness and eternal life.
    Receive our thanks.

Gracious God,
    you have given to us without counting the cost,
        not just a little but all.
    Receive our thanks.

You emptied yourself,
    taking the form of a servant,
    sacrificing your only Son for our sakes.
Receive our thanks.

And the wonder is you ask so little in return –
　　you make no extortionate demands,
　　you set no stringent conditions to your love,
　　you ask simply that we love you in return.
Receive our thanks.

Gracious God,
　　teach us to offer you our willing and joyful discipleship,
　　and to play our part in working for your kingdom.
Receive our thanks,
　　for the sake of Jesus Christ our Lord.
　　Amen.

58

GOOD FRIDAY CONFESSION

Lord Jesus Christ,
    today of all days we are reminded
        just how much we owe you,
            how great a price you were willing to pay
            to give us the gift of life.
    Forgive us for giving you so little in return,
        for shying away from discipleship
            when there is any suggestion it may be costly.
    Lord, in your mercy,
        hear our prayer.

We are reminded how you stayed true to your calling,
    despite every attempt to deflect you from it.
Forgive us that we so often take the way of least resistance,
    compromising our convictions for the sake of any easy life.
Lord, in your mercy,
    hear our prayer.

We are reminded how you stayed true
    to those who were to fail you,
        more concerned for their own safety than your welfare.
Forgive us that we so readily put self-interest
    before the interests of others,
        our loyalty depending on how much is asked of us.
Lord, in your mercy,
    hear our prayer.

We are reminded how you endured ridicule and violence
    without any attempt at retaliation,
        praying instead for those who persecuted you.
Forgive us that we lash out at the slightest provocation,
    that we are more often concerned with exacting revenge
    than offering forgiveness.
Lord, in your mercy,
    hear our prayer.

We are reminded of how you loved us so much that you died for us,
> willingly taking the Way of the Cross.
Forgive us that we love you so little,
> that we find it so hard to offer anything of ourselves.
Lord, in your mercy,
> **hear our prayer.**

Lord Jesus Christ,
> we thank you for this day and for all it calls to mind.
Help us to hear its message
> and respond to its challenge.
Lord, in your mercy,
> **hear our prayer,**
> **for in your name we ask it.**
> **Amen.**

59

GOOD FRIDAY
THE PAIN OF CHRIST

Lord Jesus Christ,
    on this day we marvel again at the extent of your love,
        and especially the pain you were ready to face
        so that we might receive life in all its fullness;
        a pain that goes far beyond anything
        we can ever imagine or understand.
    Gracious Lord, for all you willingly endured,
        we thank you.

We remember the pain of body
    as thorns were twisted into your head,
    as the lash tore into your body,
    as you staggered under the weight of the cross,
    as nails were hammered into your hands and feet,
    as you writhed in agony,
    waiting for the blissful release of death.
Gracious Lord, for all you willingly endured,
    we thank you.

We remember the pain of mind
    as you came to terms with the betrayal of Judas,
    the denial of Peter,
    the faithlessness of your followers,
    and the shouts of 'Crucify!'
    from those who just days before
    had welcomed you as their king.
Gracious Lord, for all you willingly endured,
    we thank you.

We remember the pain of spirit
>   as you bore the sins of the world on your shoulders,
>   as you experienced that dreadful sense of isolation from God,
>   as you felt yourself to be abandoned,
>   left there to face the awfulness of your fate, alone.
Gracious Lord, for all you willingly endured,
>   **we thank you.**

Lord Jesus Christ,
>   we can never begin to grasp what you went through,
>   nor ever fully appreciate
>   the scale of the suffering you endured.
But we know that yours was a love greater
>   than any we can ever show,
>   and a sacrifice more costly
>   than any we can ever offer.
Gracious Lord, for all you willingly endured,
>   **we thank you.**

Open our eyes to the wonder of this day,
>   and help us to respond in the only way we can –
>   with heartfelt gratitude,
>   with joyful praise,
>   and with loving service,
>   offered in your name and for your glory.
Gracious Lord, for all you willingly endured,
>   **we thank you.**
>   **Amen.**

60

GOOD FRIDAY INTERCESSION

Lord Jesus Christ,
    broken on the cross,
        tortured there in body, mind and soul,
        you know what it means to suffer.
So now we pray today for the broken people of our world,
    all those who have experienced something of your pain.
Reach out in love, and make them whole.

We pray for the broken in body –
    those injured in accidents,
    those maimed in war,
    those disabled by disease.
Reach out in love, and make them whole.

We pray for the broken in mind –
    those tormented by fears,
    those wrestling with depression,
    those who have suffered a mental breakdown.
Reach out in love, and make them whole.

We pray for the broken in spirit –
    those whose dreams have been destroyed,
    those whose love has been betrayed,
    those whose faith has been crushed.
Reach out in love, and make them whole.

Lord Jesus Christ,
    you came to make us all whole,
        to mend broken lives.
        to restore broken people.
Reach out in love, and make them whole,
    for in your name we ask it.
    Amen.

61

GOOD FRIDAY
LIGHT IN OUR DARKNESS

Lord Jesus Christ,
    you came to our world as light in its darkness,
        bringing life and love,
        hope and forgiveness.
    Lighten our darkness, Lord, we pray.

    You came not to condemn, but to save,
        not to judge, but to show mercy,
        and to do that
        you willingly endured darkness for our sakes –
        the darkness of loneliness and rejection,
        of betrayal and denial,
        of suffering and humiliation,
        of fear and death,
        of all our human sinfulness
        pressing down on your shoulders.
    Lighten our darkness, Lord, we pray.

Lord Jesus Christ,
    forgive us that, despite all you have done,
        we so often walk in darkness,
        preferring our way to yours,
        betraying our convictions,
        abandoning our responsibilities,
        and denying our faith through the way we live.
    Lighten our darkness, Lord, we pray.

    Teach us to walk in your light
        and to follow where you lead,
        knowing that in you
        is the Way, the Truth and the Life.
    Lighten our darkness, Lord, we pray,
        for in your name we ask it.
        Amen.

EASTER

62

EASTER WORSHIP

Almighty God,
   with joy and praise,
      with awe and wonder,
      with gladness and celebration,
      we bring our Easter worship.

We lift up our hearts,
   we lift up our thoughts,
   we lift up our voices,
   we lift up our souls,
   recognising afresh all you have done for us in Christ.

We rejoice in the message of this day,
   the Good News at the heart of our faith –
   light after darkness,
   joy after sorrow,
   good after evil,
   life after death!

Almighty God,
   speak to us again today
      through all we read,
      all we hear,
      all we sing,
      all we do.

May the truth of the resurrection inspire us with new hope.
May the victory of Christ fill us with new joy.
May the reality of his presence fill us with new faith.
And so may we serve you with new vigour
   to the glory of your name,
   through Jesus Christ our Lord.
   Amen.

63

EASTER PRAISE

Living God,
　　we thank you for this day of praise and celebration –
　　　　a day of hope after despair,
　　　　joy after sorrow,
　　　　life after death –
　　　　a day to lift up our hearts
　　　　and to offer you our praise!

Loving God,
　　we remember today all you have done for us
　　　　and for all the world –
　　　　your great victory over sin and death,
　　　　your triumph over everything that keeps us from you
　　　　and prevents us living the life you want us to lead.

Saving God,
　　we join this day with your Church in every age
　　　　to bring our Easter worship –
　　　　to acknowledge you as a God of love and power,
　　　　to welcome Christ as our living Lord.

Sovereign God,
　　breathe new life into our hearts this day.
　　Fire us with renewed confidence and enthusiasm.
　　Fill us with resurrection power,
　　　　and grant that we might meet and walk with Christ,
　　　　offering him our joyful faithful service
　　　　this and every day,
　　　　for his name's sake.
　　　　Amen.

64

EASTER PRAISE AND INTERCESSION

Loving God,
    we praise you for this day of celebration,
        this day of praise,
        this day of thanksgiving,
        a day that changes the way we think,
        the way we act,
        the way we live –
        that changes everything.
Lord of life,
    hear our prayer.

And so we pray now for change in our world,
    for change in all those places where there is human need.
We pray for the poor, the homeless,
    the sick and the hungry.
Lord of life,
    hear our prayer.

We pray for the victims of war, for refugees,
    for divided communities and countries,
Lord of life,
    hear our prayer.

We pray for the sorrowful, the fearful,
    the troubled in heart and mind.
Lord of life,
    hear our prayer.

We pray for the oppressed, the persecuted,
    the imprisoned and the exploited.
Lord of life,
    hear our prayer.

Living God,
> may the truth of Easter
>> break into each and every one of these situations,
>> bringing help and healing,
>> strength and support,
>> comfort and courage,
>> hope and help,
>> faith and freedom,
>> love and life,
>> the change that you alone can bring.
> Lord of life,
>> **hear our prayer,**
>> **through Jesus Christ our Lord.**
>> **Amen.**

65

EASTER PRAISE
THE VICTORY OF LOVE

Loving God,
    we praise you once more for all you have done in Christ,
        for your victory through him over sin and evil,
        darkness and death.
    We praise you for your love that cannot be kept down,
        whatever it may face.
May the knowledge of that love inspire us
    to keep on following you
    through good and bad.

When life seems hard,
    when good seems frustrated,
    when we feel ourselves in danger
    of being overwhelmed by trials and temptations,
    assure us once more of your love
    that will not be defeated.

When our work seems to bear no fruit,
    when our efforts go unrewarded,
    when our hopes appear unfulfilled,
    teach us to trust in your purpose
    that presses on towards fulfilment.

When the innocent suffer,
    when evil prospers,
    when hatred seems to hold sway,
    help us to keep on believing
    that good will finally win through.

Grant us a deep unshakeable confidence
    that whatever life brings,
    whatever we face,
    however things seem,
    your will shall be done and your kingdom come,
    through Jesus Christ our Lord.
    Amen.

66

EASTER PRAISE AND CONFESSION

Living God,
    we are here in the name of Christ.
    We are here to celebrate once more his resurrection,
        to rejoice once more at his victory
        over evil, hatred and death,
        to give thanks once more
        for his living presence with us now and always.
    Lord of life,
        hear us.

Receive our praise,
    our worship,
    ourselves as we come before you.
Fill us with joy and wonder
    as we hear again the message of the risen Christ,
    and as we recognise his presence among us
    through his Holy Spirit.
Lord of life,
    hear us.

Living God,
    we are here in the name of Christ.
    We are here to confess our faults and failings,
        to acknowledge our unworthiness of your love,
        to seek your mercy and forgiveness,
        and to ask for renewal in our lives.
    Lord of life,
        hear us.

Receive our confession,
    our penitence,
    ourselves as we come before you.
Cleanse and restore us through the love of Christ,
    and strengthen us through the inner power
    of your Holy Spirit.
Lord of life,
    hear us.

So may we serve you better,
    and live to your glory.
Lord of life,
    hear us,
    through Jesus Christ our Lord.
    Amen.

67

EASTER CONFESSION AND PETITION

Almighty God,
   today is the most special of days –
      a day of victory, celebration and praise!

   A day on which we remember your great triumph –
      the defeat of evil, suffering and death.

   A day on which we recall the transformation you have brought –
      joy after sorrow, hope after despair, faith after doubt.

   A day on which we give thanks for all you have given us –
      love, laughter, life!

Almighty God,
   forgive us that we lose sight of those truths.
   We are so quick to become disheartened.
   We so easily forget all you have done for us.
   Forgive us for the limits we set upon your love.
   Forgive the feebleness of our response.
   Forgive the smallness of our vision.

   Speak to us through this joyful season,
      and fill us with greater trust and deeper faith.
   So may we live not just this day but every day
      as your Easter people,
      through Jesus Christ our Lord.
      Amen.

68

EASTER THANKSGIVING AND CONFESSION

Sovereign God,
   we thank you for the victory we remember this day –
      the victory of Christ over evil, sin, hatred,
      darkness and death.

So now we come,
      confessing our many faults,
      acknowledging our weakness,
      ashamed of our lack of faith,
      but also assured of your mercy,
      rejoicing in your forgiveness,
      confident of your love,
      and certain of your renewing, restoring power.

Sovereign God,
   who makes all things new,
      fill us now with new faith, new commitment,
      new purpose and new life,
      through the power of the risen Christ.
      Amen.

69

EASTER THANKSGIVING

All-loving and all-powerful God,
  we thank you for this day and all it means –
    the assurance it brings that your love is stronger
    than anything else in heaven or earth –
    stronger than evil,
    than all human powers,
    than sorrow and suffering,
    than death itself.
  Accept our thanks for this day.
  Accept our thanks for everything.

We thank you that in our world of so much pain and sorrow
  you have shown that hope and faith is not in vain.
Your purpose is always at work,
  giving meaning to our seeking and striving after good.
Accept our thanks for this day.
Accept our thanks for everything,

All-loving and all-powerful God,
  accept our praise for all you have done in Christ –
    a mystery before which we stand in awe,
    a wonder before which we bow down in praise,
    a truth in which we live and move
    and have our being.
  Accept our thanks for this day.
  Accept our thanks for everything,
    in the name of the living and risen Christ!
    Amen.

70

GOD OF THE UNEXPECTED

Mighty God,
    we praise you for the great surprise of Easter –
        your transformation of what had seemed the end
        into a new beginning;
        your turning of what had seemed the triumph of evil
        into the victory of love.
    God of the unexpected,
        hear our prayer.

We praise you for the way you changed the lives
    of Jesus' followers –
        turning sorrow into celebration,
        doubt to faith,
        questions to answers,
        confusion to confidence,
        darkness to light.
    God of the unexpected,
        hear our prayer.

Forgive us that we too,
    like the Apostles arriving at the tomb,
    are sometimes deceived by appearances.
We make judgements based on our own limited assumptions,
    and we lose faith
    when life doesn't measure up to our expectations.
We imagine we have all the answers,
    and we are frightened when we find we have not.
We reject truths that do not fit in with our view of the world,
    and then are puzzled
    when we cannot make sense of things.
God of the unexpected,
    hear our prayer.

Forgive us for doubting your love,
>for losing sight of your purpose,
>for questioning your power.
Forgive us for ignoring your promises,
>for diminishing your greatness,
>for forgetting that your ways are not our ways
>nor your thoughts our thoughts.
God of the unexpected,
>**hear our prayer.**

We pray for all those unable to make sense
>of the situations they find themselves in,
>their hopes shattered by their experiences of life –
>those who are anxious, fearful, disillusioned, depressed,
>faced perhaps by inexplicable suffering, sorrow or evil,
>or having lost their homes, their employment,
>their livelihoods, their loved ones;
>afflicted by disease, disability, disaster,
>or exploited, oppressed,
>deprived of their basic human dignity.
God of the unexpected,
>**hear our prayer.**

May the surprise of Easter burst afresh
>into their lives and our own,
>revealing new possibilities to life
>and a new dimension to your love,
>giving new meaning to each day and every moment,
>bringing new strength and opportunities,
>offering new hope for the future
>and renewed purpose in the present.
May this day we celebrate teach us to expect the unexpected!
God of the unexpected,
>**hear our prayer,**
>**in the name of the risen and victorious Christ.**
>**Amen.**

71

EASTER VICTORY

Loving God,
we praise you once more for the Good News of Easter,
the triumphant message of resurrection –
new hope,
new joy,
new life!
Christ is risen,
he is risen indeed!

We praise you for what we see in the Easter stories –
your love that could not be kept down,
your purpose that could not be defeated,
your goodness that could not be destroyed.
Christ is risen,
he is risen indeed!

Teach us that what was true then is true now –
that resurrection is not just about life after death
but about constant new beginnings,
the way you are able to transform every part of our lives,
the way you are always bringing renewal –
and may that truth inspire us
to keep on following you
not only through the good but the bad.
Christ is risen,
he is risen indeed!

When life seems hard,
when we feel overwhelmed by trials and temptations,
when faith seems to fly in the face of reason,
assure us once more that your love will not be overcome.
Christ is risen,
he is risen indeed!

When our work seems to bear no fruit,
> when our efforts go unrewarded,
> when our hopes remain unrealised,
> teach us that your purpose will ultimately be fulfilled.
Christ is risen,
> **he is risen indeed!**

When the innocent suffer,
> when goodness is rejected,
> when evil appears victorious,
> teach us that right will finally emerge victorious.
Christ is risen,
> **he is risen indeed!**

Loving God,
> grant to us the deep inner assurance
> which only Easter can bring –
> that whatever life brings,
> whatever we face,
> however things may seem,
> your will shall be done and your kingdom come.
Christ is risen,
> **he is risen indeed!**
Thanks be to God!
> **Amen.**

72

EASTER ASSURANCE

Living God,
  we come to you on this day of celebration,
    conscious that there is so much in our lives
    that is uncertain,
    so much we cannot predict,
    so much we neither know nor understand.
  Assure us of the victory you have won in Christ.

Remind us once more through this season
    that in all the changes and chances of this world
    you are an unchanging rock,
    an unfailing deliverer,
    and an everlasting hope.
  Assure us of the victory you have won in Christ.

Remind us, as we continue to celebrate Easter in the days ahead,
    that your love continues through all things,
    your power is supreme over all things,
    and your presence is with us in all things.
  Assure us of the victory you have won in Christ.

Give us this day
    a sense of your greatness,
    a recognition of all you have done,
    and a confidence in all you shall do.
  Assure us of the victory you have won in Christ.

Living God,
    be among us now, we pray, through the risen Christ.
    Help us to hear his voice,
        to offer him our service,
        and to offer you our praise.
Assure us of the victory you have won in Christ.

We know that our hope is in you and you alone.
    Help us to accept that,
        to live in that assurance,
        and so to follow wherever you might lead us.
Assure us of the victory you have won in Christ,
    for in his name we ask it.
    Amen.

73

SHARING THE NEWS

Lord Jesus Christ,
    we thank you for the message of Easter –
        for the assurance it brings of your triumph over death,
        the proof it offers
        that love will always have the last word.
    Yet alongside that message there is another
        that perhaps we do not hear so often –
        a challenge which sometimes we can ignore,
        a call to action as well as to celebration.
    You have given us good news;
        teach us to share it.

Lord Jesus Christ,
    you appeared to your followers,
        demonstrating you had risen,
        and then you sent them out
        to proclaim your resurrection to all.
    You met with them,
        and then called them to lead others to you.
    You gave them joy,
        and then told them to share it.
    Easter was not for the few but for all,
        not just for them but the whole world!
    You have given us good news;
        teach us to share it.

Lord Jesus Christ,
    forgive us that so often we forget that.
    Having experienced your risen presence,
        we keep it to ourselves.
    Having met with you,
        we fail to introduce others to you in turn.
    Having received so much,
        we have shared so little.
    You have given us good news;
        teach us to share it.

Lord Jesus Christ,
we thank you for those who have fulfilled your call –
those who first made the Gospel known to us,
those who proclaim it to others,
those who sow, nurture, and bring to fruition
the seeds of faith.
We pray for all you have specially gifted
to proclaim the Good News –
preachers and evangelists,
ministers and missionaries,
teachers and writers.
May many meet with you through their labours
and come to know you
as their living Lord and Saviour.
You have given us good news;
teach us to share it.

Lord Jesus Christ,
you call each one of us to be your witnesses –
to tell others what we have experienced of your love,
to make known what you have done for us,
to testify to the way you have changed our lives.
Help us to do that faithfully,
to play our part in your kingdom and purpose.
And so through us may others come to meet you
and know you for themselves.
You have given us good news;
teach us to share it,
to your glory.
Amen.

74

Low Sunday
The continuing reality of Easter

Sovereign God,
  we thank you for the realities of Easter
    which we continue to celebrate today,
    realities that make such a difference to life –
    the victory of good over evil,
    love over hate, life over death;
    the turning of weakness into strength,
    fear into courage, doubt into faith;
    a new beginning where it had seemed like the end,
    new hope where there had seemed despair
    new confidence where there had been confusion.
  Teach us to live each day as your Easter people.

Sovereign God,
  we thank you that Easter
    is not just about events long ago,
    but about life now,
    not just about others, but about us,
    not just about one thing, but everything!
  Teach us to live each day as your Easter people.

Help us, we pray, to live each day in the light of Easter,
    with its joy bubbling up in our hearts,
    its laughter shining from our eyes,
    and its message always on our lips.
  So may others, seeing the difference it has made to us,
    discover the difference it can make for them.
  Teach us to live each day as your Easter people,
    to the glory of your name.
    Amen.

ASCENSION

75

ASCENSION PRAISE AND CONFESSION

Lord Jesus Christ,
  risen and ascended,
    the Word made flesh,
    before all, in all, and beyond all,
    for the lives you have given us,
    and the gift of life eternal,
    we praise you.

For all the beauty,
    the complexity,
    the variety,
    and the wonder of life that surrounds us,
    we praise you.

For all the opportunities,
    the challenges,
    the experiences,
    and the achievements life offers us,
    we praise you.

For all the things we can think and do,
    see and touch,
    hear and feel,
    smell and taste,
    we praise you.

Lord Jesus Christ,
  Lamb of the world,
    suffering servant,
    heavenly King,
    for the love that surrounds us each day,
    through family and friends,
    the fellowship of the Church
    and the inner presence of your Holy Spirit.
    we praise you.

For all the care,
   the support,
   the understanding,
   and the friendship we enjoy,
   we praise you.

Lord Jesus Christ,
   Lord of lords,
      Prince of Peace,
      King of kings,
      for your greatness that fills the universe,
      your power and majesty,
      holiness and righteousness,
      justice and mercy.
   we praise you.

For the way you have brought our world into existence,
   the way you have worked through history,
   the way you have shared our humanity,
   and the way you continue to build your kingdom,
   we praise you.

Lord Jesus Christ,
   Lord of all,
      forgive us that we have not lived our lives to the full –
      we have taken its wonder for granted,
      we have failed to appreciate its potential,
      and we have lost sight of the abundant, eternal life you offer.
   For offering us life despite all that,
   we praise you.

Forgive us that we have not responded fully
   to the love shown to us –
   we have allowed it to be poisoned
   through discord and division,
   we have starved it of nourishment
   through failing to offer our love in return,
   and we have closed our hearts to all you would offer us.
  For loving us despite all that,
   we praise you.

Forgive us that we have not begun to grasp your lordship –
 we have not kept our sense of awe and wonder before you,
 we have let our vision become stilted,
 and we have offered worship that is half-hearted,
 reflecting our weakness rather than your glory.
For calling us despite all that,
 we praise you.

Lord Jesus Christ, our Lord and Saviour,
 open our hearts as we worship you to the fullness of life,
 the fullness of your love,
 and a fuller understanding of your greatness,
 and so may we truly confess you
 as King of kings and Lord of lords.
For all you are, all you have done,
 and all you have yet to do,
 we praise you,
 this day, and for evermore.
 Amen.

76

ASCENSION CONFESSION

Lord Jesus Christ,
  We remember today
    how your apostles stood gazing into heaven,
    troubled and confused,
    fearing they had lost you,
      struggling to make sense of their experience.
Open our eyes to your glory.

We remember how in the days following your Ascension
    they remained hidden behind locked doors,
    bound by the weakness of their imagination,
    tied down by the feebleness of their vision,
    restricted by the smallness of their faith.
Open our eyes to your glory.

Instead of worshipping you
    as King of kings and Lord of lords,
    they thought you had gone from them.
Instead of rejoicing at your exaltation,
    they felt they were separated from you once again.
Open our eyes to your glory.

Despite what they had been told,
    they looked still for the man they knew and understood,
    the man who had walked the streets of Nazareth,
    who had talked with them beside the sea of Galilee,
    who had suffered and died for them in Jerusalem.
Open our eyes to your glory.

But you showed them that Jesus was greater
    than they had begun to imagine –
    not bound by space and time,
    nor tied down to one particular place,
    nor restricted to one particular people,
    but ascended to your side
    and one with you for all eternity.
Open our eyes to your glory.

Lord Jesus Christ,
    forgive us that all too often
        we make the same mistake as the apostles –
        we expect you to fit in with our own expectations,
        we assume we know all there is to know about you,
        we settle for a comfortable, cosy picture of you
        that offers much and asks little;
        and when that way of thinking
        is challenged or threatened,
        we are puzzled,
        suddenly overcome by a multitude of questions.
Open our eyes to your glory.

Forgive us that our horizons have been too narrow,
    our sights set too low,
    our expectations too limited.
Open our eyes to your glory.

Help us to glimpse the wonder of who you are
    and the untold possibilities of all you can do,
    catching our breath in awe
    and captured by a new vision of your kingdom.
Open our eyes to your glory,
    for we ask it in your name.
    Amen.

77

SERVING THE ASCENDED CHRIST

Lord Jesus Christ,
> **we greet you this day as King of kings and Lord of lords –**
> we proclaim your greatness,
> **we acknowledge your authority,**
> we celebrate your exaltation,
> **we rejoice in your triumph.**

Living Lord,
> **open our eyes to the meaning of this day –**
> broaden our vision,
> **enlarge our understanding,**
> widen our perspectives,
> **deepen our faith.**

> **Accept us now as your disciples,**
> inspire us through your Holy Spirit,
> **lead us in your service,**
> equip us for all you would have us do,
> **and so may we live to your glory**
> **and bring your kingdom nearer.**
> **In your name we pray.**
> **Amen.**

78

THE WONDER OF ASCENSION

Almighty God,
　　we come today reminded of your greatness,
　　　　your glory,
　　　　　your sovereign power and eternal purpose
　　　　　expressed so wonderfully in Jesus Christ,
　　　　　risen and ascended.
Worthy is the Lamb that was slain
　　to receive power and wealth,
　　wisdom and might,
　　honour and glory and blessing!

We thank you for the wonder of Ascension,
　　that marvellous yet mysterious moment
　　in the life of Apostles
　　which left them gazing heavenwards in confusion
　　yet departing in joy.
Worthy is the Lamb that was slain
　　to receive power and wealth,
　　wisdom and might,
　　honour and glory and blessing!

We thank you for the way it brought the ministry of Jesus
　　to a fitting conclusion,
　　testifying decisively to his oneness with you,
　　demonstrating your final seal of approval
　　on all he had done.
Worthy is the Lamb that was slain
　　to receive power and wealth,
　　wisdom and might,
　　honour and glory and blessing!

We thank you that through his Ascension
　　Jesus was set free to be Lord of all –
　　no longer bound to a particular place or time,
　　but with us always
　　and able to reach to the ends of the earth.

Worthy is the Lamb that was slain
   to receive power and wealth,
   wisdom and might,
   honour and glory and blessing!

We thank you that through his departing
   Jesus prepared the way for his coming again,
   through his Spirit,
   his Church,
   and his coming again in glory.
Worthy is the Lamb that was slain
   to receive power and wealth,
   wisdom and might,
   honour and glory and blessing!

Almighty God,
   forgive us for so often failing
      to grasp the wonder of Ascension,
      for living each day as though it had never been.
   Forgive the smallness of our vision,
      the narrowness of our outlook,
      the feebleness of our love,
      the nervousness of our witness,
      our repeated failure to recognise
      the fullness of your revelation in Christ.
Worthy is the Lamb that was slain
   to receive power and wealth,
   wisdom and might,
   honour and glory and blessing!

Give us a deeper sense of wonder,
   a stronger faith,
   and a greater understanding of all you have done.
Worthy is the Lamb that was slain
   to receive power and wealth,
   wisdom and might,
   honour and glory and blessing!

Almighty God,
    like the apostles,
        we too will never fully understand
        all Ascension means.
    We accept, but we do not fully understand.
    We believe, yet we have many questions.
    Help us, despite our uncertainty,
        to hold firm to the one great truth
        that the wonder of Christ goes far beyond
        anything we can ever imagine,
        and in that faith may we live each day.
Worthy is the Lamb that was slain
    to receive power and wealth,
    wisdom and might,
    honour and glory and blessing!
Thanks be to God!
    Amen.

PENTECOST

79

PENTECOST PRAISE

Mighty God,
  we remember this day, with awe and wonder,
    the events of that day of Pentecost long ago
    which so transformed the lives of the apostles.
  Move in us, we pray.

  We remember how in the space of a few moments
    their experience was revolutionised –
    their expectations turned upside down,
    their attitudes changed forever;
    one moment consumed by fear,
    the next radiating confidence;
    one moment uncertain of the future,
    the next sure of their calling;
    one moment wrestling with doubt,
    the next full of faith;
    one moment hiding behind locked doors,
    the next preaching boldly to the crowds.
  Move in us, we pray.

Mighty God,
  you came through your Spirit
    and life was never the same again.
  Come to us, breathing new fire into our hearts,
    new energy into our lives,
    new life into our souls.
  Transform our fear, anxiety and doubt,
    filling us with confidence and faith.
  Move in us, we pray.

  Open our minds to new horizons, new experiences
    and a new way of looking at life,
    and so may we live by the Spirit,
    bearing rich fruit to your glory.
  **Move in us, we pray,
    through Jesus Christ our Lord.
    Amen.**

80

PENTECOST CONFESSION

Living God,
  we have rejoiced again today
    at the gift of your Spirit,
    the way you breathed new hope, new faith
    and new life into your people.
  But we remember also
    that not everyone responded so gladly
    to the Spirit's coming –
    from some there was scorn, ridicule and disbelief,
    suggestions that the apostles were drunk
    or even out of their minds.
  Lord, have mercy.

Living God,
  forgive us that we too
    can be guilty of a similar response.
  Instead of welcoming the Spirit
    we greet him with cautious and suspicious hearts.
  Instead of opening our lives to the Spirit's movement
    we close our minds to anything
    which challenges our long-held preconceptions.
  Instead of gladly receiving your Spirit's gifts
    we barricade our souls against change.
  Lord, have mercy.

Living God,
>   you warn us to test what we think is the Spirit
>>   and ensure it is of you;
>>   and there are times when we need to do that,
>>   when it is right to be aware
>>   of misplaced enthusiasm and false prophecy.
>   Yet save us from ever quenching,
>>   obstructing or frustrating the Spirit.
>   Forgive us all the times we have done that,
>>   and open our lives now
>>   to your Holy Spirit's life-giving breath,
>>   so that we may live more truly as your people.
>   **Lord, have mercy,**
>>   **in the name of Christ.**
>>   **Amen.**

81

PENTECOST
OPEN TO THE SPIRIT

Almighty and loving God,
    we gather together today
        as those joined by your Holy Spirit.

We come remembering your ancient promise
    to send your Spirit upon all people,
    young and old,
    male and female,
    Jew and Gentile.
Move within us we pray.

We come remembering that first Pentecost
    when your Spirit was given to the apostles,
    renewing their faith and transforming their lives.
Move within us we pray.

We come, on this Pentecost Sunday,
    reminded of the constant work of your Spirit,
    inspiring,
    guiding,
    challenging,
    refining.
Move within us we pray.

Almighty God, Spirit of truth,
    come as you promised
        and reveal to us more of the way of Christ.
    Come and fill us with deeper faith and greater love.
    Give us the gifts we need to work for your kingdom,
        inspire us with new vision and purpose,
        and breathe your power into our lives.
Move within us we pray.

Almighty and loving God,
open our hearts and minds and souls to your Spirit,
whoever we may be,
and so equip us to live as your people,
not just this but every day,
our lives reflecting your glory
and proclaiming your love.
Move within us we pray,
to the glory of your name.
Amen.

82

Pentecost petition

Mighty God,
 come to us through your Holy Spirit,
  filling us with peace.
 Give us a love for all and a desire to serve,
  humility of mind and gentleness of soul.
 Nurture your grace in our hearts.

Mighty God,
 come to us through your Holy Spirit,
  setting us on fire with love for you.
 Fill us with a burning desire to work for your kingdom,
  and cleanse us of all that is impure
  and unworthy in our lives.
 Kindle a flame of faith in our hearts.

Mighty God,
 come to us through your Holy Spirit,
  breathing new life into our souls.
 Fill us with energy and enthusiasm in the service of Christ,
  and sweep away all in our lives
  that keeps us from living as your people.
 Instil a sense of expectation in our hearts.

Mighty God,
 forgive us that we so easily limit the Spirit,
  receiving its blessing for ourselves
  but failing to pass it on to others.
 Forgive us that we so readily quench the Spirit,
  resisting that which challenges and disturbs.
 Forgive us that we are so often closed
  to the movement of your Spirit,
  shutting it out by the narrowness of our vision.
 Come as the dove, the fire, and the wind,
  opening our lives to the peace, the power
  and the inspiration you would give us.
 Open our lives and touch our hearts,
  through Jesus Christ our Lord.
  Amen.

TRINITY

83

TRINITY APPROACH

Great and wonderful God,
  with awe and wonder we come to you.

You are greater than our minds can fathom,
    more powerful that we can ever imagine,
    beyond our highest thoughts,
    Lord of space and time,
    ruler over all.
Sovereign God,
    receive our worship.

You love us with a fierce and total love,
    valuing us for who and what we are,
    caring enough to call us your children,
    providing each day our every need,
    guiding us throughout our lives.
God the Father,
    receive our worship.

You have shared our humanity,
    identifying yourself wholly with our world,
    experiencing first-hand our joys and sorrows,
    decisively demonstrating your love in action,
    showing us the way of service.
God made flesh,
    receive our worship.

You are with us each and every day,
    constantly by our side,
    working in us and through us,
    teaching, guiding, encouraging,
    leading us to new experiences of your love.
Mighty and mysterious God,
    receive our worship.

Give us this day a sense of your greatness
    and your gentleness;
    a glimpse of your otherness
    and your nearness;
    an awareness of your eternal purpose that spans creation
    yet includes us all, here and now.
Great and wonderful God, Father, Son and Holy Spirit,
    receive our worship, in Jesus' name.
    Amen.

84

TRINITY WORSHIP

Mighty God,
   beyond all space and time,
      greater than our minds can fully grasp,
      ruler over all that is and has been and shall be,
   we worship you.

Loving Father,
   kind and merciful,
      full of goodness and compassion,
      constantly watching over us and directing our steps,
   we worship you.

Saviour Christ,
   flesh of our flesh yet the living image of God,
      sharing our humanity yet one with the Father,
      loving to the point of death yet bringer of life,
   we worship you.

Holy Spirit,
   free and mysterious,
      source of guidance and inspiration,
      filling our hearts and minds and lives,
   we worship you.

Father, Son and Holy Spirit,
   God of gods and Lord of lords,
      with awe and wonder,
      joy and gladness,
      love and praise,
      we bring this day,
      we bring our lives,
      we worship you,
      in the name of Christ.
      Amen.

85

TRINITY PRAISE

Great and loving God,
    we greet you this day with praise and wonder.
    We greet you as the creator of the ends of the earth,
        sovereign over space and time,
        greater than we can ever imagine.

Gracious and living Christ,
    we greet you this day with joy and thanksgiving.
    We greet you as our Lord,
        our friend,
        our Saviour.

Mysterious and mighty Spirit,
    we greet you this day with awe and worship.
    We greet you as our guide and inspiration,
        our source of strength and comfort,
        a living inner reality.

Almighty God, Father, Son and Holy Spirit,
    we greet you this day,
        and we praise you that you are here
        to greet us and everyone,
        today and every day,
        here and everywhere.

Help us to meet with you,
    and grow closer to you,
    through this time of worship.

Help us to glimpse your glory,
    and make it known,
    through all we say and do,
    to the glory of your name.
    Amen.

86

THE GOD WHO IS HERE, THERE AND EVERYWHERE

God beyond us,
   God with us,
   God inside us,
      we worship you.

God outside us,
   God among us,
   God within us,
      we praise you.

God above,
   God beside,
   God below,
      we thank you.

God the Father,
   God the Son,
   God the Holy Spirit,
      we honour you.

God of past,
   God of present,
   God of future,
      we bless you.

God of here,
   God of there,
   God of everywhere,
      we salute you.

God of majesty,
   God of love,
   God of power,
      we acknowledge you.

Loving God,
   Father, Son and Holy Spirit,
      for all you are,
      all you do,
      all you mean,
      we give you our thanks,
      and offer our worship,
      in the name of Christ.
      Amen.

ALL SAINTS' DAY

87

ALL SAINTS' DAY
OUR CHRISTIAN HERITAGE

Lord God of history,
    we thank you for the way you have been with your people
        across the years –
        the way you called Abraham to leave everything
        and venture out into the unknown,
        the way you chose Moses to lead the people of Israel
        out of slavery and through the wilderness
        into the Promised Land,
        the way you called judges and priests,
        rulers and prophets,
        writers and thinkers,
        to guide and challenge your people,
        teaching them more of your will
        and constantly seeking to draw them closer to you.
    One generation shall laud your works to another,
        and shall declare your mighty acts.

Lord God of history,
    we thank you for the way Jesus called twelve ordinary people
        to be his apostles,
        how through their faith and witness
        you chose countless others to become your Church,
        and how through the years since then,
        despite all its faults and weaknesses,
        its errors and misunderstandings,
        you have spoken through your Church
        to countless generations,
        ever more people day by day coming
        to living and saving faith in Christ.
    One generation shall laud your works to another,
        and shall declare your mighty acts.

Lord God of history,
　　we thank you for the way
　　　　you called our own church into being –
　　　　the way you led various individuals
　　　　to begin a new initiative in this area,
　　　　the way you guided them to this place,
　　　　the way you inspired them to persevere
　　　　despite the obstacles they faced.
　　One generation shall laud your works to another,
　　　　and shall declare your mighty acts.

We thank you for the way you have spoken
　　　　through those who have been part of this church,
　　　　the way you have taught and inspired
　　　　through pastors and teachers,
　　　　the way you made yourself known
　　　　through the life, witness, and example
　　　　of those who have gone before us,
　　　　running their race and keeping the faith,
　　　　and the way you continue to speak to us
　　　　through one another.
　　One generation shall laud your works to another,
　　　　and shall declare your mighty acts.

Lord God of history,
　　we thank you for the tradition of faith in which we stand –
　　　　the great multitude of witnesses
　　　　that surround us in past and present,
　　　　and we thank you for the history of this church
　　　　of which we are a part,
　　　　the privilege of belonging to it,
　　　　to one another and to you.
　　Help us, we pray, to learn from all that has gone before,
　　　　to contribute meaningfully
　　　　to this present chapter in our church's life,
　　　　and to work faithfully so that those who come after us
　　　　may be inspired by the legacy they inherit
　　　　to continue your work and further your cause.
　　One generation shall laud your works to another,
　　　　and shall declare your mighty acts.

Thanks be to God through Jesus Christ our Lord,
　　the same yesterday, today and forever.
　　Amen.

88

ALL SAINTS' DAY
THE GOD OF HISTORY

Lord of all,
    God of space and time,
        Ruler of history,
        Sovereign over all that is and has been and shall be,
        we acknowledge your greatness.
O give thanks to the Lord, for he is good;
    his steadfast love endures for ever!

We gather before you,
        the God of Abraham, Isaac and Jacob,
        the God who led your people across the Red Sea
        and through the wilderness,
        who guided your chosen nation into the Promised Land,
        who spoke your word through the prophets,
        who led your people out of exile back to Jerusalem,
        and above all who lived and moved and breathed
        in the person of your Son, Jesus Christ our Lord.
O give thanks to the Lord, for he is good;
    his steadfast love endures for ever!

In his name we come,
        with confidence, faith, joy and thanksgiving,
        knowing that as you have guided your people across the years
        so you will continue to guide us today,
        and knowing also that in life or in death,
        wherever we walk and whatever we experience,
        you will be there alongside us –
        a rock and a refuge,
        a constant source of strength,
        an unfailing giver of hope,
        an unquenchable fountain of life and love.
O give thanks to the Lord, for he is good;
    his steadfast love endures for ever!

Lord of all,
> for all who have gone before us,
>> and for calling us in turn
>> to be part of that great company of saints,
>> we thank you and praise you.
> O give thanks to the Lord, for he is good;
>> **his steadfast love endures for ever!**
> **Thanks be to God.**
>> **Amen.**

89

ALL SAINTS' DAY PETITION
(based on 1 Peter 2:9-10)

Eternal God,
    we thank you today that you have called us
        to share in the inheritance of your saints,
        one with you and all your people across the ages.
By your grace,
    help us to fulfil that calling.

Once we were not a people,
    but now we are the people of God.
Once we had not received mercy,
    but now we have received mercy in all its fullness.
Through you we have become a chosen race,
    a royal priesthood,
    a holy nation,
    called out of darkness into your marvellous light
    in order to proclaim your mighty acts.
By your grace,
    help us to fulfil that calling.

Teach us to put aside everything that denies our faith
    and betrays your love –
    anger,
    greed,
    envy,
    bitterness.
Teach us to act honourably and with humility,
    loving and gentle in all our actions,
    living in unity with you and one another.
By your grace,
    help us to fulfil that calling.

Help us to look towards your kingdom,
    to live as those ready for the coming of Christ
    and to offer an example to those around us,
    not superior in our attitudes
    nor thinking of ourselves more highly than we should,
    but offering ourselves in the service of others,
    proclaiming the Gospel through faithful discipleship.
By your grace,
    help us to fulfil that calling.

Eternal God,
    we come to you as ordinary, everyday people,
    nothing special about us and no particular merits to boast of,
    yet you have welcomed us into your family,
    you have called us to be your Church,
    and you have given us a place
    among the great company of saints in heaven and on earth.
By your grace,
    help us to fulfil that calling,
    through Jesus Christ our Lord.
    Amen.

90

ALL SAINTS' DAY INTERCESSION

Loving God,
> we remember today all who have gone ahead of us
>> in the journey of faith,
>> running the race set before them,
>> and holding firm to the end.

Grant to them and to us your eternal blessing.

> We remember those you called at the beginning –
>> like Abraham, Isaac and Jacob –
>> examples of faith who have been an inspiration
>> to generations since.

Grant to them and to us your eternal blessing.

> We remember those you called to lead your people
>> through adversity –
>> like Moses, Joshua, Gideon –
>> examples of commitment and determination
>> against all odds.

Grant to them and to us your eternal blessing.

> We remember those you called to speak your word –
>> like Samuel, Elijah, Elisha –
>> examples of wisdom and insight into your will.

Grant to them and to us your eternal blessing.

> We remember those you called to rule your chosen nation –
>> like Saul, David, Solomon –
>> examples of human greatness and human fallibility.

Grant to them and to us your eternal blessing.

We remember those you called
      to proclaim judgement and renewal –
      like Isaiah, Ezekiel, Jeremiah –
      examples of openness to your word
      and courage in proclaiming it.
Grant to them and to us your eternal blessing.

We remember these and so many more
      leading up to the coming of Christ,
      and we remember also your servants
      who were a part of his ministry,
      or a part of his Church.
Grant to them and to us your eternal blessing.

We remember John the Baptist, the voice in the wilderness,
      Mary, the mother of Jesus,
      the twelve apostles, his friends and confidantes,
      the women at the empty tomb, looking in vain for his body,
      and all those countless individuals
      who were touched by his earthly ministry.
Grant to them and to us your eternal blessing.

We remember Peter, the Rock of the Church,
      Paul, apostle to the Gentiles,
      and those who have followed in their footsteps,
      saints known and unknown, near and far,
      yet each a part of the great company of your people
      in heaven and on earth.
Grant to them and to us your eternal blessing.

We remember those we have known,
      those who have been part of our own church,
      who have influenced our lives,
      who have inspired and encouraged us through their lives.
Grant to them and to us your eternal blessing.

We remember those around us,
>
> the churches of our town,
> Christians across the country,
> fellow-believers throughout the world.
>
> **Grant to them and to us your eternal blessing.**

And we pray finally for those who will come after us,
>
> all who will come to faith,
> offer their service,
> and live for Christ.
>
> **Grant to them and to us your eternal blessing.**

Loving God,
>
> we remember today all who have gone before us
> in the journey of faith.
> Help us and all who follow to run the race as they did,
> holding firm to the end.
>
> **Grant to them and to us your eternal blessing,**
> **through Jesus Christ our Lord.**
> **Amen.**

PART TWO

LIFE AND FAITH

OLD AND NEW YEAR

91

WATCHNIGHT PRAISE

Mighty God,
we come together at the end of another year,
with joy and gratitude in our hearts.

We come to lift up our voices,
to sing your praises,
and to declare your faithfulness.
Lord of past, present and future,
receive now our worship.

We gather with your people across the world,
to bring you our thanksgiving,
to offer our service,
and to seek your guidance.
Lord of past, present and future,
receive now our worship.

For the love we have received,
the care you have always shown,
and the help you have invariably given:
Lord of past, present and future,
receive now our worship.

For the mercy you have displayed,
the forgiveness you have offered,
and the renewal you have brought:
Lord of past, present and future,
receive now our worship.

For all you are,
all you have been,
and all you shall be:
Lord of past, present and future,
receive now our worship.

Meet with us now through this time of worship,
    so that through being here tonight
    we may grow closer to you and one another,
    and be equipped to work for your kingdom
    in the year ahead.
Lord of past, present and future,
    receive now our worship,
    through Jesus Christ our Lord.
    Amen.

92

WATCHNIGHT THANKSGIVING

Living God,
    once more we stand on the threshold of another year –
        at the end of an old chapter
        and the beginning of a new.
    We come to recall all you have done,
        and to look to all you shall yet do.
    Lord, always you have been by our side:
        go with us now.

We thank you for everything this past year has brought us –
    the fun enjoyed,
    the friendship shared,
    the lessons learned,
    the obstacles overcome,
    the dreams realised.
Lord, always you have been by our side:
    go with us now.

We ask your help in everything the future holds –
    all the challenges we shall face,
    the opportunities we shall glimpse,
    the initiatives we shall begin,
    the successes we shall achieve,
    and the disappointments we shall endure.
Lord, always you have been by our side:
    go with us now.

Living God,
    guide us in all the days ahead,
        so that in good or bad,
        success or failure,
        joy or sorrow,
        we may walk with you and work for your kingdom,
        until that day when Jesus comes,
        and we are one with you and all your people
        for all eternity.
Lord, always you have been by our side:
    go with us now,
    in the name of Christ.
    Amen.

93

NEW YEAR THANKSGIVING

Everlasting God,
>we have come together at the start of another year
>>to worship you.
>For all you mean to us,
>>**receive our praise.**

We come remembering all you have done for us
>over these past twelve months –
>the ways you have guided and taught us,
>the times you have offered us strength and support,
>the occasions you have specially surrounded us
>with your love and compassion.
For all you have given us,
>**receive our praise.**

We come now anticipating the year ahead,
>knowing you will always be watching over us through it,
>constantly working out your purpose in our lives,
>looking to lead us to a deeper understanding of your love.
For all you promise us,
>**receive our praise.**

Touch our hearts now as we join in worship,
>as we make time to dedicate ourselves again
>to one another,
>to you,
>and to your kingdom.
For all you ask of us,
>**receive our praise.**

Strengthen us,
>inspire us,
>equip us,
>and lead us forward in your service,
>in the name of Christ.
For all you do through him,
>**receive our praise.**
>**Amen.**

94

NEW YEAR PRAISE AND PETITION

Living God,
  on this first Sunday of another year we come to praise you,
    conscious that you have watched over us
    in the months gone by.
  You have blessed us in so much that is past,
  teach us to trust you for the future.

We praise you for the countless ways
    we have experienced your love –
    the faith you have nurtured,
    the strength you have given,
    the guidance you have offered.
  You have blessed us in so much that is past,
  teach us to trust you for the future.

We praise you for the fun we have enjoyed,
    the fellowship we have shared,
    the encouragement we have given and received.
  You have blessed us in so much that is past,
  teach us to trust you for the future.

We thank you for the ventures we have begun,
    the successes we have achieved,
    and the dreams we still have.
  You have blessed us in so much that is past,
  teach us to trust you for the future.

Living God,
  You have always been by our sides,
    your love constantly surrounding us,
    your hand supporting us
    whatever we have been called to face.
  You have blessed us in so much that is past,
  teach us to trust you for the future.

Grant now your blessing on the days ahead.
Help us to make the most of the opportunities that lie before us,
    to live each day to the full,
    and to stay faithful to you through good and bad,
    serving Christ in all we say and do.
You have blessed us in so much that is past,
    teach us to trust you for the future,
    for in his name we pray.
    Amen.

REDEDICATION SERVICE

95

REDEDICATION PRAISE

Loving God,
    We have come together today for a special purpose –
        to rededicate our lives to you,
        to commit ourselves afresh to your service,
        to declare again our faith,
        and to offer you our discipleship.
Take us and use us, we pray.

We come, conscious of all you have done for us –
        of your great faithfulness,
        your constant goodness,
        your unfailing mercy,
        your awesome goodness.
Take us and use us, we pray.

We come to praise you for your amazing grace.
Though we have forgotten you,
    you have not forgotten us.
Though we have failed you,
    always you have remained true.
Though we have strayed from your side,
    patiently you have drawn us back again.
Though we have disobeyed your will,
    still your love for us continues.
Take us and use us, we pray.

We come to thank you for the assurance you have given –
        that your purpose will never be defeated,
        your compassion never exhausted,
        your mercy never withheld,
        and your love never withdrawn.
Take us and use us, we pray.

Loving God,
    receive the worship we bring you,
        and help us to offer the same dedication to you
        as you offer to us.
    Take us and use us, we pray,
        in the name of Christ.
        Amen.

96

REDEDICATION PETITION

Almighty and loving God,
    great and wonderful, true and faithful,
        we come before you with thanksgiving,
        to sing your praise
        and celebrate your unfailing love and mercy.
    Greatly you have blessed us,
        gladly we respond.

We bring you then our worship,
        as a token of our gratitude and expression of our faith;
        as a way of acknowledging your goodness and guidance,
        the many blessings you have showered upon us
        throughout our lives.
    Greatly you have blessed us,
        gladly we respond.

Loving God,
    we come today to dedicate ourselves again to your service,
        to reaffirm our loyalty to Christ and his Church,
        and especially the family here
        of which we are part.
    Greatly you have blessed us,
        gladly we respond.

Speak to us through this service, we pray,
        so that, familiar though our words may be,
        they may stir and challenge our hearts.
    Greatly you have blessed us,
        gladly we respond.

Help us to consider carefully the promises we make this day,
        so that we may mean them with all our hearts,
        and be equipped to honour them in the days ahead.
    Greatly you have blessed us,
        gladly we respond.

Be present among us in this time of worship,
    so that we catch a new sense of your purpose,
    and a new vision of the future you would lead us to.
Greatly you have blessed us,
    gladly we respond,
    through Jesus Christ our Lord.
    Amen.

WEEK OF PRAYER FOR CHRISTIAN UNITY

97

THE FAMILY OF GOD
(based on 1 Peter 2:9-10)

Loving God,
    we thank you that you have called us together in this place
        as part of the great family of your people.

We praise you for the common bond
    you have given us in Christ –
    the fact that we gather here as friends,
    in fellowship with you and one another,
    and as part of the great company of your people
    in every time and place.
In one faith we have gathered:
    bind us together in love.

We praise you that through Jesus Christ
    we have become a chosen race,
    a royal priesthood,
    a holy nation,
    your own people,
    called to proclaim your mighty acts
    in leading us out of darkness into light.
Once we were no people,
    but you have called us to be the people of God,
    chosen and precious to you.
Once we had not received mercy,
    but now we have received your mercy in all its wonder!
In one faith we have gathered,
    bind us together in love.

Loving God,
  we praise you for your awesome love,
    so great that while we were yet sinners
    you gave your Son for us.
  We praise you for your limitless patience,
    always forgiving despite our failure to serve you as we should.
  We praise you for your constant care,
    watching over us as a father watches over his children.
  In one faith we have gathered,
    bind us together in love.

Help us to call you 'our Father' not just in name but in truth –
    to be obedient to you,
    to seek your guidance,
    to accept your discipline,
    and trust your judgement.
  Help us to learn what it means to be your people,
    to appreciate just how wide and great
    is the extent of your love.
  And teach us to show that same love and care
    in all our dealings with one another.
  In one faith we have gathered,
    bind us together in love.

Loving God,
  we meet together again as your people
  May we be encouraged through being with you
    and being with one another.
  So may your family in this church and all represented here,
    in this town and every place,
    grow and flourish to the glory of your name.
  In one faith we have gathered,
    bind us together in love,
    through Jesus Christ our Lord.
    Amen.

98

OUR FAILURE TO LIVE AS A FAMILY OF GOD'S PEOPLE

Almighty God,
  we come together today reminded again
    of your call to be one people,
    the body of Christ,
    united in faith,
    working together for your kingdom.
  We have called ourselves your family,
    but all too often have been a family divided.

Forgive the divisions we allow to come amongst us,
    our lack of concern for each other's welfare,
    our blindness to one another's needs,
    our reluctance to become involved meaningfully
    in ecumenical partnership.
  We have called ourselves your family,
    but all too often have been a family divided.

Almighty God,
  forgive us our failure to look outside ourselves
    to the wider family to which we belong.
  We have failed to be concerned
    with our brothers and sisters in Christ,
    those near and far away.
  We have not met together to encourage one another.
  We have been narrow in our outlook,
    refusing to broaden our horizons,
    and we have made ourselves and others the poorer for it.
  We have called ourselves your family,
    but all too often have been a family divided.

Almighty God,
help us to recognise our unity in Christ
with all your people in every place,
and to understand that whatever may divide us,
whatever we may disagree about,
it should never destroy the fellowship we share.
We have called ourselves your family,
but all too often have been a family divided.

Give us a true concern for all,
a genuine awareness of the wider fellowship
to which we belong,
a real openness to each other,
and a deep and sincere love for your people everywhere,
that all may see the bond in Christ that makes us one.
We have called ourselves your family:
help us to be a family united.
In the name of Christ.
Amen.

99

DIVIDED CHURCHES

Loving God,
    we pray for those many churches –
        far too many –
        which have experienced divisions among themselves,
        split apart over issues of doctrine, worship and authority.
    For all that denies our unity in Christ,
        forgive us, O Lord.

We pray for those whose faith
    has been undermined by such disputes,
    who feel hurt and let down by what has taken place,
    and we pray also for those left to pick up the pieces.
For all that denies our unity in Christ,
    forgive us, O Lord.

We pray for those outside the Church
    who have witnessed such division,
    those who have been put off by what they have seen,
    seeing it as an argument against the truth of the Gospel,
    a contradiction of everything we proclaim about you.
For all that denies our unity in Christ,
    forgive us, O Lord.

Loving God,
    unite your Church in every place,
        drawing together those of different denominations,
        temperaments, outlooks and traditions.
    May there be a respect between all,
        a willingness to work together,
        and a sense of unity that speaks beyond all those differences.
    For all that denies our unity in Christ,
        forgive us, O Lord,
        in his name.
        Amen.

LEPROSY SUNDAY

100

LEPROSY SUNDAY THANKSGIVING

Loving God,
  this is a day which reminds us how fortunate we are –
    how lucky to enjoy good health,
    to have a national health service,
    to receive medical care whenever we need it,
    to be part of a country where many once common diseases
    are a thing of the past,
    to have enough and more than enough to meet all our needs.
  Lord of all, as we have received,
    so teach us to give.

But it is also a day which reminds us of those less fortunate –
    those who suffer from afflictions like leprosy,
    those for whom the good things we enjoy are only a dream,
    those who do not have the levels of care we take for granted,
    those for whom disease is still an ever-present reality,
    those who do not have the resources to help themselves.
  Lord of all, as we have received,
    so teach us to give.

Loving God,
  help us to be truly thankful for all we have received,
    and to be thankful also for those, like Leprosy Mission,
    who have the compassion,
    the will,
    the faith,
    and the resolve,
    to do something for the needy of our world.
  Lord of all, as we have received,
    so teach us to give.

Help us to recognise the difference such organisations have made
    to so many lives,
    and the difference they could make to so many more
    if only they were given the means.
So may we show our thanksgiving,
    not only in words,
    nor simply in prayers,
    but through our actions,
    giving freely of ourselves in the cause of others.
Lord of all, as we have received,
    so teach us to give.

Loving God,
    reach out to those who cry to you,
        bringing your wholeness,
        your healing,
        new hope,
        new life.
Lord of all, as we have received,
    so teach us to give,
    in the name of Christ.
    Amen.

101

LEPROSY SUNDAY INTERCESSION

Loving God,
  we bring before you today
    the sick and suffering of our world,
    and especially we pray for those
    who suffer from the disease of leprosy,
    so horrible in its effects
    and yet potentially so easy to cure and prevent.
  Lord, in your mercy,
    hear our prayer.

Forgive us that so many people continue to endure the pain,
  the disfigurement,
  and the stigma associated with leprosy,
  when in real terms it would cost so little
  to wipe this disease out for ever.
Lord, in your mercy,
  hear our prayer.

Prosper the work of all those who, like Leprosy Mission,
  strive to bring help and healing.
Give them the words to get their message across,
  the resources to treat sufferers wherever they find them,
  and support in their drive
  to make leprosy a thing of the past.
Lord, in your mercy,
  hear our prayer.

Loving God,
  we pray also today for all who through disease or the fear of infection
    find themselves ostracised by society,
    and especially we think of those who suffer from AIDS,
    so different in its effects,
    so much harder to cure,
    yet for so many still having the same stigma attached,
    and creating the same feelings of despair and hopelessness.
  Lord, in your mercy,
    hear our prayer

Give hope and courage to all those who suffer,
 and give wisdom and inspiration
 to those who labour to find a cure.
Lord, in your mercy,
 hear our prayer.

We pray for those who fear they may be at risk,
 those who are anxious that they may unknowingly carry the virus,
 those who know they have the disease,
 who are terminally ill,
 or who have lost hope in the future.
Lord, in your mercy,
 hear our prayer.

Loving God,
 support and strengthen all those
 who share in your work of healing,
 all who labour to bring relief,
 all who seek in any way to show something
 of your love and compassion.
Lord, in your mercy,
 hear our prayer.

Grant to each one your wisdom and guidance,
 and work through them,
 so that those who suffer may find strength to face life or death
 with dignity, hope, and peace.
Lord, in your mercy,
 hear our prayer,
 in the name of Christ.
 Amen.

EDUCATION SUNDAY

102

EDUCATION SUNDAY APPROACH

Loving God,
    we come together on this new day,
        this first day of a new week,
        in the name of Christ who makes all things new.
God of truth,
    renew our faith.

We come grateful for the new opportunities this day will bring,
    the new experiences of your love we shall share in,
    the new life you have given to us in Jesus,
    the new light he brings on your promises of old.
God of truth,
    renew our hearts.

And especially today, on Education Sunday,
    we come reminded of the way
    Jesus brought new insights into ancient teaching,
    the way he saw behind the letter to the spirit,
    the simple yet unforgettable way he taught the multitudes.
God of truth,
    renew our minds.

Speak to us through our hymns and songs,
    our worship and fellowship,
    and our listening to your word,
    that through it all we may be guided by your Spirit into all truth.
God of truth,
    renew our souls.

Open our hearts and lives to everything you would teach us,
    and help us to listen,
    to understand,
    and to rejoice in your love.
God of truth,
    renew our lives,
    through Jesus Christ our Lord.
    Amen.

103

EDUCATION SUNDAY INTERCESSION

Father God,
    on this Education Sunday
        we pray for all those responsible for offering instruction.
    We pray especially for teachers in our schools,
        faced in recent years by so many changes,
        so many extra demands,
        so much that is new and unfamiliar,
        so much added responsibility,
        and all too often with so little resources or support.
    Equip them with the wisdom and enthusiasm they need
        to equip others for life.
    Lord, in your mercy,
        hear our prayer.

We pray for those whose morale is low,
    who question their ability to adapt,
    who find the pressures too demanding,
    who feel themselves to be undervalued and overworked.
Lord, in your mercy,
    hear our prayer.

Grant, we pray, that the importance of education in our society
    will be fully appreciated,
    that the contribution of all who teach,
    whether in schools, colleges or universities,
    by profession or as volunteers,
    will be properly recognised and rewarded.
Lord, in your mercy,
    hear our prayer.

And grant to all teachers everywhere
    the wisdom they need,
    the dedication, commitment, skill and sensitivity required,
    to nurture those in their care,
    develop their gifts,
    and prepare them for life ahead.
Equip them with the wisdom and enthusiasm they need
    to equip others for life.
Lord, in your mercy,
    hear our prayer,
    in the name of Christ.
    Amen.

MOTHERING SUNDAY

104

MOTHERING SUNDAY PRAISE

Gracious God,
   as a mother loves her child so you love us.
   For that great truth
      we praise and thank you.

We owe our very lives to you.
You have watched over us from our birth,
      tenderly nurturing us,
      showering us with love.
When we have needed you, you have been there.
For that great truth
      we praise and thank you.

You have given us strength in times of need,
      comfort in times of distress,
      encouragement in times of despair,
      guidance in times of uncertainty.
Whatever we have faced, you have been with us.
For that great truth
      we praise and thank you.

Gracious God,
   we have not always appreciated your love,
      all too often ignoring what you would teach us,
      disobeying your instructions,
      taking you for granted and wandering far from your side.
Yet through it all your love has remained constant.
For that great truth
      we praise and thank you.

Gracious God,
   caring for us more than you care for yourself,
      sacrificing your all for our sakes,
      loving us with an unquenchable love,
      you have called us all to be your children,
For that great truth
      we praise and thank you,
      in the name of Christ.
      Amen.

105

MOTHERING SUNDAY THANKSGIVING

Gracious God,
> on this special day we thank you for mothers –
>> our own mothers and mothers everywhere.
> Lord of love,
>> **hear our prayer.**

We thank you for all they do, or once did,
> all they give, or once gave,
> all they mean, and will always mean.
Lord of love,
> **hear our prayer.**

Grant to all entrusted with the responsibility of motherhood
> your wisdom,
> your guidance,
> your support.
Lord of love,
> **hear our prayer.**

We thank you that you love us as a mother loves her child –
> passionately, fiercely, devotedly, wholeheartedly –
> and that, like a mother, you watch over us
> every moment of every day,
> seeking our welfare,
> concerned about our progress,
> equipping us for the journey of life.
Lord of love,
> **hear our prayer.**

You are always there when we need you,
> ready to comfort, encourage and reassure,
> slow to punish and swift to bless.
Lord of love,
> **hear our prayer.**

Gracious God,
    we call you 'Our Father',
        but equally you are our Mother.
    Help us to learn what that means,
        and to rejoice in that truth.
    Lord of love,
        hear our prayer,
        in the name of Christ.
        Amen.

106

MOTHERING SUNDAY
THANKSGIVING AND INTERCESSION

Loving God,
    we thank you for this day –
        this day of remembering,
        rejoicing,
        and responding.
    Lord of all,
        hear our prayer.

We thank you for our homes and all we associate with them –
        the joy of family life,
        the debt we owe to our parents,
        and especially today the love of our mothers across the years.
    Lord of all,
        hear our prayer.

We thank you for the much wider family of which we are a part –
        the family of humankind,
        of this fellowship,
        and the Church universal.
    Lord of all,
        hear our prayer.

We thank you for the love you show us –
        the same love a mother feels for her child,
        the same patience and understanding,
        the same concern and protectiveness.
    Lord of all,
        hear our prayer.

Loving God,
    grant your blessing upon all mothers and all families this day;
        upon the family of humankind the world over,
        upon the family of your Church, here and everywhere.
Lord of all,
    hear our prayer.

And grant your special care and support
        to all those deprived of a mother's love,
        and all those who have not yet come to know
        your love for themselves.
Lord of all,
    hear our prayer,
    in the name of Christ.
    Amen.

107

MOTHERING SUNDAY INTERCESSION

Gracious God,
    you know what it is to love your children –
        to watch over them tenderly, anxiously,
        proudly, and constantly.
    You know what this means,
        for you have called us your children,
        and you care for each of us
        as deeply as a mother cares for her child.

So now we pray for those
    entrusted with the responsibility of motherhood –
    all those who watch over their children in the same way,
        with the same feelings and intensity.
Grant to each one your wisdom, guidance, and strength.
Lord of love,
    hear our prayer.

We pray especially for single mothers –
    those faced with the challenge
    of raising a child or children on their own,
    with no one else to share the demands or joys of parenthood.
Give to each of them patience, devotion, and dedication.
Lord of love,
    hear our prayer.

We pray for those who have lost their mothers
    or never known them,
    those orphaned as children or given up for adoption,
    those whose mothers have died
    all for whom this day brings pain rather than pleasure.
Grant them your comfort, your support,
    and the assurance of your love always with them.
Lord of love,
    hear our prayer.

We pray finally for those who are separated from their children –
    those whose children have moved far from home,
    those who have suffered a miscarriage
    or been through an abortion,
    those who have endured the agony of a child's death.
Give to them your help, your solace, and hope for the future.
Lord of love,
    hear our prayer.

Gracious God,
    you understand what mothers face,
        what they give,
        what they feel.
    Accept our thanks for them this day,
        and grant them your special blessing.
    Lord of love,
        hear our prayer,
        in the name of Christ.
        Amen.

CHRISTIAN AID WEEK

108

CHRISTIAN AID WEEK
THANKSGIVING AND INTERCESSION

Almighty and all-loving God,
    time and again across the years we have come to you,
        asking, in the words that Jesus taught us, for daily bread.
    We thank you for the wonderful way
        you have answered this prayer,
        providing not only what we ask but far more besides.
    You have given us bread and food in plenty,
        so much that we have little idea
        what it means to go hungry.

But we think now of the many people in our world
    who are less fortunate than we are –
    those facing famine,
    the homeless,
    those overwhelmed by disease,
    victims of war and genocide,
    those with inadequate means to provide for themselves
    or improve their situation,
    the weak, the sick, and the oppressed.
Lord, in your mercy,
    hear our prayer.

Reach out to them in their need,
    and give them courage and strength,
    the conviction that someone cares,
    a reason to look forward.
Lord, in your mercy,
    hear our prayer.

Almighty and all-loving God,
   grant your blessing on all who, like Christian Aid,
     strive to help the needy,
     all who campaign for their cause –
     who supply food and clothing,
     nursing and medicine,
     education and training,
     crops and machinery,
     the will and the opportunity to help themselves.
   Lord, in your mercy,
     hear our prayer.

Grant that those who are hungry may find bread for life,
     and teach us the part we must play in bringing that to pass,
     working for your kingdom not just in heaven,
     but here on earth.
   Lord, in your mercy,
     hear our prayer,
     in the name of Christ.
     Amen.

109

CHRISTIAN AID WEEK CONFESSION

Lord of all,
    we thank you for the world we live in –
        for the rich heritage of the nations,
        the bountiful resources of this earth,
        the astonishing diversity of your wonderful creation.
    You have given us so much:
        teach us to use it wisely.

Forgive us that we have taken what is so beautiful
    and created within it so much ugliness:
    hunger,
    injustice,
    exploitation,
    poverty,
    homelessness,
    war.
You have given us so much:
    teach us to use it wisely.

Forgive us that a few dine richly,
    whilst the many go hungry;
    that the resources of our world
    are disproportionately shared.
You have given us so much:
    teach us to use it wisely.

Forgive us our poor stewardship
    of all you have given us,
    our plundering of the earth's treasures
    with little thought for tomorrow.
You have given us so much:
    teach us to use it wisely.

Lord of all,
>
> grant your blessing on all who seek to build
>> a fairer and more just world –
>> those who, like Christian Aid, work to alleviate
>> poverty and hunger,
>> who fight against oppression,
>> who strive to bring opportunity to all.
>
> You have given us so much,
>> **teach us to use it wisely.**

And grant finally your wisdom to those whose decisions
>> will affect the lives of nations –
>> teach them to work for justice,
>> to pursue peace,
>> to promote harmony,
>> looking not just to the few
>> but to the common family of humankind.
>
> You have given us so much,
>> **teach us to use it wisely,**
>> **in the name of Christ we pray.**
>> **Amen.**

110

CHRISTIAN AID WEEK INTERCESSION
LIVING AS NEIGHBOURS

Living God,
>you have taught us through Jesus
>>that our neighbours are not just those who live next door,
>>or those who live nearby,
>>but everyone, everywhere.
>And so now, once again, we pray for our world,
>>our neighbours near and far.
>Lord of heaven and earth,
>>**hear our prayer.**

We pray for the victims of injustice –
>those who live in poverty,
>or face starvation,
>or have no roof over their heads.
Lord of heaven and earth,
>**hear our prayer.**

We pray for victims of natural disasters –
>those whose homes,
>loved ones,
>and lives have been destroyed through flood,
>earthquake, or other catastrophe.
Lord of heaven and earth,
>**hear our prayer.**

We pray for victims of war,
>those who mourn loved ones,
>those maimed and wounded,
>and those forced to flee as refugees,
>leaving possessions, livelihoods,
>and everything they hold dear.
Lord of heaven and earth,
>**hear our prayer.**

Living God,
   teach us to respond –
      to reach out to our troubled, divided world,
      recognising the call of our neighbour
      in the cry of the needy;
      to see that, whatever may divide us, more unites us,
      that beyond our differences lies a common humanity.
Lord of heaven and earth,
   hear our prayer.

Help us to ensure that love triumphs over hatred,
   goodness over evil,
   justice over corruption,
   and peace over war.
Lord of heaven and earth,
   hear our prayer.

May the time come when as individuals and as nations
   we live together as neighbours –
   members together of an extended family of humankind,
   for we ask it in the name of Christ.
Lord of heaven and earth,
   hear our prayer, for his sake.
   Amen.

111

CHRISTIAN AID WEEK INTERCESSION 2

Lord of all,
    we pray today for all in our world
        who are ill-equipped to cope with what life brings them –
        the poor, the hungry and the homeless;
        the disabled, the sick and the suffering;
        the oppressed, the weak, the persecuted.
    Lord, in your mercy,
        hear our prayer.

We pray for those denied their basic human rights –
    a basic education,
    employment,
    freedom of speech and conscience,
    or the proper reward for their labours.
Lord, in your mercy,
    hear our prayer.

We pray for those living in lands racked by war,
    victims of brutality and violence,
    and we pray for refugees,
    those with no country to call their own.
Lord, in your mercy,
    hear our prayer.

Lord of all,
    we thank you for those
        who have the courage to stand up for such people –
        the courage to stand out against injustice,
        and the faith to believe something can be done about it –
        organisations like Christian Aid who work tirelessly,
        despite powerful opposition,
        frequent misunderstanding,
        and all kinds of obstacles,
        to build a fairer world.
    Lord, in your mercy,
        hear our prayer.

Give them strength to continue their work,
   and give us the will to support their cause,
   not just once each year in Christian Aid week,
   but every day,
   through the lives we live,
   the sacrifices we make,
   and the faith we proclaim.
Lord, in your mercy,
   hear our prayer.
   in the name of Jesus Christ, our Lord.
   Amen.

FATHER'S DAY

FATHER'S DAY

112

FATHER'S DAY PRAISE

Loving God,
  we come on this Father's Day,
    reminded that you are the Father of us all.
You have been with us from our birth,
    guiding, nurturing, and sustaining us.
Father God,
  we praise you.

You have taught us and brought us to maturity,
    always concerned for our welfare,
    constantly seeking the best for us.
Father God,
  we praise you.

Whenever we have needed you, you have been there,
    willing to listen and advise,
    yet giving us freedom to make our own choices
    and find our own way.
Father God,
  we praise you.

You have called us to be your family,
    a people united through your Son, Jesus Christ,
    and through him you have revealed your love,
    a love that reaches out to us day by day
    despite our failure to love you in return.
Father God,
  we praise you.

Teach us to live as your children –
    to hear your voice,
    obey your instruction,
    and respond to your goodness.
Father God,
  we praise you.

Teach us to bear your name with pride,
>to share with others,
>through word and deed,
>the joy you have given us.
Father God,
>**we praise you.**

And finally receive our thanks
>for the fathers you have given us,
>all they have meant to us,
>all they have given,
>and all they have done in so many ways.
Father God,
>**we praise you,**
>**in the name of Christ.**
>**Amen.**

113

FATHER'S DAY CONFESSION

Gracious God,
   you are the Creator of the ends of the earth,
      and yet you call us your children.
   You are greater than we can ever begin to imagine,
      and yet you invite us to call you 'Our Father'.
   Always you have loved us:
      forgive our feeble response.

You do not keep us at arm's length,
      remote in your holiness,
      but you reach out your hands in love,
      wanting us to relate to you, one to one.
   Always you have loved us:
      forgive our feeble response.

Gracious God,
   forgive us that we call you 'Our Father',
      but fail to live as your children.
   We do not trust you as we should,
      preferring instead to follow our own inclinations.
   We are reluctant to accept your will,
      repeatedly disobeying your instructions.
   We are slow to seek your guidance,
      but swift to forget you and wander from your side.
   We all too rarely thank you for what we have,
      but all too often complain
      when we do not receive what we ask for.
   Always you have loved us:
      forgive our feeble response.

Gracious God,
> we have returned your love by acting like spoilt children,
>> yet still you have kept faith.
>
> Accept our thanks that, despite our wilfulness,
>> you refuse to give up on us,
>> working instead to draw us closer.
>
> You are always there for us,
>> waiting to welcome us back
>> and set us on our feet again.
>
> Always you have loved us:
>> **forgive our feeble response.**

Gracious God, our Father,
> we praise and thank you for your undeserved goodness,
>> and we resolve today
>> to live more faithfully as your children.
>
> Always you have loved us:
>> **forgive our feeble response.**
>> **In the name of Jesus Christ, your Son, our Lord.**
>> **Amen.**

114

FATHER'S DAY PETITION

Loving God,
  we come together on this Father's Day,
    reminded not just of our earthly fathers but of you.
  You tell us that all who believe in you
    shall be called your children,
    and you invite us to address you quite simply as 'Our Father'.
  For the wonder of your love,
    we praise you.

  We praise you that, despite all our weakness and disobedience,
    you view us not as subjects,
    or as servants,
    but as children.
  And we rejoice that you want us to see you
    not as some deity remote in splendour,
    nor as a jealous God demanding our homage,
    but as a father, watching over us
    with infinite care and tenderness.
  For the wonder of your love,
    we praise you.

Loving Father,
  teach us not simply to say 'Our Father',
    but to mean it –
    to recognise that you love us as deeply,
    as dependably,
    and as devotedly as any human father,
    and infinitely more besides.
  For the wonder of your love,
    we praise you.

Teach us that we matter to you,
    that you are concerned for our welfare,
    that you delight to bless us,
    that we need only to ask and you are there.
For the wonder of your love,
    we praise you.

Teach us that it is because you care so much
    that you instruct us,
    discipline us,
    and correct us.
For the wonder of your love,
    we praise you.

Teach us that, however far we stray from you,
    however much we may reject your love
    or ignore your guidance,
    still you go on reaching out,
    longing to draw us close once more.
For the wonder of your love,
    we praise you.

Loving God,
    you are 'Our Father' and we praise you.
Teach us to be your children,
    in the name of Christ.
    Amen.

115

FATHER'S DAY INTERCESSION

Gracious God,
    you know the joy of fatherhood and also the pain,
        for you witnessed the life and death of your Son,
        and you see each day the triumphs and tragedies of us,
        your children.
Lord God our Father,
    reach out in love.

In Jesus you experienced the delight of being a father –
    as you watched him grow and mature into adulthood,
    as you saw him baptised in the Jordan,
    as day by day he responded to your guidance,
    faithful to the very last –
    a beloved son with whom you were well pleased.
Yet also you experienced agony –
    in the horror of the Cross,
    the pain, the humiliation,
    and the sorrow he endured for our sakes.
Lord God our Father,
    reach out in love.

In each of us you find pleasure –
    when we pursue what is good,
    when we honour your commandments,
    when we seek your will and respond to your guidance.
But we cause you also so much pain –
    through our weakness,
    our repeated disobedience,
    our deafness to your call and our rejection of your love.
Lord God our Father,
    reach out in love.

Gracious God,
you know the joy and the pain of fatherhood,
and so now we pray for fathers everywhere.
Help them to appreciate both the privilege
and the responsibility they bear,
and teach them to give freely of themselves
so that they may discover the happiness,
the fulfilment,
and the inexpressible rewards that fatherhood brings.
Lord God our Father,
reach out in love.

Give them wisdom, patience, and dedication,
and grant them strength to persevere
when children brings tears as well as laughter,
anxiety as well as hope,
pain as well as pleasure.
Lord God our Father,
reach out in love.

Reach out, we pray, to all fathers in such circumstances –
those who question their ability to cope,
or who fear they have failed;
those striving to offer support,
or who feel they have nothing left to give.
Lord God our Father,
reach out in love.

And finally hear our prayer for children
who on this Father's Day feel pain instead of joy –
those whose fathers have died,
those orphaned as children,
those who have been mistreated, rejected, abused,
and those from broken homes
who barely see or know their fathers.
Lord God our Father,
reach out in love,
through Jesus Christ our Lord.
Amen.

HARVEST FESTIVAL

116

Harvest celebration

Loving God,
 we come this day to praise you,
  to celebrate your great goodness.
 We come with thanksgiving, joy and wonder,
  reminding ourselves of the richness of your creation,
  and acknowledging your faithfulness
  in providing for all our needs and far beyond!
 You have blessed us beyond our deserving:
  gladly we rejoice.

Loving God,
 for the beauty of the seasons,
  the constant cycle of day and night,
  and the vital gifts of rain and sunshine,
  we praise you.
 You have blessed us beyond our deserving:
  gladly we rejoice.

For the miracle of growth,
 the wonder of life,
 and the incredible variety of harvest,
 we bring you our thanksgiving.
You have blessed us beyond our deserving:
 gladly we rejoice.

Receive then our worship,
 accept our offerings,
 bless our celebration,
 and fill us with thankfulness for all you have given.
You have blessed us beyond our deserving:
 gladly we rejoice.
 In the name of Christ.
 Amen.

117

HARVEST PRAISE AND THANKSGIVING

Almighty and eternal God,
  we rejoice this day in the greatness of your love,
    the fullness of your provision.
  We come together surrounded by the fruits of your creation,
    the rich variety and plenty of another harvest.
  Once more you have blessed us,
    and we thank you.

Receive then our worship –
    for your giving and sustaining of life,
    for the constancy of the seasons,
    for the regular pattern of day and night,
    for the wonderful riches of our world.
  Once more you have blessed us,
    and we thank you.

Receive also our praise for the human labour
    that is part of harvest –
    the preparing and sowing,
    the cultivating and growing,
    the reaping and packaging,
    the transporting and selling.
  Once more you have blessed us,
    and we thank you.

Eternal God,
  we thank you that you allow us to work hand in hand with you,
    nurturing and gathering in the fruitfulness of your creation.
  Help us to recognise the responsibility that involves,
    and so to be faithful stewards of all you have given.
  So may our lives as well as our words
    offer to you our joyful praise and heartfelt worship.
  Once more you have blessed us,
    and we thank you,
    in the name of Christ.
    Amen.

118

Harvest for All

Living God,
    creator of all that is, and has been, and shall be,
      we thank you for this glad season and this special day.
    You have blessed us in so much:
      help us to respond.

We thank you for our world
    with all its rich and wonderful variety,
    for your gift of life
    constantly being renewed by your loving hand,
    for all that you have made to grow and flourish around us,
    all that provides our food and clothing,
    all the bountiful resources of this astonishing planet.
You have blessed us in so much:
    help us to respond.

We thank you for those to whom we owe this harvest –
    workers on farms and in agriculture,
    sailors and fishermen
    who risk their lives on the seas,
    miners and engineers
    who help supply the raw materials for industry,
    scientists and technicians
    who help develop better crops,
    employees in shops and factories
    who labour to satisfy our demands,
You have blessed us in so much:
    help us to respond.

Living God,
   help us to appreciate all so many do
      to bring us the fruits of creation,
      and teach us the part we must play
      in ensuring future generations can enjoy it in turn.
   Teach us to use your gifts wisely,
      responsibly
      effectively,
      so that nothing may be needlessly wasted
      or foolishly squandered.
   You have blessed us in so much:
      help us to respond.

   Help us to remember those who do not share equally
      in the rewards of harvest –
      the poor,
      the hungry,
      the homeless,
      the oppressed,
      those overwhelmed by disaster,
      and those whose crops have failed.
   Save us, we pray, from selfish indulgence,
      looking to our comforts and ignoring their needs.
   Inspire us to share from our plenty with all who cry out for help.
   You have blessed us in so much:
      help us to respond.

Living God,
   you have provided beyond our needs,
      enough for all in every place
      to have enough and more than enough.
   Forgive us that some still go hungry,
      and forgive our part within that.
   Stir our hearts so that we may challenge
      the consciences of governments and nations,
      until the time comes at last
      when your gifts are shared and enjoyed by all.
   You have blessed us in so much,
      help us to respond,
      in the name of Christ.
      Amen.

119

HARVEST INTERCESSION

Lord of all,
  as we thank you for our harvest
    we remember those who do not celebrate –
    those whose harvest is poor or non-existent,
    those with insufficient resources to tend their land,
    those denied a just reward for their labours,
    those whose harvest has been destroyed
    in the chaos of war or by natural disaster.
  Lord, you have blessed us richly:
  teach us to remember others.

Help us, as we celebrate our plenty,
    to remember those who have so much less –
    the poor and needy of our world,
    driven by famine, disaster or civil war
    to the brink of starvation.
Help us to respond with love and concern,
    offering whatever help we can.
Lord, you have blessed us richly:
  teach us to remember others.

Lord of all,
  speak to us at this harvest time,
    so that our hearts may be stirred
    and our consciences quickened.
Teach us to share our bounty with those who have nothing,
    so that the time may one day come
    when all have enough and none too much.
  Lord, you have blessed us richly:
  teach us to remember others,
  in the name of Christ.
  Amen.

ONE WORLD WEEK

120

ONE WORLD WEEK
RESPONSIBILITY TOWARDS OUR ENVIRONMENT

Creator God,
    you have given us the privilege of participating
        in the care and nurture of this world.
    You call us to work in partnership with you and one another,
        not simply serving ourselves,
        nor looking only to short-term interests,
        but conscious of our responsibility to our children
        and those who will follow them.
Teach us to be faithful stewards of creation.

Forgive us for mistakenly imagining
    we can work independently of you,
    living and acting as we please
    with no thought of the consequences.
Teach us to be faithful stewards of creation.

Forgive us for exploiting the treasures of this earth
    as though they are ours by right,
    wantonly destroying the environment in our thirst for gain.
Teach us to be faithful stewards of creation.

Forgive us for losing our sense of wonder
    before the magnificence of your creation,
    abusing all you have given
    instead of handling it with respect.
Teach us to be faithful stewards of creation.

Forgive us for living today as if there will be no tomorrow,
    squandering finite resources,
    heedless of our responsibilities to others or to you.
Teach us to be faithful stewards of creation.

Forgive us for always seeking more while others have nothing,
    satisfying our needs while a multitude go hungry.
Teach us to be faithful stewards of creation.

Creator God,
    teach us to work not just for ourselves but for all,
        to recognise we are indeed stewards of creation
        rather than its masters,
        answerable finally to you for what we do with it.
    Teach us to give thanks for all you have given us,
        and to play our part in ensuring
        that those who come after us may share in it too.
Teach us to be faithful stewards of creation.
In the name of Christ we pray.
    Amen.

121

ONE WORLD WEEK
FAMILIES AND FELLOWSHIP

Loving God,
    We come to you today as the family of your people,
        those you have united in Christ.
        and as we come, reminded of that great truth,
        we give you thanks for all the families
        to which we belong.
    Lord of all,
        join us together in love.

We think of the families among whom we have been raised –
        those with whom we have shared so much,
        to whom we are specially close,
        and who will always be uniquely precious to us.
    Lord of all,
        join us together in love.

We think of the family of this church –
        the fellowship we find here,
        the friends we have made,
        and the encouragement we give to one another.
    Lord of all,
        join us together in love.

We think of the family of the Church as a whole –
        those across this country,
        across the world,
        across the centuries who are one with us in Christ.
    Lord of all,
        join us together in love.

We think of the family of humankind,
   the common bond that ties us together,
   the variety of peoples and nations
   of which we form a part,
   the diversity of cultures, customs.
Lord of all,
   join us together in love.

Loving God,
   we thank you that we share something in common
      with all people near and far,
      our lives interwoven, inter-related,
      interdependent, intertwined.
Help us we pray to recognise more fully what that means,
      to appreciate the responsibilities it brings
      and the opportunities to share it offers,
      and so may we learn to love our neighbours as ourselves.
Lord of all,
   join us together in love,
   for the sake of Jesus Christ our Lord.
   Amen.

122

ONE WORLD WEEK THANKSGIVING
OUR COMMON HUMANITY

Gracious God,
    we thank you for our country –
        for its history,
        its traditions,
        its culture,
        and its abundance of good things.
    You have given us much to celebrate:
        receive our praise.

We thank you for the riches we enjoy as a society –
        material comforts in abundance,
        freedom of speech and worship,
        security through our health service and welfare state,
        beautiful countryside and thriving towns and cities;
        all this, and so much more.
You have given us much to celebrate:
        receive our praise.

We thank you that we have so much
    to be proud of and grateful for.
But we thank you also today for our world –
        its rich assortment of nations,
        and the histories and traditions which are part of them,
        an awesome diversity of countries and continents,
        and languages within them;
        a fascinating mixture of people, places, customs, cultures,
        with so much to teach us and so much to offer.
You have given us much to celebrate:
        receive our praise.

We thank you for everything that contributes
  towards the world-wide community –
  the insights of different religions and philosophies,
  the interchange of ideas between races and cultures,
  the promotion of dialogue concerning global issues,
  the desire to establish justice and peace among all nations.
You have given us much to celebrate:
  receive our praise.

We thank you that we all have something to receive
  from the wider world,
  and something to offer it;
  that our horizons are constantly being stretched,
  and our thinking broadened.
You have given us much to celebrate:
  receive our praise.

Gracious God,
  you have given us one world.
Help us to live as responsible citizens within it,
  united together in our common humanity,
  and bound together in you.
You have given us much to celebrate:
  receive our praise,
  through Jesus Christ our Lord.
  Amen.

123

ONE WORLD WEEK
THE COMPLEXITY AND ORDER OF THE WORLD

Loving God,
    we thank you for the wonder of your creation –
        the beauty of our world,
        the vastness of the universe,
        and the richness of our lives.
In all you have given,
    teach us to see your hand.

We praise you for all you have made
    and the place you have given us within creation.
You have surrounded us with so much that is good,
    and we marvel at it –
    plants, animals, trees, birds,
    mountains, valleys, continents, oceans,
    towns, cities, nations and people:
    a world of infinite beauty and wonder.
In all you have given,
    teach us to see your hand.

We thank you that out of chaos you brought order,
    an order that we can depend upon, explore and understand,
    that shapes the very pattern of our universe,
    that reflects your sovereign and guiding purpose.
In all you have given,
    teach us to see your hand.

Loving God,
>help us to appreciate the wonder of your creation,
>>open to the new discoveries which research daily brings.
>Save us from closing our minds
>>to that which challenges our convictions;
>>from retreating into narrow-thinking,
>>or blind prejudice,
>>or some ivory tower removed from the real world.
>In all you have given,
>>**teach us to see your hand.**

Help us to see that as our understanding of creation grows
>so we see more of your greatness –
>our sense of awe, wonder and astonishment
>enlarged by the insights of modern science.
But help us also to recognise the limitations of scientific study –
>aware of the things it can't answer as much as the things it can,
>awake to its weaknesses as well as its strengths,
>open to spiritual reality as well as empirical truth.
In all you have given,
>**teach us to see your hand.**

Loving God,
>give wisdom to those involved in research
>>and all who must legislate upon its application,
>>and grant your guidance to all who strive
>>to improve the quality of our lives through their investigations.
>Teach them and us to use creation wisely,
>>employing its resources for good
>>rather than exploiting them for evil,
>>and thinking not simply of ourselves
>>but all who will follow us.
>In all you have given,
>>**teach us to see your hand,**
>>**for we ask it in the name of Christ.**
>>**Amen.**

REMEMBRANCE DAY

124

REMEMBRANCE DAY REFLECTION
TO THE UNKNOWN SOLDIER

(It is hard for us to imagine the full horror of what so many have been through in war, but it is vital that we try, for only then can we appreciate all we owe to the millions we remember today, and so understand the importance of maintaining peace for future generations. The following reflection, written during a visit to the war graves of Flanders, asks how it must have felt to be one of the countless young men sent out to the battlefields of 'The Great War'. It is offered as a possible introduction to the two minutes' silence and subsequent prayers of remembrance.)

How did you feel that morning
    when the call up papers came through?
Did your blood run cold, or excitement take hold
    at the thought that your country needs you?

How did you feel that morning
    when the time came to set off from home?
Did you conquer your fears, or break down in tears
    with the loved ones you'd soon leave alone?

How did you feel that morning
    when you first set foot in the trench?
Did you brush it aside, or wish you could hide
    from the horror, the carnage, the stench?

How did you feel that morning
    when your friend was blown up by a shell?
Did you rush to his aid, or just stand there, afraid
    that you'd somehow been whisked off to hell?

How did you feel that morning
    when they sent you over the top?
Did you shout with relief, or in sheer disbelief,
    vainly pray that this nightmare would stop?

How did you feel that morning
   when the bullets started to fly?
Did you think even then you might cheat death again,
   or did you know you were going to die?

How did you feel that morning
   as the lifeblood slipped slowly away?
Did you try to make sense of these crazy events
   or with one final breath try to pray?

How do I feel this morning
   in the face of such slaughter and sorrow?
Do I just stand aghast as I think of the past
   or give all for a better tomorrow?

125

REMEMBRANCE DAY REFLECTION
TEARS OF VICTORY

(For over fifty years in Britain we have enjoyed peace. There have, of course, been confrontations involving British forces, both in the Falklands and the Gulf War, but civilians at home have been largely untouched by the fighting. There is a danger that we might come to take peace for granted, forgetting the price at which it was won, and the ease with which it could be lost. The following reflection, again offered as an introduction to the time of silence and subsequent prayers of remembrance, reminds us of the celebrations which followed the declaration of peace after two world wars, but speaks also of the personal tragedies which for many scarred that peace for ever.)

There were crowds in the streets of London the day the peace was signed,
    they sang in exultation; they danced, they wined, they dined;
    for the dreadful war was over, the slaughter at an end,
    and now at last a broken world could slowly start to mend.
But among the celebrations, the cheerful, happy cries,
    a multitude were weeping, no laughter in their eyes.
For these there was no reason to share the festive mood,
    their hearts were bowed with sorrow, their every thought subdued.
For while the throng around them gave vent to shouts of joy,
    they grieved a loving husband, they mourned their precious boy,
    they thought of dads or brothers, of cousins, nephews too,
    of uncles, colleagues, trusted friends, so many they once knew.

So when some talk of glory, of mighty deeds once done,
    think also of the suffering with which it all was won.
And when they speak of victory upon that glorious day,
    remember all those buried in fields so far away.
It's true that time's a healer, and it was all long ago,
    it's true we've learned to live with the ones we once called foe;
    but many still are haunted by thought of those they lost,
    still struggling with their feelings, still counting out the cost.
So if you would pay tribute and honour those who fell,
    then work for peace and justice, and make your freedom tell.
There is no way more fitting we can repay the debt,
    nor better way of saying that we will not forget.

126

REMEMBRANCE DAY APPROACH

Almighty God,
   we come this day to remember and learn –
      to remember the lessons of the past:
         the cost of war,
         the price of peace,
         the scope of human depravity,
         the extent of human self sacrifice.
   Remind us of all we owe,
      lest we forget.

Help us to learn those lessons –
      to live and work for peace,
      to fight only what is evil and corrupt.
      to serve and not to count the cost,
      to give our all in the cause of a better world.
   Remind us of all we owe,
      lest we forget.

Almighty God,
   we come to remember all you have done –
      your creative acts,
      your mighty deeds throughout history,
      your dealings with your people,
      your gift of Christ,
      your love experienced daily in our lives.
   Remind us of all we owe,
      lest we forget.

Forgive us that so often and so easily we do forget.
We fail to remember your sovereign transforming power,
      to remember you in the good times as well as the bad,
      to see you in the fellowship of your Church,
      to count our many blessings,
      to recognise your hand at work in every moment of our lives.

Almighty God,
through all things you remember us –
help us to remember you!
Remind us of all we owe,
lest we forget.
We ask it in the name of Christ.
Amen.

127

REMEMBRANCE DAY CONFESSION

(This prayer may be used following the traditional time of silence and words of remembrance.)

Loving God,
  once more we have been reminded
    of the terrible cost of war,
    the suffering and sacrifice of so many,
    the depths of inhumanity some have sunk to,
    and the heights others have climbed in the service of others.
  Teach us to remember,
    not just today but always.

We have heard again today words
  which have been spoken so many times over the years,
  words which we ourselves have shared time and again:
  'Lest we forget.'
Yet the tragedy is we do forget, all too easily –
  this annual remembrance all too easily a token gesture,
  observed sincerely and respectfully
  but then over and done with for another year.
Teach us to remember,
  not just today but always.

We forget how fortunate we are to live in freedom,
  how lucky we are to enjoy peace.
We forget how some still suffer from the wounds of battle,
  and others even now mourn their loved ones.
Teach us to remember,
  not just today but always.

Loving God,
forgive us that, despite our words and best intentions,
we have so often forgotten the lessons of the past.
Speak to us through all we have heard and shared today,
so that we can truly say,
and truly mean,
'We will remember them.'
Teach us to remember,
not just today but always,
for we ask it in the name of Christ our Lord.
Amen.

128

REMEMBRANCE DAY THANKSGIVING

Almighty God,
    we thank you today for all those
        who across the ages have been examples of courage,
        all whose words and actions
        have given inspiration to subsequent generations.
    In glad thanksgiving,
        we will remember them.

We thank you for those who have had the courage
        to stand up for their convictions, come what may;
        to fight against evil and injustice,
        even at the cost of their own lives;
        to live out their faith and share it with others
        in the face of bitter opposition.
    In glad thanksgiving,
        we will remember them.

And especially this day we thank you
        for those who displayed such courage
        in all the horror of war –
        those who fought so bravely,
        who served so faithfully,
        and who sacrificed so greatly
        for the cause they believed in.
    In glad thanksgiving,
        we will remember them.

We give thanks for the freedom we enjoy
        through their sacrifice,
        we salute their courage,
        we acknowledge again the debt we owe them,
        and we remember, so that the lessons of the past
        may not be forgotten or the sacrifices wasted.
    In glad thanksgiving,
        we will remember them.
    Thanks be to God.
        Amen.

129

REMEMBRANCE DAY PETITION

Living God,
    on this day we are called to remember the past –
        all those who lost their lives in the course of wars,
        the horror they endured,
        the determination they displayed
        to defend the values we hold so dear today,
        the sacrifices they made
        so that we now might enjoy lasting peace.
    Lord, in your mercy,
        hear our prayer.

Living God,
    forgive us that, despite our words, all too easily we forget –
        we fail to learn the lessons of the past,
        we forget the debt we owe,
        we take for granted the security we enjoy,
        we do not work for the kind of world
        so many gave their lives for.
    Lord, in your mercy,
        hear our prayer.

Living God,
    let there be peace in our world where now there is war,
        and grant that the time will come
        when nations will live together,
        justly,
        openly,
        and harmoniously
        in a common fellowship of humankind.
    Lord, in your mercy,
        hear our prayer
        in the name of the one who came in peace,
        Jesus Christ our Lord.
        Amen.

130

REMEMBRANCE DAY INTERCESSION

Living God,
   we are here to remember –
      to remember again the awful cost of war,
      to remember the millions
      who gave their lives for the cause of freedom,
      to remember the courage and heroism,
      fear and pain, tragedy and grief of so many.
   At the going down of the sun, and in the morning,
   we will remember them.

Living God,
   we are here to remember all of this, and much more besides –
      those who still mourn the loved ones they lost,
      those whose lives even now are blighted by war,
      those scarred in body, mind or spirit,
      those for whom warfare has meant
      life can never be the same again.
   At the going down of the sun, and in the morning,
   we will remember them.

And we remember also those who strive
      to establish and maintain peace –
      governments and world leaders,
      United Nations' forces and diplomats,
      pressure groups and ordinary people;
      all who in different ways strive
      to promote harmony between nations,
      giving victims of war the opportunity
      to live a normal life once more.
   At the going down of the sun, and in the morning,
   we will remember them.

Living God,
  we remember today the cost of war,
    and the price of peace.
  Help us to go on remembering, tomorrow and every day,
    and to do all in our power to work for your kingdom,
    here on earth.
  At the going down of the sun, and in the morning,
    we will remember them,
    in the name of Christ.
    Amen.

SONGS OF PRAISE/
MUSIC SERVICE

131

MUSIC SERVICE
MAKING MUSIC

Living God,
    you tell us to sing your praises,
        to make music in our hearts,
        to lift up our voices in joyful adoration.
    We come with gladness:
        receive the worship we offer.

We bring you this service of celebration –
    our hymns,
    our songs,
    our music –
    and we offer them gladly to you,
    as an expression of thanksgiving,
    an outpouring of praise,
    and a token of our love.
We come with gladness:
    receive the worship we offer.

Living God,
    uplift us through this time together.
    May it speak to us of all you have done
        and continue to do through Christ,
        and so may there always be a song of praise on our lips,
        and music in our hearts.
    We come with gladness:
        receive the worship we offer,
        through Jesus Christ our Lord.
        Amen.

132

SONGS OF PRAISE
OFFERING OUR WORSHIP

Loving God,
  we come this day with a song in our hearts,
    to celebrate your gift of music,
    to lift up our voices in glad thanksgiving,
    to make a joyful noise to you!
  With all the company of heaven,
    we sing your praise.

You have given us so much to celebrate,
    so much to rejoice in.
It is good to give thanks,
    right to be glad,
    fitting to show our joy in music and song.
With all the company of heaven,
    we sing your praise.

So now we bring you this service –
    as an act of worship,
    an expression of thanksgiving,
    and an outpouring of our love.
With all the company of heaven,
    we sing your praise.

Receive our praise,
    accept our songs,
    and fill our hearts with joy and thanksgiving,
    as we remember the wonder of your love,
    and rejoice in all you have done for us.
With all the company of heaven,
    we sing your praise,
    through Jesus Christ our Lord.
    Amen.

133

SONGS OF PRAISE
INTERCESSION FOR THOSE WITH NOTHING TO CELEBRATE

Loving God,
   we have come to you in song,
      expressing our joy and gratitude
      for all you have done,
      and all you have given.
   But we come now to pray for all in our world
      who feel they have nothing to sing about,
      nothing to celebrate or rejoice over –
      the poor, the sick and the hungry,
      the homeless, the unemployed, the downtrodden,
      the weak, the vulnerable and the oppressed,
      the lonely, the unloved and the unwanted,
      the sorrowful, the depressed and the despairing,
      the sick, the diseased, the dying.
   Lord, in your love, put a new song into their hearts –
      a song of hope instead of despair.

We pray for those for whom life brings intolerable demands –
      those facing famine,
      fleeing as refugees,
      suffering persecution,
      enduring war,
      struggling against injustice,
      terrified of the future,
      haunted by the past.
   Lord, in your love, put a new song into their hearts –
      a song of victory instead of defeat.

Loving God,
  reach out in compassion to all in such circumstances,
    assuring them that despite appearances you are there,
    sharing their pain,
    anxious for their welfare,
    hungry to bless.
  Lord, in your love, put a new song into their hearts –
    a song of life instead of death.

May the day come when they, with us,
  join in singing songs of praise,
    to the glory of your name.
    Amen.

CHURCH ANNIVERSARY

134

CHURCH ANNIVERSARY PRAISE

Loving God,
    on this day of thanksgiving and celebration
        we praise you for who and what you are.
    We marvel at your great goodness,
        the love and care, mercy and forgiveness
        you have so faithfully shown to us;
        the strength, support, guidance and inspiration
        you have so freely given.
    Loving God,
        for all the ways you are with us,
        we praise you!

Gracious God,
    on this day of memories as we recall the past
        we praise you for all you have done for us –
        the lessons we have learned,
        the blessings we have received,
        the friends we have loved,
        the goals we have reached,
        the faith that has grown.
    Gracious God,
        for all the gifts you have showered upon us,
        we praise you!

Living God,
    on this day of looking forward and anticipating the future
        we praise you for everything you shall yet do among us –
        all that life continues to offer,
        all we have still to attempt and experience,
        all who in time will become part of our fellowship,
        all that will test and challenge us,
        and all which will bring us joy and fulfilment
        in the years ahead.
    Living God,
        for all you still hold in store,
        we praise you!

Almighty God,
    for all you are,
        all you have been,
        and all you shall be,
        we praise you,
        in the name of Christ!
        Amen.

135

CHURCH ANNIVERSARY
THANKSGIVING FOR OUR PAST

Loving God,
  we thank you for all you have done in our lives –
    the ways you have taught us,
    helped us,
    and provided for us so wonderfully.
  Take us now,
    and lead us forward.

We thank you for all you have done in our church –
    the fellowship you have created,
    the service inspired,
    and the faith nurtured.
  Take us now,
    and lead us forward.

We thank you for those who have helped to shape our lives –
    all who have inspired,
    challenged,
    and guided us across the years.
  Take us now,
    and lead us forward.

We thank you for those who have helped build up this church –
    its founders,
    its ministers,
    and its successive generations of believers.
  Take us now,
    and lead us forward.

Loving God,
  we thank you for our past,
    and we ask your guidance for the future.
  Help us to learn from everything that has been,
    so that we can make the most of what is,
    and work wisely towards what shall be.
  Take us now,
    and lead us forward,
    in the name of Christ.
    Amen.

136

ANNIVERSARY SUNDAY
GOD'S FAITHFULNESS

Gracious God,
    on another Anniversary Sunday
        we come to celebrate again your great faithfulness,
        to remember everything you have done for us,
        and so to look forward with confidence
        to all the future yet holds.
For the assurance of your continuing goodness,
    we praise and thank you, O Lord.

Always you have been with us,
    seen or unseen, acknowledged or unacknowledged,
    your spirit at work in our lives,
    surrounding us with your love,
    delivering us from evil,
    nurturing our faith,
    leading us to a deeper awareness
    of your eternal purpose in Jesus Christ.
For the assurance of your continuing goodness,
    we praise and thank you, O Lord.

You have been with us as a church from the beginning,
    calling us into being,
    directing our life and witness,
    speaking your word,
    renewing our commitment,
    binding us together in fellowship,
    and sending us out in faith.
For the assurance of your continuing goodness,
    we praise and thank you, O Lord.

Inspire us today through the example of those
    who have run the race before us.
Help us to play our part in continuing what they have begun.
May our love for you be equally as real,
    our worship as sincere,
    our witness as faithful,
    and our faith as strong.
For the assurance of your continuing goodness,
    we praise and thank you, O Lord.

Gracious God,
    we stand today between the past and the future.
Help us to grasp the present and live it to your glory,
    in the name of Christ.
    Amen.

137

ANNIVERSARY CELEBRATION

Loving God,
    we are here today to celebrate,
        to offer our thanks
        for your immeasurable and inexpressible goodness.
    Greatly you have blessed us;
        gladly we rejoice.

For leading us throughout our lives,
        patiently unfolding your will and revealing your love,
        we thank you.
Greatly you have blessed us;
        gladly we rejoice.

For leading this church from its earliest days,
        helping your people here to grow
        in faith and commitment,
        we thank you.
Greatly you have blessed us;
        gladly we rejoice.

For all who have been part of our history,
        all who have served this church so faithfully
        in past and present,
        we thank you.
Greatly you have blessed us;
        gladly we rejoice.

For those who have been an inspiration to us,
        offering an example to follow,
        we thank you.
Greatly you have blessed us;
        gladly we rejoice.

For the fellowship we share in Christ,
    the joy of growing and working together through him,
    we thank you.
Greatly you have blessed us;
    gladly we rejoice.

For all the past has given and all the future holds,
    the certainty that nothing finally
    shall ever separate us from your love,
    we thank you.
Greatly you have blessed us,
    gladly we rejoice.

Loving God,
    help us, as we celebrate another year in the life of our church,
    to appreciate all you have done,
    trust in all you will yet do,
    and recognise all you are doing, here and now.
Greatly you have blessed us,
    gladly we rejoice,
    in the name of Christ.
    Amen.

138

ANNIVERSARY REMEMBRANCE

Lord God our Father,
    we thank you today for all who have contributed
        to the life of this church over the years.

We remember those who have served as ministers,
    and we thank you for the guidance,
    leadership and pastoral care
    each has offered in their own special way.
God of past, present and future,
    receive our praise.

We remember those who have held positions of responsibility
    within this fellowship,
    and we thank you for the faithful work
    they have performed among us.
God of past, present and future,
    receive our praise.

We think of those who have worked behind the scenes,
    often unnoticed,
    and we thank you for the vital contribution
    they have made to our life together.
God of past, present and future,
    receive our praise.

We think of those whose vision it first was
    to start this church,
    and we thank you for the labour and sacrifice
    that went into turning that dream into reality.
God of past, present and future,
    receive our praise.

We think of those who in a multitude of ways
    have shared their faith with others,
    and we thank you for all
    who have come to know you as a result.
God of past, present and future,
    receive our praise.

We think of all we have known in this church,
    enriching us by their presence,
    and we thank you for the example
    of their faith and commitment.
God of past, present and future,
    receive our praise.

For all that has been done,
    and all we have received,
    may we be truly thankful.
God of past, present and future,
    receive our praise,
    in the name of Christ.
    Amen.

139

ANNIVERSARY PETITION

Loving God,
   we thank you for this building set aside for you,
      this place in which we come together to worship,
      to celebrate,
      and to share fellowship in Christ.
   Lord of the Church,
      hear our prayer.

We thank you for all that lies behind this building –
      the sacrifices that have gone into its upkeep,
      the efforts over the years to maintain and improve it,
      the people who have given their time, money, and energy
      to make it what it is today.
   Lord of the Church,
      hear our prayer.

We thank you for the memories this place holds,
      the special events we have shared here,
      the activities which have taken place within these walls,
      the times of praise and worship shared together.
   Lord of the Church,
      hear our prayer.

Loving God,
   teach us to play our part in looking after this sanctuary,
      ensuring it may serve the generations to come
      as well as it has served us.
   Teach us to give generously when the need is put before us,
      so that it may always be honouring to you.
   Lord of the Church,
      hear our prayer.

But teach us also always to remember
    that your Church is not finally about a building
    or bricks and mortar,
    but about people –
    the fellowship we share,
    the people we are,
    the things we do
    and the way we live.
Lord of the Church,
    hear our prayer.

So above all today we thank you
    for those who have been part of this church –
    members,
    worshippers,
    congregation,
    all who contributed
    towards the life of the fellowship here.
Lord of the Church,
    hear our prayer.

We thank you for those who have inspired us,
    offering an example to follow,
    and we praise you for the enrichment we have found
    simply through sharing together,
    united in love and faith.
Lord of the Church,
    hear our prayer.

For all that has been attempted,
    all experienced,
    and all accomplished,
    we offer you our praise.
Lord of the Church,
    hear our prayer.

Loving God,
>help us to live as your people –
>>to draw closer to you and one another,
>>to appreciate the gifts you have given to us and to all,
>>to recognise what you call us to be,
>>and why you call us to it.
>Lord of the Church,
>>**hear our prayer.**

Help us never to allow bricks and mortar
>to obscure our view of people,
>our concern with fabric
>to overshadow our concern for your kingdom.
But help us also to recognise that the way we care for our building
>will speak to many of how much we care for you.
Receive then our worship,
>accept our thanksgiving,
>bless our gifts,
>and use all that we offer this day,
>both people and building,
>towards the growth of your kingdom.
Lord of the Church,
>**hear our prayer,**
>**in the name of Christ.**
>**Amen.**

CHURCH MEETINGS

140

MEETING TOGETHER

Living God,
   we come, as your people across the years have come,
      seeking your guidance,
      hungry to know your will and understand your purpose.
   You have called us to be your people;
      help us to hear your voice.

We come bringing the life of our fellowship before you –
      our practical and spiritual needs,
      our hopes and fears,
      joys and sorrows,
      successes and failures.
   You have called us to be your people;
      help us to hear your voice.

Give us faith and wisdom to discern your will,
      vision and courage to respond to it.
Give us patience and understanding in our discussions together,
      openness to other opinions,
      and a spirit of love where we disagree.
   You have called us to be your people;
      help us to hear your voice.

Living God,
   we do not think only of ourselves
      but also those not with us at this time –
      those prevented from coming by ill-health,
      age, infirmity, or other commitments;
      those who have lost their faith
      or their sense of belonging to this fellowship;
      those still uncertain of their commitment;
      those who have not yet reached the point
      of expressing their faith.
   Teach us to respond sensitively to each one,
      making real our love in Christ,
      and showing a genuine concern for all.
   You have called us to be your people;
      help us to hear your voice.

Living God,
we thank you for the privilege of meeting together.
Open our hearts to you,
to one another,
and all around us,
so that we may truly meet in heart and mind and soul.
You have called us to be your people;
help us to hear your voice,
through Jesus Christ our Lord.
Amen.

141

CHURCH MEETINGS
SEEKING GOD'S GUIDANCE

Gracious God,
   once more we bring to you the life of our church.

We ask for your guidance as we look to the future –
   help us grow in faith,
   in fellowship,
   and in numbers.
Lord of your Church,
   hear our prayer.

We ask for guidance in our daily living –
   help us to draw closer to you,
   to learn more each day of your love,
   and to show the truth of what we believe in our lives.
Lord of your Church,
   hear our prayer.

We ask for guidance in our life together –
   help us to draw closer to one another,
   to show genuine care and concern in all our dealings,
   to support each other wherever possible.
Lord of your Church,
   hear our prayer.

We ask for guidance in our witness –
   help us to draw closer
   to the community around our church,
   to serve wherever we see need,
   and to proclaim the Good News of Christ
   whenever the opportunity arises.
Lord of your Church,
   hear our prayer.

We pray for those who specially need your guidance,
    those facing problems unknown to us,
    those for whom advancing years
    bring illness or infirmity,
    those who have drifted away from us and from you,
    those for whom life is dark and difficult.
Lord of your Church,
    hear our prayer.

May each in their different situations feel your presence,
    and know your support,
May they know they are still remembered and valued,
    and find encouragement in that knowledge.
Lord of your Church,
    hear our prayer.

Gracious God,
    we thank you for this opportunity to meet together
        and discuss affairs large and small.
    And we thank you for the assurance
        that Christ is here among us as we gather in his name.
    Speak to us,
        through your word, your Spirit,
        and the fellowship we share,
        so that in all our thinking, talking, planning and deciding
        we may discern your will
        and work more effectively to fulfil your purpose.
    Lord of your Church,
        hear our prayer,
        in the name of Christ.
        Amen.

142

CHURCH MEETINGS
GOD'S PEOPLE TOGETHER

Loving God,
    we thank you for the privilege of meeting together,
        for all we can give and receive at times like these –
        the happiness,
        the support,
        the encouragement,
        and the inspiration that comes through sharing fellowship.
    We come in the name of Christ:
        meet with us now.

We thank you for everything we have experienced together –
    the times of worship,
    of study and reflection,
    of sharing our faith,
    of simply enjoying each other's company.
We come in the name of Christ:
    meet with us now.

Loving God,
    forgive us that we have sometimes made the mistake
        of merely meeting,
        rather than meeting together.
    Forgive us that we have sometimes
        gone through the motions of fellowship,
        when in reality we have lost sight of its true meaning.
    Forgive us that we have sometimes
        been so concerned about ourselves or our church,
        that we have forgotten about each other.
We come in the name of Christ,
    meet with us now.

Open our hearts now to you and to one another.
Give us a willingness to trust and be trusted,
    a readiness to listen and to understand,
    an openness of mind and spirit,
    an attitude of compassion and consideration.
May we always be conscious of Christ among us,
    and in meeting together with him
    may we come together ourselves.
We come in the name of Christ,
    meet with us now,
    for his name's sake.
    Amen.

143

ANNUAL GENERAL MEETING (BEGINNING)

Gracious God,
    we come together today recognising once again
        that you have called us to fellowship,
        that each of us has a place, a role,
        a ministry within the body of Christ,
        all with something to offer to one another,
        and something to receive.
Guide us therefore as we meet now
        to consider the past and plan for the future.
Open our hearts to you,
    and our minds to one another.

Give us the ability to hear your voice
    and discern your will,
        to recognise the gifts you have given us,
    and to show our appreciation
        of all the work undertaken over this last year.
Open our hearts to you,
    and our minds to one another.

Give us insight into your will,
    inspiration through your Holy Spirit,
    and instruction through your word.
Open our hearts to you,
    and our minds to one another.

Give us wisdom to see the opportunities before us,
    courage to grasp them,
    and perseverance to see them through to fulfilment.
Open our hearts to you,
    and our minds to one another.

Gracious God,
    we thank you for all that has been accomplished
        in and through this church,
        for all those who have contributed to what it is today;
        and we pray you will enable us in our different ways
        to build together for the future,
        open to the prompting of your Spirit,
        guided by the love of Christ,
        and working for your glory.
Open our hearts to you,
    and our minds to one another,
    through Jesus Christ our Lord.
    Amen.

144

ANNUAL GENERAL MEETING (END)

Loving God,
  once more we thank you for our church
    and the fellowship we share with one another.
  We praise you for all whose contribution to our life together
    we have recognised and acknowledged this evening –
    all who have served this church over the years,
    who have nurtured and encouraged our faith,
    who have been part of our continuing life and witness.
  You have called us into the body of Christ;
    help us to honour that calling.

  We pray now for all who have offered their service this day:
    those who have taken on new positions of responsibility
    at this meeting –
    equip them to fulfil their duties wisely and faithfully;
    those who will continue in work
    they have already been undertaking –
    give them renewed inspiration and vigour in their work;
    those who have stood down from positions of office –
    may they know their labours have been appreciated
    and may they find new ways to be of service;
    and finally those who have not been elected to posts
    they would gladly have taken on –
    may they not feel undervalued or rejected
    but find new avenues in which they can use their gifts.
  You have called us into the body of Christ;
    help us to honour that calling.

Loving God,
  we pray not just for these but for us all.
  Help us to recognise
    what you would have us do in the days ahead,
    to grow closer to you,
    to look to you for strength and guidance,
    and to serve you more faithfully,
  You have called us into the body of Christ;
    help us to honour that calling,
    for his name's sake.
    Amen.

CHURCH MEMBERSHIP

145

CHURCH MEMBERSHIP
BELONGING

Father of all,
   you have called us to be your people.
Through your grace you have welcomed us
      into your family, united in Christ.
By faith we have become members one of another.
Teach us that we belong together.

We thank you for the great community to which we belong,
      and above all for the fellowship here
      in which we are able to work out our membership
      through concrete words and actions.
Teach us that we belong together.

Help us, we pray,
      through the love and service
      we offer to one another and to the world,
      to show what our membership means.
Teach us that we belong together.

Help us constantly to discover
      new avenues of service to one another,
      new opportunities to further your kingdom,
      new ways in which we can make known your love.
Teach us that we belong together.

Save us from nominal discipleship,
      from selfish faith,
      from seeing the Church as existing
      solely for our own benefit.
Teach us that we belong together.

Help us to give as well as to receive,
    to put in as much as we take out,
    to serve as much as be served.
Teach us that we belong together.

Help us to be your people together,
    here in this place,
    united in love and faith.
**Teach us that we belong together,
    through Jesus Christ our Lord.
    Amen.**

146

Church membership
The amazing call of Christ

(For *AB* insert the name of the candidate for membership)

Lord Jesus Christ,
 we remember today how you chose
  twelve ordinary people to be your disciples –
  calling them to follow you,
  entrusting them with the message of the Gospel,
  expecting them to make your love known to all people.
 Loving Lord,
  we praise you for your call.

We remember how you chose one of those men, Simon Peter,
  to be the rock on which you would build your Church –
  a man, like us, so clearly human,
  weak and fallible,
  the spirit willing but the flesh all too weak.
 Loving Lord,
  we praise you for your call.

We remember how across the centuries
  you have chosen people to serve you –
  people from all walks of life,
  from different cultures and backgrounds,
  with contrasting characters, temperaments and gifts.
 Loving Lord,
  we praise you for your call.

Time and again you have chosen the most unlikely people
  to be your Church.
 Loving Lord,
  we praise you for your call.

Lord Jesus Christ,
    we rejoice today that you have chosen us in turn –
        to be your people,
        your children,
        your disciples.
Loving Lord,
    we praise you for your call.

And especially we rejoice that you have called *AB*
        into the life of our fellowship,
        to be part of the great company of saints
        in heaven and on earth.
Fill *him/her* with your Holy Spirit,
        equip *him/her* for service,
        inspire *him/her* with vision,
        nurture *his/her* faith,
        and guide *him/her* always in your ways.
Loving Lord,
    we praise you for your call,
    in the name of Christ.
    Amen.

147

CHURCH MEMBERSHIP
SHINING LIKE STARS

Almighty God,
  you call us to shine like stars in the world,
    to shed light like a lamp set upon a lampstand.
Help us, and all your Church,
    to fulfil at least a little of that calling –
    through our words, our actions,
    our living, and our loving,
    to share something of what we have received from you.
Where there is darkness,
  let us bring light.

Teach us to speak openly and honestly of our faith,
    not falling into the language of jargon or cliché,
    but testifying in our own words
    to what Jesus means to us.
Where there is darkness,
  let us bring light.

Teach us to work with our fellow Christians
    of all denominations and none,
    recognising the need to learn from one another,
    and working together in the cause of the Gospel.
Where there is darkness,
  let us bring light.

Teach us to love those around us,
    not simply other believers, nor merely in words,
    but all people, and through actions that speak
    unmistakably of our sincerity.
Where there is darkness,
  let us bring light.

Almighty God,
>   it is easy to talk of being your people;
>   >   much harder to live as though we are.
>   Equip us and enable us to respond to that challenge,
>   >   and reach out in love to the world.
>   Where there is darkness,
>   >   **let us bring light,**
>   >   **to the glory of your name.**
>   >   **Amen.**

MISSIONARY SERVICES

148

MISSION AND MISSIONARIES

Loving God,
   you call us all to the task of mission,
      to make known the Good News of Christ,
      to proclaim the Gospel to all we meet
      through word and deed.
   Teach us what that means,
      and to be ready to fulfil that calling
      when the opportunity arises.
   Grant your wisdom, guidance and inspiration,
      so that many will hear and respond.

Loving God,
   you call us all to be witnesses for Christ,
      but there are some you set apart for a particular calling –
      evangelists,
      ministers,
      preachers and teachers of your word,
      each with a special responsibility to lead others to you.
   Grant your wisdom, guidance and inspiration,
      so that many will hear and respond.

   You call others to more specialised ministries –
      working in industry or shops, prisons or hospitals,
      the armed forces, sport, youth work, charities,
      or ecumenical projects.
   Grant your wisdom, guidance and inspiration,
      so that many will hear and respond.

   You call others again to missionary service,
      either at home or overseas,
      to share the Gospel through their preaching and teaching,
      or through offering practical skills
      as a testimony to the love and compassion of Christ.
   Grant your wisdom, guidance and inspiration,
      so that many will hear and respond.

Loving God,
> we thank you for all who in different ways
>> strive to fulfil the great commission,
>> taking the Gospel to the ends of the earth.
> Teach us to see their work as our work,
>> their needs as our needs,
>> their opportunities as our opportunities;
>> and so challenge us and your people everywhere
>> to support them always,
>> through our prayers, our money and our love,
>> demonstrating our appreciation of their work
>>> and our concern for your kingdom.
> Grant your wisdom, guidance and inspiration,
>> **so that many will hear and respond,**
>> **in the name of Christ.**
>> **Amen.**

149

MISSIONARY SERVICES
A BROADER VISION

Loving God,
   you have called us into this church,
      to share fellowship with each other,
      to be your family in this place,
      to be one people bound together in love.
   Together we are the body of Christ:
      bind us together in love.

But we come today recognising
      you have called us also to a wider fellowship,
      a fellowship which extends across denominational differences,
      beyond geographical boundaries,
      out and into the world.
   Though we may never meet in person,
      we are one with fellow Christians everywhere,
      united by one faith,
      sharing the common goal
      of taking the Good News of Christ
      to the ends of the earth.
   Together we are the body of Christ:
      bind us together in love.

We come then now to listen and learn,
      to hear of all you are doing across the world,
      and to respond with gratitude,
      to recognise all we can receive from the wider Church,
      and all we can contribute to it.
   Together we are the body of Christ:
      bind us together in love.

Open our horizons through this time together,
    broaden our vision,
    enlarge our understanding,
    and help us to glimpse more fully
    the extent of your purpose,
    the wonder of your love,
    and the richness of the Christian family
    to which we belong.
Together we are the body of Christ:
    bind us together in love,
    through Jesus Christ our Lord.
    Amen.

INFANT BAPTISM/DEDICATION

150

THANKSGIVING ON THE BIRTH OF A CHILD

(For *A* insert the name of the child; for *C* and *D* the names of the parents)

Creator God,
    We worship you today for the gift of a new life.
    We come with joy in our hearts,
        to thank you for this child,
        to praise you for all *his/her* birth means to us,
        and all it means to you.
    Lord of life,
        hear our prayer.

We thank you for the love that has brought *A* into being,
        the care that surrounds *him/her*,
        the excitement *his/her* arrival has brought,
        and the happiness that *he/she* has given
        to those around *him/her*.
    Lord of life,
        hear our prayer.

Grant your blessing upon *A*.
Watch over *him/her*.
Guide *his/her* footsteps.
Protect *him/her* from danger.
Bless *him/her* with health.
Fill *him/her* with joy.
And in the fullness of your time
        may *he/she* come to know your love,
        and respond to you in faith,
        discovering the joy and peace
        that you alone can offer.
Lord of life,
    hear our prayer.

Creator God,
    We pray also for *C* and *D*,
        whom you have entrusted
        with the responsibilities of parenthood –
    Give them wisdom,
        patience,
        devotion,
        and dedication.
    Lord of life,
        hear our prayer.

May *A* enrich their lives in immeasurable ways,
    and may they in turn offer *A* the security
    of a loving, caring home in which to grow.
Help them, through their words and actions,
    to sow the seeds of your love in *A*'s heart,
    and then to give *him/her* space
    to make *his/her* response in *his/her* own time and own way.
Lord of life,
    hear our prayer.

Creator God,
    we thank you for this day,
        this child,
        and this family.
    And we thank you for your love which surrounds us all,
        this day and always.
    Lord of life,
        hear our prayer,
        in the name of Christ.
        Amen.

151

BLESSING OF A CHILD

Gracious God,
    you have brought this child into being –
        go with *him/her* now in their journey of life.
    May *he/she* know joy,
        health,
        and peace.
    May *he/she* grow in love,
        wisdom,
        and faith.
    Direct *his/her* steps,
        keep *him/her* from evil,
        and help *him/her* to live life in all its fullness,
        this day and always.
In the name of Christ.
Amen.

152

THANKSGIVING AND INTERCESSION

Gracious God,
    we thank you for your gift of children,
        for the joy, the laughter,
        and the fun they bring in so many ways.
    We thank you for their innate zest for life –
        the interest, excitement and fascination they find
        in so much we count ordinary.
    We thank you for their special qualities –
        their innocence, trust, enthusiasm, energy,
        and sheer hunger to learn.
    We lift them now to you:
        open your heart to all.

Gracious God,
    we pray for this child presented to you this day,
        and for children everywhere,
        so precious to us,
        so precious to you.
    Watch over them,
        protect them, guide them and bless them.
    We lift them now to you:
        open your heart to all.

And hear also our prayer for those who are childless,
    or who long to conceive another child.
Reach out to them in their pain, their frustration,
    their disappointment, their anger.
Help them not to lose hope until all hope is past,
    and if that time finally comes
        give them the comfort you alone can bring,
        and courage to channel their love to those around them.
We lift them now to you:
    open your heart to all.

Finally we pray for disadvantaged children –
    those who are disabled, abused, orphaned,
    undernourished, unloved, unwanted –
    so many denied the start in life they deserve
    and the care they need.
We lift them now to you:
    open your heart to all.

Loving God,
    in Christ you welcomed little children,
        demonstrating their importance to you,
        their special place in your heart.
Prosper the work of all who care for children today –
    all who strive to give them a better life,
    a brighter future,
    a safer world in which to grow.
Use them, and us, to make real your care for all.
We lift them now to you:
    open your heart to all,
    for we ask it in the name of Christ.
    Amen.

BELIEVERS' BAPTISM/
CONFIRMATION

153

BAPTISMAL/CONFIRMATION PRAISE

(For *AB* insert the full name of the candidate)

God of majesty,
   you are the beginning and the end of all,
      higher than our highest thoughts,
      greater than we can ever begin to imagine,
      defying expression in human terms.
   There is nothing you are unable to do,
      no one you are unable to change –
      always you are at work within us,
      reaching out to transform our lives.
   Receive our praise,
      in the name of Christ.

God of love,
   we praise you for all you have done for us –
      the good things we have received from your hands,
      the guidance you have so faithfully given.
   Though you are sovereign and wholly other,
      yet you care for us all,
      constantly striving to draw us closer,
      longing to bless us with life in all its fullness.
   Receive our praise,
      in the name of Christ.

God of grace,
   we praise you for your coming in Jesus Christ –
      for speaking so powerfully of your love
      through his birth and ministry,
      his death and resurrection,
      his ascension and exaltation.
   We praise you for his continuing presence with us now
      through his Holy Spirit,
      nurturing our faith,
      calling us to service,
      and filling us with joy.
   Receive our praise,
      in the name of Christ.

God of mercy,
    We praise you for the forgiveness you offer us
        despite our failure to live as your people.
    Though we repeatedly disobey you,
        often ignore you,
        and daily forget you,
        still you continue to reach out,
        calling us back and renewing us through your grace.
    Receive our praise,
        in the name of Christ.

God of life,
    we thank you for accepting us as we are,
        with all our faults and weaknesses,
        and we thank you today
        that you have called *AB* to faith in you,
        leading *him/her* to this moment
        through which *he/she* will publicly testify
        to all that you mean in *his/her* life.
    We thank you that as you welcome *him/her*,
        so also you long to welcome each of us.
    Receive our praise,
        in the name of Christ.

Loving God,
    meet with us now in this time of worship.
    Help us to sense your nearness and hear your voice,
        responding freely and gladly in faith,
        not holding back or putting off,
        but accepting your love
        and rejoicing in all you have done for us.
    Receive our praise,
        in the name of Christ.
        Amen.

154

BAPTISMAL/CONFIRMATION THANKSGIVING

(For *AB* insert the full name of the candidate; for *A* insert Christian name only)

Loving God,
  we thank you that you have brought *AB* to this point
    of publicly declaring *his/her* faith in you.
  We thank you for the joy and fulfilment
    he/she has found in Christ,
    discovering in him the way, the truth
    and the life for themselves.
  We praise you for all the ways you have guided,
    nurtured and spoken to *A;*
  for all the strength you have given, love you have shown,
    and help you have offered.
  You are constantly reaching out in love,
    and we praise you for it.

Loving God,
  we thank you for *A,*
    and all this moment means to *him/her.*
  And we thank you that you invite each of us in turn
    to make our own individual response.
  You call us, as you have called *A,*
    not through any goodness on our part,
    nor because we have all the answers and no questions,
    but because you love us
    and are ready to accept us as we are.
  You are constantly reaching out in love,
    and we praise you for it.

Loving God,
    speak to us through this service,
        so that we may hear your voice
        and respond to your challenge.
    You are constantly reaching out in love,
        and we praise you for it,
        in the name of Christ.
    Amen.

CHRISTIAN MARRIAGE

155

OPENING PRAYER 1

(For A and C insert the Christian names of the bride and groom)

Living God,
    we praise you for this day of joy and celebration,
        love and commitment,
        nostalgia and anticipation.
    For all that this day means,
        we thank you.

We thank you for all A and C have shared,
    and all they will share –
    for the happiness they have found in each other,
    and their desire today before us and you
    to bear witness to that happiness.
For all that this day means,
    we thank you.

We thank you for the love this service speaks of –
    the love A and C have for each other,
    the love of family and friends,
    the love you have for us.
For all that this day means,
    we thank you.

Living God,
    open our hearts, we pray, to all you would say to us.
    May this be a day for A and C to remember with gratitude,
        the first of many days and many years of lasting fulfilment.
    And may this for us all be a day
        when we recognise more clearly
        the greatness of your love,
        and in glad thanksgiving make our response.
    For all that this day means,
        we thank you,
        in the name of Christ we pray.
        Amen.

156

OPENING PRAYER 2

(For *A* and *C* insert the Christian names of the bride and groom)

God of love,
> we come together on this special day
>> to give you thanks,
>> to celebrate,
>> and to worship.
> Gracious God,
>> **hear our prayer.**

We come remembering everything
> that has made this day possible –
> the love that has surrounded *A* and *C* since their birth,
> the experiences that have shaped their characters,
> the events that have brought them together
> and cemented their relationship.
> Gracious God,
>> **hear our prayer.**

We come looking forward to everything the future holds –
> the joys *A* and *C* will share,
> the dreams they will work to fulfil,
> the love that will continue to grow.
> Gracious God,
>> **hear our prayer.**

We come rejoicing in everything this present moment has to offer –
> the reunion of family and friends,
> the fun, laughter and happiness we share,
> the joining together before you of husband and wife.
> Gracious God,
>> **hear our prayer.**

God of love,
    this is a precious day –
        a time for thanksgiving, celebration, and worship.
    Accept our praise for everything you have done,
        and everything we are privileged to witness today.
    And grant your blessing on all the future holds,
        so that all we hope for and more besides
        may be realised over the years to come.
    Gracious God,
        hear our prayer,
        through Jesus Christ our Lord.
        Amen.

157

THANKSGIVING

(For *A* and *C* insert the Christian names of the bride and groom)

Loving God,
    we thank you for this special day –
        this day of rejoicing, celebration, expectation
        and new beginnings.
    Lord of love,
        hear our prayer.

We thank you for this couple –
    all they mean to us,
    all they mean to each other,
    and all they mean to you.
Lord of love,
    hear our prayer.

We thank you for bringing them together,
    for the love they share,
    and the life they look forward to.
Lord of love,
    hear our prayer.

Enrich both them and us through being here today.
May the making of vows,
    the exchanging of rings,
    the reading of your word,
    and the offering of our worship,
    speak powerfully of the gift of human love,
    and more powerfully still of your eternal love
    that unfailingly encircles us.
Lord of love,
    hear our prayer.

Loving God,
 grant your blessing upon *A* and *C*,
  so that in everything the future holds,
  for better or for worse,
  for richer for poorer,
  in sickness and in health,
  they may continue to cherish each other,
  and their love continue to grow.
 Grant that the closeness they feel now
  may be just as real, as sure, and as special
  tomorrow and in the years to come as it is today.
 Lord of love,
  hear our prayer,
  in the name of Christ.
  Amen.

158

THE GIFT OF LOVE
(based on 1 Corinthians 13)

(For *A* and *C* insert the Christian names of the bride and groom)

Living God,
    there is so much to enjoy in this day,
        not simply this service now, central though it is,
        but everything else that is part of this occasion:
        the giving and receiving of gifts,
        the taking of photographs,
        the making of speeches,
        the fun of the reception,
        the excitement of family and friends,
        the prospect of time away on honeymoon –
        so much happiness,
        so much laughter,
        so much to celebrate.
    And we thank you for it all with glad and joyful hearts.
    Lord, in your love,
        hear our prayer.

But we pray that through it all
    you will save us from losing sight
    of what this day is really all about –
    your gift of love;
    and not just love in the sentimental way we use that word,
    but the way the Apostle Paul used it
    when he spoke to the Corinthians –
    patient and kind,
    never insisting on its own way,
    nor arrogant, rude, irritable or resentful,
    but rejoicing in truth,
    bearing all things,
    believing all things,
    hoping all things,
    enduring all things.
Lord, in your love,
    hear our prayer.

Living God,
    help us to enjoy this day,
        celebrating every part of it enthusiastically
        as your gift to us.
But help us also to remember that without love at its heart
    this day would be nothing.
And so grant your blessing upon A and C,
    and upon each of us in our own relationships,
    so that whatever we may face
    our love may continue to grow,
    this day and always.
Lord, in your love,
    hear our prayer,
    in the name of Jesus Christ our Lord.
    Amen.

159

RENEWAL OF WEDDING VOWS
OPENING PRAYER

(For *AB* and *CD* insert the full names of the bride and groom; for *A* and *C* insert Christian names only. The words printed in italics may be used as an optional response by the couple.)

Gracious God,
>we are here to celebrate your love,
>>and rejoice in your great faithfulness.

>*You have been always good to us,*
>>*always true,*
>>*always by our side,*
>>*and we praise you for it.*
>Receive our praise,
>>**in the name of Christ.**

>*Day by day you have held us close,*
>>*sharing with us in the good times and bad,*
>>*our surest and dearest friend,*
>>*and we thank you for it.*
>Receive our praise,
>>**in the name of Christ.**

Gracious God,
>we are here to celebrate your gift of love,
>>the love that *AB* and *CD* have shared over so many years,
>>the faithfulness they have shown to each other –
>>the closeness that has grown between them.
>Receive our praise,
>>**in the name of Christ.**

We are here to celebrate how you have sustained them,
    through joy and sorrow,
    hopes and fears,
    trials and temptations,
    good and bad.
Receive our praise,
    in the name of Christ.

Gracious God,
    we are here to celebrate,
    with you,
    with *A* and *C*,
    and with one another.
Speak to us through the vows renewed in this service,
    of the love you have for us,
    and help us to pledge our love in return to you.
Receive our praise,
    in the name of Christ.
    Amen.

160

RENEWAL OF WEDDING VOWS
THANKSGIVING PRAYER

(For *A* and *C* insert the Christian names of the bride and groom)

Eternal God,
    we come today to celebrate the gift of love –
        your love for us,
        and the love of *A* and *C* for each other.
You have blessed us,
    and we thank you.

We thank you that though all else may change,
    though heaven and earth may pass away,
    your love continues unchanging,
    constant and dependable,
    always the same,
    always certain.
You have blessed us,
    and we thank you.

We thank you for the way you have been with *A* and *C*
    throughout their lives –
    the way you brought them together,
    the way you have guided them,
    nurtured and enriched their relationship,
    and blessed them and their loved ones.
You have blessed us,
    and we thank you.

We thank you for their commitment to each other,
    to their family,
    to us,
    and to Christ.
You have blessed us,
    and we thank you.

Go with them now,
  watch over them,
  and grant them many more years
  of health and happiness together,
  until that day when you unite them and all your people
  in your everlasting kingdom
  and the joy of your unchanging presence.
You have blessed us,
  and we thank you,
  in the name of Christ.
  Amen.

CHRISTIAN BURIAL

161

CALL TO WORSHIP

(For *AB* insert the full name of the deceased)

We are here to express sorrow that a life is ended,
    to give thanks for a life well-lived.
We are here grieving that a life is over,
    but rejoicing that life eternal has just begun.
We are here conscious of separation,
    yet confident we shall meet again.
We are here remembering what has been,
    and looking forward to what shall be.
We are here to pay tribute to all *AB* has meant to us,
    to remind ourselves of all *he/she* means to God.
We are here to entrust someone we have greatly loved
    to his eternal keeping,
    and to entrust ourselves to the same God
    who so greatly loves us.
Listen then to words of Scripture and tribute,
    bring your pain, your shock and sadness,
    offer to God this time of worship,
    and receive the comfort he longs to give you,
    in the name of Christ.
    Amen.

162

APPROACH

(For *AB* insert the full name of the deceased;
for *A* insert Christian name only)

Loving God,
> we come today struggling for words to express our feelings,
>> lost for words to express our thanks
>> for all *AB* has meant to us.
> We come with sorrow as we think of our loss,
>> with gratitude as we recall the person *A* has been,
>> with praise as we remember
>> all you have done through *him/her*,
>> with faith as we commit both *A* and ourselves
>> to your eternal care.

Loving God,
> draw near to us as we draw near to you.
> Speak to us through the words of Scripture,
>> through our prayers,
>> through all we shall share,
>> so that, believing in the Gospel and trusting in Christ,
>> we may receive the comfort, peace and strength
>> you long to give us,
>> and find hope in this life,
>> and the life to come.
> **Through Jesus Christ our Lord.**
>> **Amen.**

163

OPENING PRAYER 1

Lord,
   someone we have loved has died,
      someone special to us,
      precious,
      irreplaceable.
And we know there are no words we can say at this moment
      to express what we are feeling,
      no words that can alleviate our sorrow
      or take away our pain.

So we come today simply to bring you the grief,
      the shock and the pain,
      the emptiness, the anger and the despair,
      the loneliness, the fear and the uncertainty
      which overwhelms us at this time.
We come bringing those honestly before you,
      and asking for strength in this time of darkness.
Hold on to us,
      even when we find it hard to hold on to you.
Be very near,
      even when we feel you to be very far.
Support us in the days ahead,
      and grant the comfort you have promised,
      until the time finally comes when we can look back
      not just with pain but thanksgiving –
      not just with sorrow but with joy.
Through Jesus Christ our Lord,
      the Resurrection and the Life!
      Amen.

164

Opening prayer 2

(For *AB* insert the full name of the deceased;
for *A* insert Christian name only)

Loving God,
  we come today to express our sorrow but also our joy,
    to remember but also to anticipate,
    to mourn but also to give thanks.
Lord, in your mercy,
  hear our prayer.

We come with gratitude in our hearts
    for all *AB* has meant to us,
    for all *he/she* continues to mean to us,
    for all *he/she* will always mean to you.
Lord, in your mercy,
  hear our prayer.

We come to acknowledge a life well-lived.
    and in faith to commit both *A* and ourselves
    to your eternal care.
Lord, in your mercy,
  hear our prayer.

Loving God,
  draw near to us as we draw near to you.
  Speak to us through the words of Scripture and tribute,
    through our hymns and prayers,
    through all we share,
    so that believing in the Good News of Christ,
    and trusting in him,
    we may receive the comfort he promises,
    the peace that passes all understanding,
    and the assurance of everlasting life,
    through Jesus Christ our Lord.
  Lord, in your mercy,
    hear our prayer,
    for in his name we pray.
    Amen.

165

THANKSGIVING 1

(For *AB* insert the full name of the deceased;
for *A* insert Christian name only)

Gracious God,
we thank you for the person *AB* has been to us.

We thank you for *his/her* love and friendship,
honesty and integrity,
kindness and thoughtfulness,
wisdom and humility.

We thank you for *his/her* faithful service in so much,
his/her dedication at work,
to *his/her* family,
to our church,
to Christ.

We thank you for *his/her* faith,
his/her commitment,
his/her discipleship,
his/her witness to the love of Christ.

Gracious God,
we thank you that *A* has enriched our lives,
that *he/she* has brought happiness to many,
that *he/she* has earned our love and respect,
that our sorrow now is deep and our loss genuine.

But most of all we thank you that our confidence,
our hope and our trust now is real,
for *A* has run the race and kept the faith
and is now with you and all your people
in your heavenly kingdom.

Watch over *A* and bless *him/her*,
    until that time when we shall meet again,
    and live together in the light of your everlasting love,
    through Jesus Christ our Lord.
    Amen.

166

THANKSGIVING 2

*(For AB insert the full name of the deceased;
for A insert Christian name only)*

Living God,
    we bring you our thanks for *AB*,
        for the person *he/she* has been,
        for all *he/she* has meant in so many innumerable ways.

We thank you for *his/her* warmth and love,
    his/her enthusiasm and zest for life,
    his/her courage and cheerfulness,
    his/her many interests and abilities.

We thank you for all the happiness *A* has brought
    to those around *him/her*,
    and especially to *his/her* family.
We thank you for all the special times shared;
    those moments which will live on in our minds
    as enduring memories,
    bringing pain in their remembering but also joy.
We thank you for the convictions *A* has held
    throughout *his/her* life,
    those things *he/she* has believed in and worked for.
And we thank you for the faith
    which has given *him/her* such support,
    and which offers us the same support now.

Give us confidence in the victory over death
    you have won through Christ,
    certainty that your kingdom will come,
    conviction that nothing will finally separate us from your love,
    and so may we find strength not just for today,
    but for tomorrow and all that the future holds.
In the name of Christ we ask it.
    Amen.

167

A PRAYER FOR THOSE WHO MOURN 1

(For *A* insert Christian name of the deceased)

Loving God,
    you have promised that those who mourn shall be comforted.
    So we pray now for each of us here today,
        bringing before you the sorrow we all feel at this moment.
    Lord, in your mercy,
        hear our prayer.

We pray especially for *A*'s family,
    in their shock and grief,
    their pain and loneliness,
    the turmoil of emotions which death inevitably brings
    to those left behind.
    Lord, in your mercy,
        hear our prayer.

We pray for all those who counted *A* as a friend,
    those in this church,
    those who worked with *A*,
    who lived near to *him/her*,
    who shared *his/her* hobbies and interests –
    all those whose lives were, in different ways,
    touched by *A*'s presence.
    Lord, in your mercy,
        hear our prayer.

Loving God,
>we bring before you now our sense of emptiness,
>>separation and sorrow.
>Give us your support as we struggle
>>to come to terms with our loss.
>Give strength to face the days ahead.
>Give courage when life seems dark.
>Give hope when the future seems without purpose.
>Lord, in your mercy,
>>**hear our prayer.**

Help us to know that your love for *A* and for us
>continues beyond death,
>>that you are with us in this moment and always,
>>and may that knowledge bring comfort and hope
>>today and in the days ahead.
>Lord, in your mercy,
>>**hear our prayer,**
>>**in the name of Christ.**
>>**Amen.**

168

A PRAYER FOR THOSE WHO MOURN 2

(For *A* insert Christian name of the deceased)

Loving God,
   you tell us to look forward to a day
      when your kingdom shall come
      and your will be done;
      a new age when there will be no more suffering,
      sorrow or death;
      a place where there will be no more mourning and weeping,
      every tear wiped away from our eyes.
Help us to find comfort in your love.

We thank you for that promise,
      and we look forward to that time,
      but we pray also for your help now,
      for today our grief is all too painful,
      and the fact of death an all too stark reality.
Help us to find comfort in your love.

So we ask you to reach out to us
      and to all whose lives have been enriched
      by *A*'s presence –
      family,
      friends,
      neighbours,
      colleagues –
      each so much the poorer for *A*'s passing.
Help us to find comfort in your love.

Loving God,
   reach out now into the darkness of this moment,
      the blackness of our sorrow,
      and grant your light which nothing can overcome,
      your peace that defies understanding,
      and your hope which will never be extinguished.
   Help us to find comfort in your love,
      through Jesus Christ our Lord.
      Amen.

PART THREE

ORDINARY SUNDAYS

PRAYERS OF APPROACH

169

HONEST TO GOD

Gracious God, Lord of all,
    we thank you that we can come to you in prayer,
        that for all your greatness, and wonder, and holiness,
        we can speak with you as to a friend.
Hear now our prayer.

We thank you that we can open our hearts to you,
        that we can pour out our innermost souls
        and share our deepest thoughts,
        in the knowledge that you are there,
        always ready to listen and understand.
Hear now our prayer.

So now once more we lay our lives before you,
        open to your gaze –
        the bad as well as the good,
        the doubt as well as the faith,
        the sorrow as well as the joy,
        the despair as well as the hope.
Hear now our prayer.

We bring the anger as well as the peace,
        the hatred as well as the love,
        the confusion as well as the certainty,
        the fear as well as the trust.
Hear now our prayer.

Gracious God,
    we bring these,
        not with pride or any sense of arrogance,
        but honestly,
        recognising that you know us through and through.
Hear now our prayer.

Help us to be truthful to ourselves and truthful to you,
and so may we discover the renewing love
which only you can offer –
a love that frees us to live as you would have us live,
and allows us to be the people you would have us be!
Hear now our prayer,
in the name of Christ.
Amen.

170

THE INGREDIENTS OF WORSHIP

Almighty and all-loving God,
  in awe and reverence we come to worship you –
    to proclaim your greatness,
    to acknowledge your power,
    to recognise your sovereignty,
    to declare your goodness.
  Lord of all, hear our prayer.

Compassionate and caring God,
  with grateful hearts we come to praise you -
    for your love that constantly surrounds us,
    for all the blessings of our lives,
    for the wonder of our world,
    for the hope of our faith in Christ.
  Lord of all, hear our prayer.

Merciful and forgiving God,
  in sorrow and shame we come before you –
    to confess our unworthiness of your goodness,
    to confess we have not loved you
    or one another as we should,
    to confess we have failed to appreciate your many gifts,
    and broken your commandments.
  Lord of all, hear our prayer.

Living and life-giving God,
  in faith and trust we come to petition you –
    to pray for ourselves, for one another, and for our world;
    to bring the concerns of daily life before you;
    to lift our loved ones into your presence;
    to commit the affairs of our world into your hands.
  Lord of all, hear our prayer.

Lord of all,
>we offer you this time of worship –
>>our praise,
>>our thanksgiving,
>>our confession,
>>our petition.
>**Lord of all, hear our prayer.**

Respond to us we pray –
>touch our hearts with your living presence
>and fill our lives with your grace,
>so that our love for you may grow,
>our faith be deepened,
>and our service strengthened.
>**Lord of all, hear our prayer,**
>>**in the name of Christ.**
>>**Amen.**

171

WANTING TO WORSHIP

Almighty and all-loving God,
   we would bring you our praise;
      we would offer you our worship;
      we would open to you our hearts;
      we would tell of all you mean to us;
      we would proclaim your name
      in a way that does justice to your greatness.
   Hear our prayer.

Eternal and all-powerful God,
   we hunger to meet with you,
      to hear your voice,
      to know your will,
      to learn more of you,
      and to offer you a commitment
      that does justice to your love.
   Hear our prayer.

Gracious and all-forgiving God,
   help us then to acknowledge our faults,
      to confess our sins,
      to recognise our many weaknesses,
      to see all that is wrong in our lives,
      and to be a people who do justice to your mercy.
   Hear our prayer.

Great and all-transforming God,
   enable us to serve you more faithfully,
      love you more deeply,
      know you more fully,
      obey you more completely,
      and live in a way
      that does justice to your renewing power.
   Hear our prayer.

Everlasting God,
  you know what we are,
    and you know what we want to be.
  Hear our prayer,
    receive our worship,
    and so help us to become the people
    ***you* would have us be,**
    to the glory of your name.
    Amen.

172

RECOGNISING CHRIST IS AMONG US

Loving God,
    we are here in the name of Christ.

We come to bow our heads,
    to lift up our hearts,
    and to offer you our praise.

We come to confess Jesus Christ as Lord,
    to enthrone him in our lives,
    and to offer him our commitment.

We come to seek his will,
    to hear his word,
    and receive his blessing.

Loving God,
    we praise you for all you have done through Christ –
        his revelation of your great love and glory,
        his obedience and faithfulness even to the Cross itself,
        his victory over death and exaltation to your side,
        his promise to come again
        as King of kings and Lord of lords.

Help us as we worship
    to recognise Christ is here amongst us.
Help us to glimpse your glory through him,
    to hear his voice through this service,
    to feel his love through our fellowship,
    and to see more clearly where we can serve him
    in the needs of our world.
Help us to bear his name faithfully,
    and live each day
    to the glory of his name.
    Amen.

173

OVER-FAMILIARITY WITH GOD

Eternal God,
>   we come once more to this familiar place
>>   at this familiar time,
>>   among familiar faces.
>   We come as we have come so many times,
>>   to sing well-loved hymns,
>>   to meet well-loved people,
>>   and listen again to well-loved words of Scripture.

Speak to us through all we know and love so well.

Eternal God,
>   we thank you for all that is familiar;
>>   all that has become so much a part of our lives.
>   But save us, we pray, from ever becoming over-familiar –
>>   over-familiar with you, so that we lose the sense of awe
>>   we should feel in your presence;
>>   over-familiar with one another,
>>   so that we lose sight of the worth in each one of us ;
>>   over-familiar with our faith,
>>   so that we come to see only what we expect
>>   rather than everything you would show us;
>>   over-familiar with the world about us,
>>   so that we fail to glimpse your hand at work
>>   in the wonder of creation.

Speak to us through all we know and love so well.

Eternal God,
>   open our eyes to your greatness,
>>   our hearts to one another,
>>   our lives to all your people in every place,
>>   and our souls to the work of your kingdom across the world.
>   Deepen our insight,
>>   increase our love,
>>   enlarge our vision,
>>   widen our horizons.

Speak to us through all we know and love so well.

And so, inspired by all you have done,
   all you are doing,
   and all you have yet to do,
   may we worship you more truly,
   and serve you more faithfully,
   to the glory of your name.
   Amen.

174

BEFORE GOD

Great and wonderful God,
  we come before you in humility,
    in awe,
    in faith,
    in hope,
    in love,
    in worship.
  In your mercy, hear our prayer.

We come to praise you,
    to bless you,
    to adore you,
    to acknowledge you,
    to salute you,
    to thank you.
  In your mercy, hear our prayer.

We come recognising your power,
    your authority,
    your wisdom,
    your faithfulness,
    your goodness,
    your love.
  In your mercy, hear our prayer.

We come confessing our weakness,
    our unworthiness,
    our faults,
    our failings,
    our faithlessness,
    our lack of love.
  In your mercy, hear our prayer.

We come seeking your mercy,
    your guidance,
    your strength,
    your renewal,
    your inspiration,
    your word.
In your mercy, hear our prayer.

We come to commit ourselves to your service,
    your purpose
    your kingdom,
    your will,
    your people,
    your world.
In your mercy, hear our prayer.

Great and wonderful God,
    we come to you now, in the name of Christ.
    Receive the worship we offer this day.
    In your mercy, hear our prayer.
        Amen.

175

BRINGING OURSELVES

Loving God,
> we join together in your house to worship you.

We come once more reminded of all you are
> and all you have done –
> **of the love with which you surround us,**
> the grace you have shown us through Jesus Christ,
> **and the purpose you have for our lives.**

We come to offer you our praise,
> **to declare again your mighty acts,**
> to marvel at your greatness,
> **and to commit ourselves to your service.**

We come to give thanks,
> **to rejoice in all you have given us,**
> to respond to your goodness,
> **and to offer our love in return.**

We come to make our confession,
> **to admit our faults and failings,**
> to recognise our weakness,
> **and to ask your forgiveness.**

We come to pray for ourselves,
> **to seek your guidance,**
> to discover your will,
> **and to find the strength we need to live as your people.**

We come to pray for others,
> **our loved ones with all their joys and sorrows,**
> our world with all its suffering,
> **and your Church as it seeks to express your compassion in action.**

We come to make our offering,
    to bring our time,
    our money,
    our talents,
    our service,
    and ourselves.

Loving God,
    we come to worship you in the conviction
        that you are here with us now,
        that you are by our side always,
        that you hold all things and all people in your hands.
    As we reach out to you,
        reach out to us, we pray,
        and fill every moment of every day
        with the light of your love,
        and the peace of your presence,
        through Jesus Christ our Lord.
        Amen.

176

COMING TO WORSHIP

Living God,
  we have come together to worship you,
    to meet here with Christ,
      not simply because we feel we should do,
    nor because it is expected of us,
    but because we want to praise you.
Meet with us now, we pray.

We have come not merely to share fellowship
    with one another,
    nor just to meet with friends,
    but to encounter you.
Meet with us now, we pray.

Help us to bring you our heartfelt worship –
    to reflect on you and not ourselves,
    to think about your love rather than our problems,
    to seek your will for us rather than our expectations of you.
Meet with us now, we pray.

Help us to draw close to you,
    rejoicing in your presence,
    receiving your love,
    reviving our faith.
Meet with us now, we pray.

Help us to put aside everything that comes between us –
    our foolish deeds,
    our trivial concerns,
    our evil desires.
Meet with us now, we pray.

Living God,
    there is so much in our lives that is not as it should be,
        not as it could be,
        and not as it would be
        if only we walked more closely with you.
Meet with us now, we pray.

Forgive us the unkind words,
    thoughtless actions,
    and unworthy thoughts,
    that deny our faith.
Meet with us now, we pray.

Forgive us the self-centred lifestyles,
    half-hearted commitment,
    and careless discipleship,
    that undermine our witness.
Meet with us now, we pray.

Forgive us the lack of devotion,
    lack of faith,
    and lack of love,
    that demean your name.
Meet with us now, we pray.

Living God,
    we gather together in the name of Christ.
    Assure us, as we worship you,
        of the forgiveness,
        the guidance,
        the love,
        and the life you offer through him.
Meet with us now, we pray.

So may we worship you
    not just through our words but in our lives,
    not merely now but always,
    not simply here but everywhere.
To the glory of your name.
    Amen.

177

DRAWING NEAR

Loving God,
  Father of Jesus Christ, the Word made flesh,
    Lord of all the earth,
    Friend and guide to your people across the ages,
    with joy and gladness we praise you.

  You have redeemed your people.
  You have shown your mercy.
  You have revealed your love.
  You have spoken through your prophets.
  You have lived amongst us.
  You have shared our life and death.
  You offer to all who truly seek you
    the assurance of your everlasting life.

Loving God,
  as we draw near to you,
    draw near to us.
  As we seek your word,
    speak to us.
  As we confess our faults and failings,
    have mercy upon us.
  As we acknowledge the weakness and faithlessness
    of our discipleship,
    cleanse us through the saving love of Christ.
  As we are reminded of all you have done for us,
    challenge us to make our response.
  As we recognise our lack of vision and courage,
    inspire us through your Holy Spirit.

Loving God,
 we come to study your word,
  and to discover your will.
 Guide our reading, our listening, and our thinking,
  so that your message of old
  may be ever new in our hearts!
 Through Jesus Christ our Lord.
  Amen.

178

THE FAITHFULNESS OF GOD

Almighty and loving God,
    we thank you for the assurance we have
        that you are always with us,
        that in you we will find help and strength
        in times of trouble,
        that whatever we face
        you will always be there to reach out and save us.
    Great is your faithfulness,
        from one generation to another.

We thank you that you are present
        not only here but everywhere,
        that no one is outside your love,
        and no place beyond your concern.
Great is your faithfulness,
    from one generation to another.

We thank you that you hold firmly to us,
        even when we try and struggle from your grasp.
Great is your faithfulness,
    from one generation to another.

We thank you that your mercy never runs dry,
        despite our repeated faithlessness.
Great is your faithfulness,
    from one generation to another.

We thank you that your patience is never exhausted,
        no matter how many times we let you down.
Great is your faithfulness,
    from one generation to another.

So now we worship you,
    you who alone are God,
    worthy of all praise and honour.
Great is your faithfulness,
    from one generation to another.

We come with gladness and thanksgiving,
    joy and celebration.
Great is your faithfulness,
    from one generation to another.

We come in awe and wonder, hope and faith.
Great is your faithfulness,
    from one generation to another.

We come to make our confession,
    offer our petition, and bring our intercessions.
Great is your faithfulness,
    from one generation to another.

Almighty and loving God,
    take our faith, weak though it is.
    Kindle the sparks of life within us
        and fan a new flame of love within our hearts;
        and so may we set out into another week
        with renewed purpose,
        resolved to live and work for you,
        in the assurance that you are with us,
        now and always.
Great is your faithfulness,
    from one generation to another.
Thanks be to God.
    Amen.

PRAYERS OF PRAISE

179

RESPONDING TO THE WONDER OF GOD

Loving God,
  all-good,
    all-true,
    all-powerful,
    almighty,
    we worship you.

Gracious God,
  all-loving,
    all-merciful,
    all-faithful,
    all-compassionate,
    we thank you.

Mighty God,
  always active,
    always leading,
    always calling,
    always knowing,
    we commit ourselves to you.

Saving God,
  always forgiving,
    always restoring,
    always teaching,
    always encouraging,
    we confess our faithlessness to you.

Sovereign God,
  all in all,
    now and always,
    we praise you,
    we worship you,
    we lift up our hearts before you.

Father God,
    we celebrate your goodness,
        we rejoice in your blessings,
        we marvel at your mercy,
        we thank you for your guidance,
    we offer our lives in response to you.

Living God,
    take this service,
        this day,
        this church,
        our lives.
    Use them for your purpose and your kingdom.
    Through Christ our Lord.
        Amen.

180

THE VICTORY OF LOVE

Loving God,
  we praise you once more for all you have done in Christ,
    for your victory through him over sin and evil,
    darkness and death.
  May that triumph shape our living and our thinking.

  We praise you for your love which cannot be kept down,
    whatever it may face,
    whatever may conspire against it.
  **May that confidence inspire us to keep on following you
    through good and bad.**

  When life seems hard,
    when good seems frustrated,
    when we feel ourselves in danger
    of being overwhelmed by trials and temptations,
    **assure us once more of your power
    that will not be defeated.**

  When our work seems to bear no fruit,
    when our efforts go unrewarded,
    when our hopes appear unfulfilled,
    **teach us to trust in your purpose
    that presses on towards fulfilment.**

  When the innocent suffer,
    when evil prospers,
    when hatred seems to hold sway,
    **help us to keep on believing
    that good will finally win through.**

Grant us a deep unshakeable confidence that,
  whatever life brings,
  whatever we face,
  however things seem,
  your will shall be done and your kingdom come,
  through Jesus Christ our Lord.
  Amen.

181

THE WONDER OF CREATION

Loving God,
　　creator of the ends of the earth,
　　　　source of all that is and has been and will be,
　　　　giver of life,
　　　　we join together to worship you.

We praise you for the wonder of our world
　　and for the vastness of the universe;
　　for all that you have made,
　　and for the place you have given us within your creation.
Loving God,
　　we join together to worship you.

We marvel at the beauty and variety of this earth –
　　its wonderful mixture of plants, animals, trees, birds,
　　mountains, valleys, streams, oceans,
　　and so much else besides.
Loving God,
　　we join together to worship you.

We thank you for everything that lifts our spirit,
　　that moves us to wonder,
　　that holds our attention,
　　that captures our interest.
Loving God,
　　we join together to worship you.

We rejoice that out of chaos you brought order –
　　an order we can see throughout the universe;
　　which we can depend upon, explore and understand;
　　an order that reflects your sovereign purpose
　　and reveals your guiding hand.
Loving God,
　　we join together to worship you.

Loving God,
    creator of life in all its fullness,
        we bring you our praise,
        we offer you our worship,
        we make our response,
        in joyful celebration.
We join together to worship you,
        in the name of Christ.
        Amen.

182

OFFERING OUR WORSHIP

Eternal and gracious God,
  we have come before you in the name of Christ,
    setting aside time and space in our lives
    to reflect on your greatness,
    to rejoice in your goodness,
    and to respond to you with gladness.
Receive once more our worship.

We come in awe,
  in wonder,
  reverence,
  and humility.
Receive once more our worship.

We come with praise,
  with thanksgiving,
  joy and celebration.
Receive once more our worship.

We come to share fellowship,
  to make our confession to you and one another,
  to pray for ourselves, our world and our loved ones,
  to offer our gifts and our service.
Receive once more our worship.

We come gladly,
  obediently,
  hungrily,
  confidently.
Receive once more our worship.

We come seeking your presence,
  your guidance,
  your strength,
  and your mercy.
Receive once more our worship.

Loving God,
    we are here before you in the name of Christ.
    Receive our worship.
    Receive our faith.
    Receive ourselves.
    And help us to receive all you would give us,
        through Jesus Christ our Lord.
        Amen.

183

THE GREATNESS OF GOD

Loving God,
    we are glad to come and worship you,
        glad to stand in your presence
        and give you the honour due to your name.
Praise and glory, thanksgiving and worship
    are yours by right.

You are greater than our highest thoughts,
    mightier than we can ever comprehend,
    before all, in all, and beyond all.
Praise and honour, thanksgiving and worship
    are yours by right.

So we come,
    acknowledging your greatness,
    marvelling at your power,
    rejoicing in your love,
    celebrating your blessings,
    and praising you for all the mercy you have shown to us
    throughout our lives.
Praise and honour, thanksgiving and worship
    are yours by right.

Accept now our songs of praise,
    our words of prayer,
    the thoughts of our hearts,
    this act of worship.
Praise and honour, thanksgiving and worship
    are yours by right.

Teach us more of all you have done
    and will continue to do,
    and help us to show the sincerity of what we offer now
    by the way we live our lives tomorrow
    and in the days beyond.
Praise and honour, thanksgiving and worship
    are yours by right,
    now and for evermore.
    Amen.

184

ALL GOD HAS DONE

Sing to the Lord a new song,
  for he has done marvellous things. (Psalm 98:1)

Almighty and everlasting God,
  we join with the Psalmist of long ago
    in giving you our praise and worship –
    you have done marvellous things for us
    and we are glad.
  You are the source and sustainer of our lives,
    from you all things come
    and to you all things lead!
  Wherever and whoever we are,
    you are always with us,
    surrounding us with your love.
  Though we forsake you,
    you do not forsake us.
  Though we fail you,
    you do not fail us.
  Despite our repeated faithlessness,
    still your faithfulness continues,
    unchanging and undiminished.

Almighty and everlasting God,
  we thank you for your constant kindness,
    your unfailing love,
    your ceaseless provision of all our needs.
  We thank you for your mercy,
    your forgiveness,
    your amazing grace offered to us in Jesus Christ.
  We thank you for the joy,
    the hope,
    and the life you have given to us in him.

So now we offer to you this service,
our singing,
our praying,
our reading,
our thinking,
as a token of our thanksgiving,
and a symbol of the joy
you have given to us through Christ.

Loving God,
you have done marvellous things for us
and made us glad.
In you we put our trust,
now and for ever.
Amen.

185

LET ALL THE WORLD
IN EVERY CORNER SING

Almighty God,
we come before you to worship you.
We come with all your people in heaven and on earth,
to lift up our hearts and voices,
and give the praise and honour due to you,
our God and King.

We know that our words can never fully express your greatness,
that our minds can only begin
to recognise something of your wonder,
but we bring what we are,
and we bring this time of worship,
offering all to you as a sign of our love,
and a simple expression of our praise.

We praise you again for our world –
all the beauty of your creation.
We praise you for the life you have given us –
so full of blessings.
We praise you for all you have done in Christ –
for the richness of life you offer through him.
We praise you for your love upon which we can depend –
your love that is always with us.

Almighty God,
accept our worship.
Touch our hearts with the nearness of your presence,
deepen our faith,
strengthen our commitment,
and broaden our vision,
so that we may grow as your people,
and play our part in working for your kingdom,
through Jesus Christ our Lord.
Amen.

186

THE SOVEREIGNTY OF GOD

Almighty and sovereign God,
  we join together once more to worship you.
  Yours is the hand that shaped the universe.
  Yours is the power that guides and controls the nations.
  Yours is the love that moves and works through all things.
  Yours is the purpose that has called us here,
    that has redeemed us from our sins,
    that has opened up the way to life,
    that has been most perfectly and wonderfully revealed in Christ.

Mighty God,
  we worship you.
  We offer you our praise.
  We bring you our joyful thanksgiving.
  We acknowledge you as Lord and master of our lives.
  Come amongst us this day with new power,
    inspire us with new vision,
    fill us with new hope,
    and send us out in your service with new purpose.
  So may we truly live and work for you and your kingdom,
    in the name of Christ our Lord.
    Amen.

187

BRINGING ALL TO GOD

Almighty and everlasting God,
    we are here to worship you.
    Meet with us afresh this day.

We come to reflect on your greatness,
    your otherness
    your righteousness,
    and your holiness.
Meet with us afresh this day.

We come to praise you for your faithfulness,
    your goodness,
    your kindness,
    and your forgiveness.
Meet with us afresh this day.

We come through the grace of Christ,
    and in the power of your Holy Spirit,
    recognising you as our God,
    our Father,
    and our Creator.
Meet with us afresh this day.

We come to bring ourselves, all we are and do,
    to bring our loved ones, all they mean to us and others,
    to bring our fellowship, in all its variety and richness,
    to bring our world, with all its joy and all its sorrow.
Meet with us afresh this day.

Almighty and everlasting God,
>we come to speak,
>>to listen,
>>to seek,
>>and to find.
>**Meet with us afresh this day,**
>>**filling us with the knowledge of your presence,**
>>**and so help us to walk each day**
>>**in the light of your love,**
>>**through Jesus Christ our Lord.**
>>**Amen.**

188

THE GOD WHO DOES MORE
THAN WE CAN EVER ASK OR THINK!

Sovereign God,
    we praise you that you are able to do more
        than we can ever ask or imagine –
        where we can do so little, you can do so much,
        when we can do nothing, you can do everything.
Teach us to believe that,
        not just with our heads but in our hearts.

When life seems dark,
        the future frightening,
        our problems insurmountable,
        and our resources to meet them all too few,
        we praise you
        that you are able to see us through.

When life feels good,
        the days ahead full of promise,
        our worries are few,
        and our joys many,
        we praise you
        that you are able to offer more still.

When loving is hard,
        caring involves pain,
        sharing means sacrifice,
        and believing entails cost,
        we praise you
        that you are able to give us strength.

When loving is easy,
   our relationships bring joy,
   our friends bring pleasure,
   and our faith brings rewards,
   we praise you
   that you are able to bring yet greater happiness.

When hopes are dashed,
   dreams lie broken,
   visions have faded,
   and plans are thwarted,
   we praise you
   that you are able to bring new purpose.

When opportunities excite us,
   prospects beckon,
   possibilities unfold,
   and challenges present themselves,
   we praise you
   that you are able to help us grasp them.

Sovereign God,
   in these things and so many more,
      you are able not simply to meet our needs
      but to transform our lives –
   able to bless us beyond words.

Receive our praise,
   and teach us that whatever we face,
   whether good or bad,
   whether we feel able to meet it or not,
   you are able to do more
   than we can ever ask or think of!
   Amen.

PRAYERS OF PRAISE
AND CONFESSION

189

God's Greatness

Almighty and sovereign God,
  great and wonderful,
    all-powerful,
    all-loving,
    all-good,
    all-forgiving,
    once more we make time to worship you.

We come to remind ourselves of all you have done –
  your mighty acts across the years,
  your coming to our world in Christ,
  your transforming of countless lives won for him.

We come to rejoice in all you are still doing –
  your faithful love reaching out to all people everywhere,
  your mercy offering new beginnings
  where before there was only despair,
  your saving purpose constantly being fulfilled.

Almighty God,
  forgive us for losing the sense of awe we once had.
  Forgive us for forgetting how great you are.
  Forgive us for bringing you down to our level,
    rather than rising up to yours.
  Forgive us the smallness of our vision,
    the feebleness of our worship,
    the weakness of our faith.

Enlarge our vision.
Deepen our faith.
Renew our trust.
Restore our sense of wonder before you.
Teach us that you are a great God above all gods,
  Lord of the nations,
  sovereign over space and time.

So may we offer to you our worship,
  with glad and grateful hearts,
in Jesus name.
Amen.

190

THE MAJESTY OF GOD

Almighty and most wonderful God,
    unsearchable and inexhaustible,
        greater than we can ever imagine,
        higher than our highest thoughts,
        enthroned in glory and splendour,
        we come to give you our worship,
        to offer our praise,
        and to make our confession,
        recognising that your ways are not our ways,
        and your thoughts are not our thoughts.
Lord, have mercy upon us!

Forgive us our misplaced pride and arrogance –
        we have been full of our own importance,
        preferring our ways to yours,
        imagining we know all there is to know about you,
        trusting in our own wisdom instead of your guidance,
        setting ourselves up in your place.
But your ways are not our ways,
        and your thoughts are not our thoughts.
Lord, have mercy upon us!

Forgive us our narrow vision and closed minds –
        we have tied you down to our own understanding,
        closing our hearts to anything
        which challenges our restricted horizons,
        losing sight of your greatness,
        failing to listen to your voice or the voice of others,
        refusing to accept that others besides ourselves
        have insights to share.
But your ways are not our ways,
        and your thoughts are not our thoughts.
Lord, have mercy upon us!

Almighty and most-wonderful God,
 remind us that you have always more to say,
  more to reveal,
  and more to do.
 Open our eyes,
  our minds,
  and our hearts to who and what you are.
 Remind us that your ways are not our ways,
  and your thoughts are not our thoughts.
 Lord, have mercy upon us!

And so fill us with awe and wonder,
 joy and thanksgiving, praise and worship,
  now and for evermore.
  Amen.

191

GLIMPSING GOD AT WORK

Living and loving God,
    once more we bring you our praise and worship.
    We acknowledge you as our God.
    We recognise your greatness and power.
    We marvel at your love and compassion.
    We come before you with awe and wonder.

You are Lord of heaven and earth,
    of space and time,
    of this world and all of the universe,
    of life and death.

Living and loving God,
    draw near to us
        and help us to draw near to you.
    Come to us through your Holy Spirit
        and help us to open our hearts to the risen Christ.
    Speak to us through the worship we offer this day,
        and through it all deepen our faith.

Living God,
    we praise you that there is so much
        that speaks to us of your love and purpose –
        so much in our lives,
        in our daily experience,
        in the world around us,
        in the vastness of the universe,
        in the fellowship we share with one another,
        and in the relationship we enjoy with you,
        through which you teach and guide and challenge us.
    Forgive us that we do not sometimes hear your voice,
        that often we do not want to hear.
    Forgive us that sometimes we refuse to listen,
        that often we are closed to anything
        but our own words.

Open our hearts
    to all the ways you are at work.
Open our eyes
    so that we may glimpse your purpose more fully.
Open our ears
    so that we may hear your voice more clearly.
Open our minds
    to receive your truth more completely.
Help us to see everything that points to your activity
    in our lives,
    in our fellowship,
    in your Church,
    and in the world.
And speak through us as we work and witness for you,
    that others may come to know you for themselves.
    Amen.

192

TRUE WORSHIP

Loving God,
    this is the day you have made
        and we thank you for it.
    We thank you for all the good things which surround us –
        our homes,
        our families,
        our friends,
        our church,
        the vastness of the universe,
        the beauty of the natural world,
        the sights and sounds of daily life.
    For all you have given,
        we praise and worship you.

We thank you for all the interest,
    and opportunities,
    and pleasures this day will bring.
For all you have given,
    we praise and worship you.

We thank you for the love of Christ encircling us,
    his Spirit guiding us,
    and your eternal purpose constantly inspiring us.
For all you have given,
    we praise and worship you.

We thank you for this day set aside
    so that we might praise you,
    so that we might bring our lives before you,
    and consecrate every day to your service.
For all you have given,
    we praise and worship you.

Loving God,
    we bring you our praise.
    Gladly and reverently we offer our worship –
        we declare your greatness,
        we acknowledge your faithfulness,
        we rejoice in your goodness,
        we marvel at your holiness.
    All we have and all that is we owe to you.
    For all you have given,
        we praise and worship you.

    You are ever at work in our lives and our world,
        striving to help and strengthen,
        heal and comfort,
        forgive and restore,
        undo wrongs and establish right.
    For all you have given,
        we praise and worship you.

Loving God,
    forgive us that we have sometimes lost sight
        of your great love,
        that we have been forgetful of you,
        greeting some days with indifference,
        even reluctance,
        instead of welcoming them as your gift.
    We have failed to count our blessings
        or appreciate how fortunate we really are.
    We have even made this time of worship
        a duty or tradition, rather than a privilege.
    For all our faults,
        forgive us, O Lord.

Loving God,
    we know we have failed you in much –
        we have not given you due recognition,
        we have not shown thanksgiving in our hearts,
        we have not lived as your people.
    For all our faults,
        forgive us, O Lord.

Have mercy on us,
   cleanse us from all our weaknesses,
   pardon our sins,
   renew our faith and restore us to your side.
For all our faults,
   forgive us, O Lord.

And so with your help,
   through the grace of Christ,
   and in the power of the Holy Spirit,
   may we be enabled to live more faithfully
   as your servants,
   through Jesus Christ our Lord.
   Amen.

193

THE OTHERNESS OF GOD

Sovereign God,
 great and wonderful,
  almighty and all-powerful,
  in grateful praise we bring you our worship.

We praise you that you are greater
 than our minds can grasp –
 higher than our highest thoughts,
 beyond expression in words.
In grateful praise we bring you our worship.

We praise you that you are the source
 of all that is and has been,
 that you are at work in our world and in our lives,
 always seeking to fulfil your purposes,
 never resting until your will is accomplished.
In grateful praise we bring you our worship.

We praise you that you came to our world in Christ,
 and that through him you come to us again,
 revealing your love,
 renewing our faith,
 showing your mercy,
 giving us life.
In grateful praise we bring you our worship.

Forgive us that we have not appreciated all you have done –
 we have not kept our first sense of wonder
 at your greatness;
 we have not given you the praise
 that is rightfully yours;
 we have presumed to limit you
 to our own expectations;
 we have been closed to your Holy Spirit's prompting;
 we have kept Christ at arm's length
 when his challenge has disturbed us.

Yet you have shown mercy to us,
    constantly reaching out to cleanse and renew.
In grateful praise we bring you our worship.

Come to us now as we worship you,
    and through your loving mercy
    give us guidance for the days ahead.
Help us to grow stronger in faith,
    more committed in discipleship,
    more faithful in the service of Christ,
    until that day when he is all and in all.
In grateful praise we bring you our worship,
    to the glory of your name.
    Amen.

194

FAILURE TO LIVE AS GOD'S PEOPLE

Sovereign God,
    again we come as part of the great company of your people
        to offer you our worship,
        to give you the praise and the glory,
        the honour and thanksgiving,
        that you and you alone deserve.
Lord of all, hear our prayer.

We come with awe and wonder,
    humility and reverence,
    joy and celebration,
    for you are a great God above all gods,
    gracious and loving,
    the creator of the ends of the earth,
    the giver of life in all its fullness.
Lord of all, hear our praise.

But we do not just bring our praise –
    we bring also our confession
    for we have failed you in so much.
We have not worshipped you as we should.
We have not shown proper gratitude
    for all you have given us.
We have not looked to you for guidance,
    nor have we always followed it when you give it.
We have not loved one another or our neighbours
    as much as we love ourselves.
We have been thoughtless, careless, selfish,
    and so much else we should not have been.
Lord of all, hear our confession.

We come with sorrow and a sense of shame,
> throwing ourselves once more upon your mercy,
> depending on your grace to lift us up
> and renew us once more.
Grant us your forgiveness,
> and do not hold our faults against us.
Give to us time for repentance,
> and the strength to turn from our sins back towards you.
Use now this time of worship to touch our hearts,
> to speak to our minds,
> to transform our lives.
Lord of all, hear our cry,
> **through Jesus Christ our Lord.**
> **Amen.**

195

CELEBRATING GOD'S GIFTS

Loving God,
    we thank you for this new day you have given us –
        for the opportunities it brings,
        the things we will enjoy in it,
        the times we will share with family,
        with friends and with you,
        the beauty we will see in the world around us,
        the people we will meet,
        and the life we will live.
Loving God, receive our thanks.

We praise you that we have so much to thank you for –
    so much that is good,
    that brings us pleasure,
    that causes us to rejoice.
We praise you that you are always looking to bless us,
    to help us celebrate life in all its fullness.
Loving God, receive our praise.

Forgive us that we sometimes fail to count our blessings –
    that we let familiarity blind us
    to how fortunate we are,
    and fail to thank you for your many gifts.
Forgive us that we fail
    to make the most of all we have received,
    constantly seeking more and more
    instead of appreciating what we have,
    squandering our inheritance
    rather than using it wisely.
Loving God, receive our confession.

Lord of all,
 assure us, once more, of your loving mercy,
  your constant forgiveness,
  your continuing love,
  and teach us to accept everything you have given us
  with heartfelt gratitude,
  showing our thanks not just in these words
  but in our daily living –
  in celebrating and sharing the wonder of life!
 Loving God, receive our worship,
  in the name of Christ.
  Amen.

196

FAITHLESSNESS IN DISCIPLESHIP

God of all,
  we come to proclaim your greatness,
    to sing of your might,
    to declare your majesty,
    and to rejoice in all that you have done.
  You are a God of love and mercy,
    and we praise you.

We come to hear again of your great acts across history,
    your wonderful deeds amongst your people,
    all you have accomplished in Christ.
  You are a God of love and mercy,
    and we praise you.

We come to lift up our hearts
    to lift up our voices,
    and to celebrate again the Gospel.
  You are a God of love and mercy,
    and we praise you.

But as we bring our praise so also we bring our confession.
Confession that too often our praise has been hollow,
    our worship restricted to Sundays
    and to these four walls.
That when the chance has come to speak for you
    we have kept silent,
    and when the opportunity has arisen to serve you
    we have held back.
That when we have known what we should do
    we have failed to do it,
    and when we have known what not to do
    we have gone ahead and done it.

That we have forgotten you are always ready
    to forgive and renew us,
    and consequently have burdened ourselves
    with feelings of guilt and despair.
You are a God of love and mercy,
    and we praise you.

Merciful God,
    forgive us now for failing to practise what we preach,
    for denying what we proclaim by the way we live,
    for letting you down in so many ways
    through our weak and feeble discipleship.
You are a God of love and mercy,
    and we praise you.

Help us to live in such a way
    that our words and actions may be one,
    and our faith seen to be real.
And so may all we say,
    all we do,
    and all we are,
    witness to you and the wonder of your love
    shown through Jesus Christ our Lord.
You are a God of love and mercy,
    and we praise you,
    in his name.
    Amen.

197

RESPONSIBILITY TOWARDS GOD AND OTHERS

Living God,
  we praise you for your love shown to us in Christ –
    your love that goes on seeking us out,
    caring,
    guiding,
    protecting,
    forgiving,
    despite our lack of love for you,
    and our failure to live as Jesus' disciples.
  Teach us to respond by loving you and others.

Living God,
  forgive us our feeble faith.
  Forgive us for caring so little about you,
    so little about others,
    and so much about ourselves.
  Forgive us for turning the Christian faith
    into something we receive,
    rather than something we share.
  Teach us to respond by loving you and others.

Living God,
  help us more truly to live as your people.
  Give us a due sense of our responsibility towards others –
    the poor, the hungry, the sick, the homeless,
    the oppressed, the lonely, the weak, the sorrowful.
  Teach us to respond by loving you and others.

Help us to recognise our responsibility
    towards you and the world you have given us,
    so that in everything we think and say and do
    we may live for your glory and work for your kingdom.
  **Teach us to respond by loving you and others,
    in the name of Jesus Christ our Lord.
    Amen.**

198

GOD'S CREATION

Lord of all,
  we praise you for our universe
    with its infinite fascination,
    for our world with all its wonder.
    for our countryside with all its beauty,
    for life itself in all its incredible variety.
  Loving Lord,
    hear our prayer.

There is so much that gives us pleasure,
    that offers us fulfilment,
    that captures our imagination,
    that challenges and inspires,
    that gives us cause to look forward with anticipation,
    that speaks to us of your great love.
  Loving Lord,
    hear our prayer.

Forgive us for so often abusing all you have given –
    for despoiling our world,
    for failing to appreciate it as we should,
    for losing our childlike sense of wonder and enquiry,
    for treating it as ours by right
    rather than entrusted as your gift,
    for being blind to your loving hand moving behind it all.
  Loving Lord,
    hear our prayer.

Open our eyes to the countless blessings
    and inexhaustible riches you have so freely given,
    and help us to show our appreciation
    by being faithful stewards of your creation.
  Loving Lord,
    hear our prayer,
    in the name of Christ.
    Amen.

PRAYERS OF CONFESSION

199

UNFULFILLED INTENTIONS

Gracious God,
  you have called us to deny ourselves,
    to put ourselves last rather than first.
Forgive us that we find that so hard,
  that we fail you so often.
Lord, in your mercy,
  hear our prayer.

Forgive us for those things we should have done
    but have left undone –
    the acts of kindness we never found time for,
    the thoughtful word never spoken,
    the message of encouragement or concern never sent,
    the helpful deed never attempted.
Lord, in your mercy,
  hear our prayer.

Forgive us for all the opportunities we have missed –
    the plans we never made,
    the dreams we never brought to reality,
    the possibilities we never imagined,
    the gifts we never used.
Lord, in your mercy,
  hear our prayer.

Forgive us for our failure to serve you as we promised –
    the prayers we never offered,
    the sacrifices we never made,
    the faith we never had,
    the commitment we never gave.
Lord, in your mercy,
  hear our prayer.

Forgive us for so often having time only for self –
    for being self-centred,
    self-important,
    self-righteous,
    self-interested,
    self-indulgent,
    self-opinionated.
Lord, in your mercy,
    hear our prayer.

Forgive us for forgetting each other here,
    for forgetting those around us,
    for forgetting you.
Lord, in your mercy,
    hear our prayer.

Gracious God,
    save us from being a people of unfulfilled intentions.
    Help us to translate our thoughts into actions,
        to put our preaching into practice,
        to turn our good intentions into good deeds.
    Lord, in your mercy,
        hear our prayer.

Help us to learn from Jesus
    who laid down his life for others,
    and, in growing closer to him,
    may our lives speak not of ourselves,
    but of you.
Lord, in your mercy,
    hear our prayer,
    for in his name we pray.
    Amen.

200

BARREN SOIL

Almighty and loving God,
    we thank you for all the ways
        you have sown the seed of your word in our lives –
        through the living relationship we share with Christ,
        through the movement of the Holy Spirit within our hearts,
        through the preaching and reading of the Scriptures,
        through the fellowship of the Church,
        through the daily experience of your love
        in the world around us.

Forgive us for all those times
    when your word has failed to take root.
Forgive us the shallowness of our faith
    and our unwillingness to dig deeper.
Forgive our failure to prepare ourselves for worship,
    our carelessness in making time for you,
    our laziness in discipleship,
    our preoccupation with all that distracts us
    from our true calling,

Loving God,
    forgive us that our lives have been barren
        when they should have borne lasting fruit.
Sow afresh your word in our hearts
    and nurture it within us,
    so that we may grow in grace
    and yield a rich harvest of your Spirit,
    through Jesus Christ our Lord.
    Amen.

201

CLOSED MINDS

Gracious God,
> you speak to us in all kinds of ways,
>> through all kinds of people –
>> **forgive us that we are sometimes closed**
>> **to what you have to say.**

> Forgive us that we avoid that which challenges,
>> disturbs or unsettles us,
>> **preferring to criticise and condemn**
>> **rather than face the issues raised.**
> Forgive us that we are swift to find fault
>> with those we don't agree with,
>> **shutting our ears**
>> **rather listening to their point of view.**
> Forgive us that we are often reluctant
>> to accept new and unfamiliar ideas,
>> **taking refuge instead**
>> **in what is tried and trusted.**
> Forgive us that we can become so bogged down
>> in what we think is right,
>> **so sure of our own convictions and set in our ways**
>> **that we resent anything new.**
> Forgive us that we sometimes go through the motions of faith,
>> **outwardly rich but inwardly barren.**

Gracious God,
> **open our hearts this day to the living reality of Christ.**
> Open our minds to the sweeping breath of your Holy Spirit.
> **Open our souls to all that you would do and say.**
> And so, assured of your mercy and renewing power,
>> **help us to live truly as your people,**
>> **in the name of Christ.**
>> **Amen.**

202

MERCY OF GOD

Almighty God,
  as we remember your faithfulness
    so we are made more conscious of our faithlessness.
  Forgive us, O Lord.

Forgive us for the smallness of our vision –
  our failure to worship you as you deserve,
  our carelessness in discipleship.

Forgive our faults and failings –
  our failure to learn from past mistakes,
  our preferring our way to yours.

Forgive us all the opportunities to serve you we have missed –
  all we could and should have done but failed to do,
  all the chances to advance your kingdom we have wasted.

Almighty God,
  we bring our confession with sorrow and shame,
    but also with confidence,
    for we know you are a gracious God,
    a God of mercy and compassion,
    slow to anger and abounding in steadfast love.

Assure us now, we pray, of your continued forgiveness,
    and help us to amend our lives,
    through Christ our Lord.
    Amen.

203

DECEIVING OURSELVES

All-seeing and all-knowing God,
   forgive us for so often deceiving ourselves
      and trying to deceive you –
         refusing to admit or accept our mistakes.
Forgive us the excuses we make for not following you
   or accepting the way of the Cross –
      blaming anything but ourselves when we let you down.
Forgive us for pretending to be better than we really are –
   avoiding that which we find hard to accept
   or do not wish to understand.
Forgive us for willingly accepting half-truths,
   and for deliberately inventing untruths.

Almighty God,
   we find it so easy to deceive ourselves
      and so hard to see ourselves as we really are,
         yet you see us as we are in all our sinfulness,
         and still you love us!
Help us to accept the freedom your love brings,
   and, in being honest with ourselves,
   to be honest with you.
Help us to come to you, just as we are,
   and find true forgiveness, real peace,
   and strength to live as your people.
In the name of Christ.
   Amen.

204

TRUSTING IN OUR OWN STRENGTH

Lord of heaven and earth,
    of all that is and has been and will be –
        forgive us for trusting in our own strength
        rather than in yours.

Forgive us for thinking our way is best,
    for claiming honour that is rightly yours,
    for seeking our ends rather than your kingdom,
    for putting our confidence in things
    which have no power to save or satisfy.
Forgive us for trusting in our own strength
    rather than in yours.

Forgive us for all the challenges we have ignored,
    the opportunities we have missed,
    the work we have failed to do,
    all through refusing to trust you fully.
Forgive us for trusting in our own strength
    rather than in yours.

Forgive us for the people we have let down,
    the circumstances we have despaired of,
    the opportunities we have wasted,
    all because we have trusted our judgement before yours.
Forgive us for trusting in our own strength
    rather than in yours.

Lord of all,
    teach us that when we feel most weak and helpless
        you are at your strongest,
        that what the world counts powerless
        is often most powerful.
Save us from closing our lives to your mighty presence.
Forgive us for trusting in our own strength
    rather than in yours.

Give us renewed faith,
    greater trust,
and deeper confidence in all that you are able to do.
Teach us to trust your strength
    rather than our own,
        and so may we attempt new things in your name
    and fulfil them to your glory,
    through Jesus Christ our Lord.
    Amen.

205

FAILURE TO LISTEN

Living God,
  we thank you for our world
    full of so many wonderful sounds –
    the sound of children laughing,
    babies crying, and people talking,
    the sound of birds singing or an orchestra playing,
    the sound of wind blowing in the trees
    and waves crashing on the seashore,
    the sound of everyday life in a busy street,
    and the sound of silence.
  Lord of all,
    teach us to listen.

In all kinds of ways you speak to us,
  but so often we fail to listen to what you are saying.
We come to you in prayer,
  but we do not wait to hear your answer.
We give ear to a multitude of voices clamouring for attention,
  but we do not hear the still small voice within.
Lord of all,
  teach us to listen.

Forgive us that we close our minds
  to what we don't want to hear,
  or that we are sometimes too busy to hear,
  or that we hear only with our ears
  and not with our souls.
Lord of all,
  teach us to listen.

Living God,
  we thank you for speaking to us.
  Teach us to listen,
    in Christ's name.
    Amen.

206

FAILURE TO SEE

Gracious God,
we thank you for the great gift of sight,
and for all there is
in this wonderful world of ours to see.
We thank you that we can look around
and feast our eyes on so much that is good,
fascinating,
memorable,
and beautiful.
Gracious God, open our eyes.

We thank you that besides this
there are other kinds of sight –
foresight,
hindsight,
insight –
each enabling us to see behind outer appearances
to a deeper reality within.
Gracious God, open our eyes.

Forgive us for so often failing to see beneath the surface,
for overlooking the ways you are at work in our lives.
for being blind to all you would reveal to us.
Gracious God, open our eyes,
and help us to see!
In the name of Christ we pray.
Amen.

207

FAILURE TO MAKE CHRIST KNOWN

Lord of all,
    you call us to go out into the world,
        to share our faith and show your love.
    You call us to go out in the name of Christ,
        to make known his name and make real his presence.
    You call us to go out through the power of your Spirit,
        to live for you and for others.

Forgive us that so often we *come* to you
    but fail to *go* for you.
Forgive us that so easily we turn in on ourselves
    and away from others.
Forgive us that having received so much
    we give so little.

Renew us now through your Spirit.
Restore us through the love of Christ.
Remake us in your likeness.
Assure us of your forgiveness.
And send us out to live and work for your kingdom,
    to the glory of your name.
        Amen.

208

SEEING ONLY THE OUTSIDE

Loving Father,
  we ask your forgiveness
    for so often being more concerned with the outside
    than the inside –
    for taking pride in external appearances
    whilst neglecting our inner selves,
    for putting on a good show
    with nothing behind it,
    for seeming virtuous on the surface
    whilst being full of ugliness underneath.
  Father God, hear our prayer.

Help us to realise that beauty is more than skin-deep,
    that faith is more than simply appearance,
    that serving you is more than looking the part.
  Father God, hear our prayer.

Help us to understand that you see us as we really are
    rather than as we like to imagine,
    that you see behind the masks we wear for the world
    into our innermost selves,
    that nothing can be hidden from your gaze.
  Father God, hear our prayer.

Loving Father,
  cleanse our hearts,
    transform our minds,
    renew our spirits
    and help us to walk with Christ.
  Father God, hear our prayer.

Clothe us with joy, peace, patience, kindness,
generosity, faithfulness, gentleness, self-control,
and, above all, love.
So lead us, through your Holy Spirit,
into the way of salvation.
Father God, hear our prayer,
through Jesus Christ our Lord.
Amen.

209

WEAKNESS IN DISCIPLESHIP

Gracious and merciful God,
   as we remember the great love and sacrifice of Christ,
      we come seeking your forgiveness and help.
   In so many ways we have failed you:
      Lord, have mercy upon us.

We have not lived faithfully as your disciples,
   or obeyed your commandments.
We have not loved you as you love us,
   or our neighbours as ourselves.
We have not taken up our cross to follow Jesus.
In so many ways we have failed you:
   Lord, have mercy upon us.

We have been narrow in our horizons,
      weak in our commitment,
      careless in our worship,
      half-hearted in our service.
In so many ways we have failed you:
   Lord, have mercy upon us.

We have preferred our ways to yours,
   and wandered far from you.
We have been concerned with our own advancement
   rather than your kingdom.
In so many ways we have failed you:
   Lord, have mercy upon us.

Gracious God,
   renew our spirits,
      strengthen our wills,
      deepen our faith,
      and send us out forgiven and restored
      to live and work for you,
      in the name of Christ.
      Amen.

210

RESISTING JESUS

Loving God,
> you have come to us in Jesus Christ,
>> offering us life through his love,
>> calling us to live as his disciples,
>> speaking to us through his life and ministry,
>> his death and resurrection.

Help us to open our lives to him.

Forgive us that all too often we do not want to hear.
Forgive us that all too frequently we refuse to listen.
We claim to be followers of Jesus Christ,
> and there is so much that draws us to him,
> but when his message is too demanding –
> when he asks from us what we would rather not face,
> when his words make us feel uncomfortable,
> striking too near the mark –
> we try then to resist him,
> closing our ears and pushing him away.

Help us to open our lives to him.

Loving God,
> forgive us for following only when it is convenient,
>> only when it fits in with our own assumptions,
>> only when little is asked of us.
> Give to us real faith and true commitment,
>> so that we will be ready to hear what is painful to hear,
>> ready to listen to what is challenging and unwelcome,
>> and ready to respond when Jesus calls
>> even when our every impulse is to shy away.

Help us to open our lives to him.

Loving God,
> you have come to us in Christ.
> **Help us to open our lives to him.**
>> **Amen.**

211

RUNNING FROM GOD
(inspired by the story of Jonah)

Living God,
  we thank you that you have called us to faith in Christ,
    to fellowship in your Church,
    to Christian discipleship.
  Help us to hear your voice.

We thank you that you keep on calling us
    to new avenues of service,
    new ways of serving you,
    new ways of working towards your kingdom.
  Help us to hear your voice.

Forgive us that we are sometimes slow
    or unwilling to respond –
    we do not always understand what you are asking of us,
    we resist when your call is too demanding,
    we run from that which we would rather not do,
    we prefer our way to yours.
  Help us to hear your voice.

Living God,
  we praise you that, though we ignore or disobey your call,
    still you seek us out,
    gently and lovingly leading us back to your way,
    and entrusting to us, despite our faithlessness,
    the message of the Gospel.
  Help us to hear your voice.

We praise you that you deal with us and all people in mercy,
    always ready to give a second chance,
    repeatedly showing your patience,
    demonstrating your awesome grace
    time and time again.
  Help us to hear your voice.

We praise you that you are a God full of mercy,
    slow to anger,
    abounding in steadfast love,
    your nature always to forgive.
Help us to hear your voice.

Living God,
    help us to hear your voice clearly,
        to accept your will humbly,
        and to respond to it gladly,
        in the name of Christ.
        Amen.

212

JUDGEMENT AND GRACE

Gracious and righteous God,
we praise you that you are always active –
moving throughout history,
working in our individual lives,
striving to work out your purposes.
You are not remote or detached from our world,
holding yourself aloof from our human condition,
unconcerned about our daily affairs,
but intimately involved in every aspect of our experience.
Gracious and righteous God,
we rejoice in your eternal purpose.

We praise you for your immeasurable love,
always watching over us,
constantly reaching out to bless,
daily by our sides.
You are a God full of mercy,
always ready to forgive,
always prepared to give us the benefit of the doubt,
always eager to wipe the slate clean and start again.
Gracious and righteous God,
we rejoice at your amazing grace.

Forgive us that because of all that
we can sometimes become over-familiar with you –
losing sight of your holiness,
forgetting your commandments,
becoming careless in our discipleship.
Forgive us that we can lose our sense of wonder –
no longer open to all you can do amongst us,
no longer expecting the unexpected,
no longer a people with the courage to dream dreams.
Gracious and righteous God,
we rejoice in the forgiveness you offer.

You are all-good and all-righteous –
    stretching out your hand in judgement,
    punishing wrong-doing,
    destroying evil.
You are all-loving and all-powerful –
    reaching out your hand to bless,
    to reward faithfulness,
    to vindicate truth.
Gracious and righteous God,
    we rejoice in your awesome goodness.

Save us from becoming complacent
    about judgement and grace –
    from imagining our thoughts or actions
    do not matter to you,
    from becoming apathetic or defeatist in our mentality,
    from losing heart when evil appears to triumph over good.
Help us to recognise the destructive consequences
    of our sinfulness,
    to see our faults and to confess them honestly to you,
    to discover the joy that comes from being at one with you,
    and to look forward to that day
    when your will shall be done and your kingdom come,
Gracious and righteous God,
    we rejoice in the certainty of your final triumph,
    through Jesus Christ our Lord.
    Amen.

213

PRIDE

Sovereign God,
    we confess to you with shame
        that sometimes, all too often,
        we have been guilty of the sin of pride.
    We have thought of ourselves more highly than we should,
        boasting of our own achievements,
        and looking down on those around us.
    Have mercy upon us.

We have not listened as we should to your voice
    or to the voice of others,
        believing that we know best,
        preferring our own way,
        trusting in our judgement alone.
    Have mercy upon us.

And we have been guilty of pride in more subtle ways,
    trying to be independent of those around us,
    hiding our frailties behind a mask of self-sufficiency,
    denying our fears and refusing support
    when it has been offered.
    Have mercy upon us.

Sovereign God,
    forgive us when we try to live life alone,
        when we think more of ourselves than of you,
        when we put ourselves before others.
    Have mercy upon us.

Give to us true humility and true lowliness of heart –
   the ability to take proper pride in ourselves
   where it is due,
   but a willingness also to listen to your voice
   and the voice of others,
   accepting our faults, recognising our limitations,
   and confessing our mistakes.

Sovereign God,
   have mercy upon us.
      through Jesus Christ our Lord.
      Amen.

214

WHAT GOD REQUIRES
(inspired by Micah 6:8)

Loving God,
    you call us to live as your people –
        to walk each day by your side,
        seeking your will,
        pursuing what is right,
        and showing your love in our attitudes towards others.
Teach us what you would have us do.

Forgive us that we sometimes make your call so complicated,
    losing sight of the things you really require.
Forgive us that we become preoccupied with the trappings of faith,
    rather than focusing on the essentials.
Forgive us that we are often good at being religious,
    but poor at doing justice, loving kindness,
    and walking humbly with you.
Teach us what you would have us be.

Loving God,
    help us to offer you the sort of lives you want to see,
        and to be the people you would have us become.
Teach us what you require,
    and by your grace may we live as your people,
    to the glory of your name.
    Amen.

215

LIVING FOR OURSELVES

Merciful God,
    once more we bring you our confession,
        conscious of our many faults and failings –
        forgive us that we have been unfaithful to you.
    We have had eyes only for ourselves,
        seeing no further than our own small concerns –
        forgive us that we have been unfaithful to you.
    We have acted with no thought of your will
        and no heed to your guidance –
        forgive us that we have been unfaithful to you.
    We have broken your commandments
        and failed miserably to follow in the way of Christ –
        forgive us that we have been unfaithful to you.

Merciful God,
    day by day you have remained faithful to us –
        forgive us that we have been unfaithful to you.
    You have forgiven us our repeated disobedience –
        forgive us that we fail to forgive others half as freely.
    You have offered us your guidance in all the decisions of life –
        forgive us that we have been slow to follow
        where you would lead.

Merciful God,
    through your grace have mercy upon us.
    Renew our faith, restore us to your side,
        teach us your ways.
        and help us to live more truly as your people,
        in the name of Christ.
        Amen.

216

SELF-INTEREST

Loving God,
>you have called us to be your servants –
>>to offer our service to Christ,
>>to one another,
>>to your Church,
>>to your world.

Forgive us that so often we have failed you.

Forgive us that we are concerned to serve only ourselves –
>our own interests,
>our own needs,
>our own desires,
>our own ends.

Forgive us that so often we have failed you.

Forgive us that we are sometimes more concerned
>with what we can get out of our faith
>than with what we can put into it;
>more concerned with what you can do for us
>than what we can do for you;
>more concerned with what we can receive from others
>than what we can give to them.

Forgive us that so often we have failed you.

Teach us to serve seeking no reward,
>to love without expecting love in return,
>to give without counting the cost,
>to follow without holding back.
>to live each day as your people,
>offering ourselves in glad and joyful service.

Amen.

PRAYERS OF THANKSGIVING

217

THANKS FOR FORGIVENESS

Almighty God,
>we thank you that we can come now before you,
>>that you are here waiting to meet with us and speak to us.
>We thank you that though we have no claim on your love,
>>and no right to expect any mercy,
>>you are always reaching out to us,
>>eager to forgive and forget.

Gracious God, open our hearts to your love.

We thank you that though we repeatedly fail you,
>and though we resist your will,
>you go on wiping the slate clean,
>offering us a new beginning, a fresh start.

Gracious God, open our hearts to your love.

We thank you that you love and care about each one of us,
>that for all our faults and weaknesses
>you accept us just as we are.

Poor though our faith may be,
>you are always ready to guide,
>to help,
>and to bless.

Gracious God, open our hearts to your love.

Almighty God,
>help us to open our lives to you,
>>to be honest with you, ourselves and others.
>Help us to see ourselves as we really are,
>>the good and the bad, the strengths and the weaknesses,
>>the lovely and the unlovely.
>Help us to recognise our sins and to confess them,
>>throwing ourselves upon your mercy.

Gracious God, open our hearts to your love.

And so may we receive the cleansing,
   the renewal
   and the forgiveness you long to show us.
Gracious God, open our hearts to your love.
   in the name of Christ.
   Amen.

218

THE WONDER OF LIFE

Loving God,
    we thank you for the world you have given us
        and all within it that speaks of you.
You have blessed us in so much,
    and we are glad.

We thank you for all that is beautiful;
        all that causes us to catch our breath in wonder
        and points to your hand in creation.
You have blessed us in so much,
    and we are glad.

We thank you for the gift of love, given and received,
        speaking to us of your own great love for us.
You have blessed us in so much,
    and we are glad.

We thank you for family life,
        reminding us of the great family of your people
        to which we belong.
You have blessed us in so much,
    and we are glad.

We thank you for our food, our clothes, our homes;
        all the comforts we enjoy,
        and the innumerable ways you provide for us.
You have blessed us in so much,
    and we are glad.

We thank you for this new morning,
        for the warmth of the sun and the richness of life,
        giving a foretaste of your gift of eternal life.
You have blessed us in so much,
    and we are glad.

Loving God,
open our eyes to your presence around us,
to your love that surrounds us each day,
and to your hand that is always at work.
You have blessed us in so much,
and we are glad.

Speak to us through both the ordinary
and the special things of life,
that through them we may know you more fully
and serve you more truly.
You have blessed us in so much,
and we are glad.

Receive then our praise and thanksgiving,
**for we offer them to you
in the name of Christ our Lord.
Amen.**

219

THANKSGIVING FOR FELLOWSHIP

Loving God,
   we thank you again today
      for the fellowship we share in this church –
      for all it offers, all it means
      and all the ways it enriches our lives
      and enlarges our experience.

We thank you for the unity we have discovered in Christ,
      for the love that binds us together.
We thank you for the experiences we have shared over the years,
      for the bond they have created between us.
We thank you for the care we have been able to show,
      and the care we have in turn received.
We thank you for the opportunities we have had to discuss our faith,
      and the way our understanding of you has grown as a result.
We thank you for the way we can talk together openly and honestly,
      and know that our friendship will not only continue but flourish.

Loving God,
   We do not claim to be a perfect family,
      for we are all too conscious of our weaknesses
      as individuals and as a family.
But we praise you that you have called us here as one people,
      in fellowship with you and one another,
      through Jesus Christ our Lord.
      Amen.

220

OUR GIFTS

Lord of life,
    we thank you for the gifts you have given us –
        the things we can do well
        and enjoy doing,
        the things that bring happiness to us,
        and contribute to the happiness of those around us.
    Lord of life, teach us to use the gifts you have given us;
        to play our part in the life of our fellowship and our society.

We thank you for the gifts of others –
    those things they can do which we can't,
    the talents they have which we haven't,
    the skills they can offer which complement our own,
    and the qualities they display
    which in so many ways enrich our lives.
Lord of life, teach us to appreciate the gifts of those around us;
    to appreciate the contribution they make to our lives.

Lord of life,
    teach us to recognise those things we can do well,
        and those things others can do better.
    Teach us that we belong together;
        that all have something to give and something to receive.
    Teach us to see the worth of every human being,
        and to understand you have a special place for each of us
        in the body of Christ,
        for in his name we pray.
        Amen.

221

HOPE IN DESPAIR

Gracious God,
    we thank you that you are always with us,
        in the bad times as well as the good,
        the difficult as well as the easy,
        the sad as well as the happy.
Lord of all hopefulness,
    hear our prayer.

We thank you that, though we have sometimes
        been unsure of the way ahead,
        you have always been there to guide us,
        though we have felt discouraged,
        you have offered us fresh inspiration,
        though we have been in despair,
        you have given us hope.
Lord of all hopefulness,
    hear our prayer.

We thank you for the assurance this brings us
        that your steadfast love never ceases,
        that your mercies are new every morning,
        that great is your faithfulness.
Lord of all hopefulness,
    hear our prayer.

May that conviction give us confidence in the days ahead,
        so that whatever problems we face,
        whatever disappointments we experience,
        whatever sorrows may befall us,
        we will still find reason to look forward,
        reason to believe in the future,
        and reason to hope.
Lord of all hopefulness,
    hear our prayer,
    in the name of Christ.
    Amen.

222

HOPE AFTER DIFFICULTIES

Loving Father,
    we thank you for your guidance
        during these past difficult days,
        for leading us safely through a time
        when the future seemed dark
        and the present uncertain.
    Whenever we have needed you,
        you have been there.

We thank you for the support you have given
        when we have felt disheartened,
        the courage to keep on believing
        when we have been tempted to doubt,
        the strength to persevere despite adversity.
    Whenever we have needed you,
        you have been there.

Loving Father,
    may all we have experienced renew our trust
        in your continuing purpose for us.
    May it give us food for faith
        in times of difficulty yet to come.
    May it inspire us to serve you
        just as you have served us.
    Whenever we have needed you,
        you have been there.

Lead us forward, we pray,
        and help us to continue in the path you set before us,
        secure in the assurance that, whatever we face,
        your grace will be sufficient for us.
    Whenever we have needed you,
        you have been there.

Thanks be to God!
Amen.

223

LAUGHTER

Loving God,
>we thank you for the things in life that make us laugh,
>>**the things that bring a smile to our faces.**
>We thank you for a sense of humour
>>helping us to see the funny side of life,
>>>**enabling us to share a joke**
>>>**even when it is on ourselves.**
>We thank you for those with the special gift
>>of bringing laughter to others,
>>>**bringing a little light relief**
>>>**into the seriousness of our world.**

Loving God,
>there is a time to weep and a time to laugh,
>>a place for solemnity and a place for humour.
>Help us to get the balance right in our lives.
>**Teach us to appreciate your gift of laughter,**
>>**and to share it with those around us,**
>>**in the name of Christ.**
>>**Amen.**

224

GOD'S GUIDANCE THROUGH HISTORY

Almighty God,
 we acknowledge you as Lord of all,
  the Alpha and Omega,
  the source and goal of all creation.

 Yours is the purpose
  that brought the world and universe into being,
  that created humankind in your image.
 Yours is the purpose
  that guided Abraham to set out in search of a new country,
  that led your people through the wilderness
  to the Promised Land.
 Yours is the purpose
  that supported and sustained them across the ages,
  fulfilled finally in Christ
  through whom you reconciled all things to yourself.

Almighty God,
 we thank you for your involvement in human history,
  for your purpose that will not be defeated.
 We thank you that we are part of that purpose,
  each having a place in your kingdom,
  that in all the vastness of space and time
  we **matter to you!**
 Help us to understand where you would lead us
  and what you would have us do,
  and give us faith to trust
  in the ultimate triumph of your will,
  through Jesus Christ our Lord.
  Amen.

225

The call of God

Almighty and all-seeing God,
throughout history you have called people
to respond to your challenge and follow you.
Today we thank you for those who have heard that call
and in faith responded–
Abraham, called to venture into the unknown,
trusting in your promise;
Moses, called to lead your people from slavery
to the Promised Land, against all odds;
Joshua, called to trust in you and you alone;
Samuel, called by you to a life of service
even before he realised it was you calling;
the prophets, called to proclaim your word of judgement
regardless of the cost to themselves;
John the Baptist, called to be a messenger in the wilderness,
preparing the way of Christ;
the twelve disciples, called to leave the security
of their livelihoods to follow Jesus;
the Apostle Paul, called to preach the Gospel to all nations.
Almighty God,
help us to hear your call,
and in faith to respond.

We thank you for these and all in subsequent generations
who have heard your voice and responded in faith,
offering to you their service undaunted by the cost.
We thank you for those we have known
whose discipleship has been an inspiration to us,
all those who offer an example of what it means
to live and walk in faith.
Almighty God,
help us to hear your call,
and in faith to respond.

Above all we thank you for your Son, Jesus Christ –
   for his perfect revelation of you,
   his total love,
   his supreme sacrifice!
We thank you for his willingness to take the Way of the Cross,
   despite the failure of his closest and most trusted friends
   to stay true,
   despite being rejected and scorned
   by the world he came to die for.
Almighty God,
   help us to hear your call,
   and in faith to respond.

Help us to learn from the example
   of those who have gone before us,
   and to respond as faithfully, as willingly,
   and as courageously as they did.
Give us ears to hear whenever you call,
   and faith to follow wherever you lead.
Take us and use us, through the power of your Holy Spirit,
   so that your will may be done
   and your kingdom come through our lives.
Almighty God,
   help us to hear your call,
   and in faith to respond,
   through Jesus Christ our Lord.
   Amen.

226

THE CALL TO DISCIPLESHIP

Lord Jesus Christ,
> we thank you for your call that comes to us –
>> **the call to discipleship,**
>> **to service,**
>> **to sharing in the work of your kingdom.**

> We thank you that you call us as we are –
>> **with all our faults,**
>> **all our doubts,**
>> **and all our sin.**

> We thank you that you chose us
>> not through our own deserving,
>> **but through your grace,**
>> **your love,**
>> **and your mercy.**

> We thank you that as you chose your people Israel,
>> your disciples,
>> and your Church,
>> **so also you have chosen each of us.**

> And we thank you that though we fail you repeatedly,
>> though we disobey your will,
>> and turn away from you,
>> **yet your purpose for us continues**
>> **and your love endures.**

Lord Jesus Christ,
> we thank you for calling us,
>> and we ask very simply,
>> but also sincerely,
>> **help us to respond,**
>> **in the name of Christ.**
>> **Amen.**

227

GOD'S CONSTANT PRESENCE

Living God,
   we thank you for your promise
      that when we come together in the name of Christ,
      he is here among us.
   We thank you that he is here now,
      ready to speak, listen, forgive, teach and love.

He is present here in one another,
   in the fellowship we share together.
He is present through the Scriptures,
   constantly speaking to us in new ways.
He is present in the sharing of bread and wine,
   **those timeless reminders of his life, his death
   and his resurrection.**
He is present in the world around us,
   in the beauty of creation and the people we meet.
He is present every moment of every day,
   through his life-giving and life-transforming spirit.

Living God,
   we thank you that whoever we are, wherever we are,
      whatever we may be doing,
      you are with us through Christ,
      constantly by our side,
      travelling with us,
      and looking to lead us forward
      into new experiences of your love.
   In the name of Christ we praise you.
   Amen.

228

THE GOD WHO GOES THE WHOLE WAY

Gracious God,
  we thank you that you are a God
    whose nature it is always to have mercy;
    a God of constant patience, love, and forgiveness.
  You have shown us grace throughout our lives,
    forgiving and renewing us
    despite our disobedience and hardness of heart.
  You have kept on reaching out to us,
    even when we have turned our backs on you.
  You love each of us as we are,
    and not for what we might become.
  You have gone the whole way for us through Jesus Christ,
    offering your life in him for the life of the world.

  Give us, we pray, that same love for you and for one another,
    a love that keeps on flowing, come what may.
  Help us to love you without reserve,
    seeking no reward except the joy of knowing you.
  Help us to love one another from our hearts,
    even when love is met with rejection.
  Help us to forgive those who cause us pain,
    even when there is no suggestion of remorse.
  Help us to swallow our pride
    and take the first step in bringing reconciliation,
    even when we may feel ourselves to be the injured party.
  Help us, like you, to go not simply part way,
    but the whole way,
    in the name of Christ.
    Amen.

229

THE GOD WHO HAS TIME FOR US

Living God,
    we thank you that you are a God of love and compassion,
        slow to anger and full of mercy,
        a God of infinite patience,
        infinite goodness,
        infinite care –
    with infinite time for each one of us.
Help us to make time for you.

We thank you that though we so often fail to make time for you,
    and so often fail to find time to serve you,
        yet you are always ready to receive us,
        to accept us,
        to respond to us,
        and to help us in our time of need.
Help us to make time for you.

Teach us to create space in our lives for you,
    for one another and for ourselves.
Help us to measure time not by our standards but yours,
    and so may we live our lives
    as you would have us lead them,
    in the name of Christ.
    Amen.

230

COUNTING OUR BLESSINGS
(based on Philippians 4:11-13)

Loving God,
    we thank you for the countless blessings we have received,
        the innumerable good things
        that surround us every moment of each day –
        so much beauty, variety and interest
        to inspire and instruct us.
     Loving God, for all you have given,
     receive our praise.

We thank you for everything you have given to us
        through Jesus Christ,
        for everything we see of you through him –
        your great love constantly reaching out to us,
        your care and compassion that never ceases,
        your mercy that is never exhausted,
        your eternal purpose which slowly but surely
        is coming to fulfilment.
     Loving God, for all you have given,
     receive our praise.

Loving God,
    forgive us that we are so rarely content,
        that we fail to appreciate how fortunate we are,
        that we lose sight of what we have
        through dwelling on what we might have had.
     Loving God, for all you have given,
     receive our praise.

Teach us to count our blessings,
>to recognise all that is good around us,
>to be truly content in all circumstances,
>to realise that your love will never fail us,
>and your grace will be sufficient for all our needs.
>Loving God, for all you have given,
>>**receive our praise,**
>>**in the name of Christ.**
>>**Amen.**

231

GOD'S FAITHFULNESS

Gracious and loving God,
we thank you for your great faithfulness,
your wonderful and constant love,
your care that is never exhausted,
and your purpose that will not be defeated.
Loving God,
you have been our refuge
from one generation to another,
and we thank you.

We thank you for the way you have chosen
and called your people throughout history –
Abraham, called to walk in faith to an unknown future;
Moses, called to lead your people out of Egypt;
the prophets, called to proclaim your word
and make known your will;
the disciples, called to leave everything
and follow Jesus Christ;
and countless other individuals,
called across the years and throughout the world
to be your Church.
Loving God,
you have been our refuge
from one generation to another,
and we thank you.

Gracious and loving God,
we thank you that though your faithfulness
has so often been returned with faithlessness,
your love so often met with rejection,
and your purpose so often frustrated,
you have not let us go,
but continue to call us your children,
delighting in our response, poor though it may be.
Loving God,
you have been our refuge
from one generation to another,
and we thank you.

Gracious and loving God,
receive our thanks,
and help us to follow
where you would lead us.
In the name of Christ.
Amen.

232

GOD'S UNFAILING PURPOSE

Loving God,
　we thank you
　　that in all the changing circumstances of our lives
　　you are a God we can depend on –
　　always faithful,
　　always true,
　　always loving,
　　always merciful.
For all your mercies,
　we praise and thank you.

We thank you that you are a God who is **constantly at work** –
　in our day-to-day lives,
　in our fellowship,
　in the Church,
　in the world.
For all your mercies,
　we praise and thank you.

Day by day,
　week by week,
　year by year,
　you are working out your purposes.
For all your mercies,
　we praise and thank you.

Seen or unseen,
　recognised or unrecognised,
　appreciated or taken for granted,
　you are moving through your Spirit,
　striving to build your kingdom and fulfil your will.
For all your mercies,
　we praise and thank you.

Loving God,
> you do not work alone,
>> but have invited us to play a part in your purpose.
> In your mercy,
>> **teach us to respond in faith.**
> Help us to keep our side of the bargain –
>> to do our bit as you do yours,
>> to be a people whose lives clearly witness to your love,
>> to live in a way that is consistent with what we believe
>> and honouring to you.
> In your mercy,
>> **teach us to respond in faith.**

> Help us to make the most of everything you have given us,
>> to use our gifts,
>> to grasp our opportunities,
>> and to offer our time, our money and our talents
>> freely in your service.
> In your mercy,
>> **teach us to respond in faith.**

> And help us finally,
>> having played our part,
>> to leave all things in your hands,
>> knowing that, though all else may fail,
>> your love never will.
> **Thanks be to God.**
>> **Amen.**

233

THE GIFT OF LOVE

Almighty God,
we thank you for your great gift of love –
the love which we are able to share with those around us,
which gives us a sense of self-worth and belonging,
which enriches our lives in so many ways.
You have opened your heart to us –
help us to do the same to you.

We thank you for your love which defies all expression,
constant, total, inexhaustible,
flowing out to us like a never-ending stream.
You have opened your heart to us –
help us to do the same to you.

Almighty God,
we thank you for loving us before we ever loved you,
and for continuing to love us
even when we fail to love you in return.
You have opened your heart to us –
help us to do the same to you.

Deepen our love for you and one another.
Help us to be faithful and true in all our relationships,
and most especially in our relationship with you.
You have opened your heart to us –
help us to do the same to you,
in the name of Christ.
Amen.

234

UNLIKELY CHOICES

Lord Jesus Christ,
  we thank you for all those
    who have heard your call across the ages –
    all those from different walks of life
    who have come together,
    at different times,
    in different ways,
    and in different places,
    to be your people.
Lord Jesus, for your surprising call,
  receive our thanks.

We thank you for the way
  you have consistently brought together
  the most unlikely of individuals –
  from different races,
  different cultures,
  with different characters,
  and different gifts,
  to become your Church.
Lord Jesus, for your surprising call,
  receive our thanks.

And, above all, we thank you that you have called us here,
  with our different outlooks,
  contrasting temperaments,
  diverging backgrounds,
  and variety of experiences,
  to be your Church in this place.
Lord Jesus, for your surprising call,
  receive our thanks.

Lord Jesus Christ,
    teach us that whoever we are you can use us –
        you can use anyone and everyone for your kingdom.
    Help us to accept one another and ourselves
        as we really are –
        united in our diversity by one common cause.
    Take us and use us just as we are,
        to demonstrate your transforming love
        and to work for the coming of your kingdom.
    Lord Jesus, for your surprising call,
        receive our thanks,
        for in your name we pray.
        Amen.

OFFERTORY PRAYERS

235

Gracious God,
    you have blessed us beyond our deserving.
        You have given us more
            than we could ever have dared ask for,
            loving us with a love that refuses to count the cost,
            showering us with good things too many to number.
Gracious God,
    for your generous and wonderful gifts we praise you,
        and we bring this our offering
        as a token of our thanksgiving,
        in the name of Christ.
        Amen.

236

Gracious God,
    we can never repay all we owe you,
        or even a fraction of what we have received
        from your loving hand.
So we bring you these gifts,
        not as any settling of a debt,
        but as a gesture of gratitude
        and an expression of our love,
        offered to you in joyful worship,
        through Jesus Christ our Lord.
        Amen.

237

Gracious God,
   we thank you that you are a God
      who gives to us and goes on giving,
      day after day after day;
      a God who shared our humanity
      so that we might share your eternity,
      who offered your own Son
      so that we might become your children,
      who was ready to die for us
      so that we might live for you.
   For that amazing truth,
      we praise you!

Forgive us that we find it so hard to give
      even a little in return,
      carefully and sometimes grudgingly
      measuring out our response,
      giving what we can afford rather than what you deserve,
      putting ourselves first and you second.
   Thank you that, despite this,
      still you love us and care for us.
   For that amazing truth,
      we praise you!
      Amen.

238

Gracious God,
   for all you have given us,
      all you will give us,
      and all you give us here and now,
      we offer you our thanks and praise,
      in the name of Christ.
      Amen.

239

God of love,
    we bring to you this day our money,
        not as a collection
        but as an offering,
        not given out of duty
        but gladly,
        not brought out of habit
        but out of love.
    Receive what we offer in the spirit that we offer it,
        for we would tell you simply through these gifts
        how much we love you
        and how much we want to thank you
        for all we have received.
In the name of Christ.
    Amen.

240

God of love,
    we offer these gifts,
        small though they are.
    We offer our worship,
        imperfect though it may be.
    We offer our faith,
        weak though it is.
    We offer our love,
        poor though it seems compared to yours.
God of love,
    take all we offer this day
        flawed though we know it to be,
        and use it in ways beyond our imagination
        for your kingdom and glory.
        Amen.

241

Lord of all,
>as we make our offering today
>>we do not just bring you our money –
>>**we bring ourselves,**
>>we bring our fellowship,
>>**we bring your Church everywhere,**
>>praying that you will use all we do,
>>**all we say,**
>>and all we are,
>>**for the growth of your kingdom**
>>and the fulfilment of your will,
>>**through Jesus Christ our Lord.**
>>**Amen.**

242

Loving God,
>we bring you these gifts,
>>not because we must
>>**but because we may,**
>>not because we have to
>>**but because we want to,**
>>not because it is our duty
>>**but because it is our privilege,**
>>not because it is expected
>>**but because it is invited.**
We present our offering freely to you,
>**just as you freely offered yourself for us in Christ.**
In his name we pray.
>**Amen.**

243

Gracious God,
   there are no words deep enough
      to thank you for all your goodness,
      no deeds great enough
      to thank you for all your love,
      no gifts costly enough
      to thank you for your gift in Jesus Christ.
   But we want to make some kind of response,
      to express our gratitude for all you have done for us.
   So we bring you now this money
      as a token of our love,
      a sign of our worship,
      and a symbol of our discipleship,
      offered to you, through Christ our Lord,
      in joyful and grateful praise.
      Amen.

244

Living God,
   you have poured out your blessings upon us,
      day after day.
   You have filled our lives with good things
      so that they overflow with plenty.
   You have met our needs and more than our needs,
      giving us a world of infinite variety and pleasure.
   Receive now these our gifts,
      receive our worship
      receive our faith,
      for we bring them to you
      as a small but simple way of saying thank you
      for all you have done in Christ.
   In his name we pray.
      Amen.

245

Loving God,
    so often we fail to thank you for all we have received.
    We are quick to ask for more
        but slow to appreciate what we have already received.
    We are quick to bring our requests
        but slow to show gratitude when they are granted.
    We are quick to complain when life is hard
        but slow to rejoice when it is good.
Loving God,
    forgive us,
        and receive now these gifts,
        offered to you as our way of saying
        what we should have said so many times before:
        Thank you for everything!
        Amen.

PRAYERS FOR OURSELVES

246

Following Jesus

Lord Jesus Christ,
 you call us, as you called your first disciples,
  to follow you –
  not simply to believe,
  not merely to declare our faith
  and confess you as Lord,
  but to keep on following wherever you lead.
Lord Jesus, help us!

Help us to follow you eagerly,
  faithfully,
  devotedly,
  seeing where you are at work
  and staying close to you.
Lord Jesus, help us!

Help us to follow in your footsteps,
  pursuing the way of love,
  and accepting the road of sacrifice.
Lord Jesus, help us!

Help us to follow after you,
  letting your presence fill our hearts,
  and trusting you so completely
  that your love shines through us.
Lord Jesus, help us!

Help us to follow through the life of discipleship,
  not allowing ourselves to become distracted,
  or to lose heart so that we wander away from you,
  but keeping faith to the end.
Lord Jesus, help us!

Lord Jesus Christ,
  you call us, as you call all your people,
    to follow you.
  Teach us what that means,
    and by your grace help us to respond
    and be followers of your way.
  Lord Jesus, help us,
    for we ask it in your name.
    Amen.

247

God's transforming power

Gracious God,
    we praise you that day by day you are at work in our lives,
        transforming them beyond all our expectations.
    We praise you for the way that despite ourselves
        you have called us to faith,
        breaking through our doubts,
        our stubbornness,
        our selfishness,
        and pride,
        drawing us to Christ.
    Gracious God,
        continue to change us, we pray.

Help us to keep firm hold of the conviction
    that you can continue to change us –
    that whoever we are,
    whatever we do,
    whatever we face,
    nothing is outside the scope of your renewing power.
Gracious God,
    continue to change us, we pray.

Help us to remember you can change others –
    that however hopeless a case may seem,
    however much a person may be opposed to you,
    however far from you they may appear,
    you are able to make a new creation of them.
Gracious God,
    continue to change us, we pray.

Help us to realise that as you have spoken to us
    so you can speak to others –
    that no matter how closed someone may be,
    how unwilling to listen,
    how indifferent,
    you are able to stir their heart
    and challenge their spirit.
Gracious God,
continue to change us, we pray.

Gracious God,
    save us from ever losing sight of that fact,
    from retreating into pessimism,
    fatalism,
    defeatism.
Gracious God,
continue to change us, we pray.

Save us from so forgetting all you can do
    that we become disheartened,
    expecting nothing,
    attempting nothing,
    achieving nothing.
Gracious God,
continue to change us, we pray.

Help us separately and together,
    through our words and our actions,
    to speak of how you have changed us,
    so that in turn you may change others.
Gracious God,
continue to change us, we pray,
through Christ our Lord.
Amen.

248

ANGER

Living God,
  we rejoice that you are a God who is slow to anger
    and full of steadfast love,
    infinitely patient, understanding and merciful,
    always seeking to forgive, to forget, to restore and renew.
  Yet do not let us become complacent,
    for there are times when even your patience
    is tested to the limit
    and your anger blazes against us –
    when we wilfully and stubbornly disobey you,
    when our actions, or failure to act, causes harm to others,
    when our faithlessness becomes a stumbling block
    to those who seek you.
  Forgive us those times,
    and help us put right our mistakes.
  Lord, in your mercy,
    hear our prayer.

Living God,
  help us to recognise there are occasions
    when you have no choice but to feel angry,
    and help us to recognise sometimes
    that we should feel the same.
  Help us to know when those occasions are.
  Lord, in your mercy,
    hear our prayer.

Teach us when anger is unjustified, foolish, petty, selfish,
    when it is more about our hurt pride than right and wrong,
    when it says more about ourselves
    than the cause we attribute anger to.
Save us then from the errors it might lead us into –
    thoughtless words, careless deeds,
    and destructive attitudes –
    and help us then to control our anger.
Lord, in your mercy,
    hear our prayer.

But teach us also when we ought to be angry.
When we are faced by anything
    that denies full living,
    that demeans and destroys,
    that feeds injustice or exploitation,
    that cheats, corrupts, wounds or hurts,
    that leads the innocent astray,
    that divides people from one another and from you,
    teach us then to feel a genuine fury
    and to express that with proper passion,
    translating anger into action,
    speaking out against falsehood,
    working to right wrongs,
    overcoming evil with good,
    giving all for your kingdom.
Lord, in your mercy,
    hear our prayer,
    in the name of Christ our Lord.
    Amen.

249

BREAKING DOWN THE BARRIERS

Sovereign God,
    there is so much in our lives that separates us from you –
        our selfishness, our pride, our greed, our envy,
        our thoughtless actions, our foolish words,
        our evil desires, our selfish natures.
    So much about us that runs contrary to your will
        and reflects everything you are not.
    Merciful God, hear our confession,
        and draw near to us.

We praise you that despite our sin you have come to us,
        opening the way to your presence,
        offering us the opportunity of knowing you for ourselves,
        establishing a living relationship between us
        and opening the way to true happiness.
    Merciful God, hear our praise,
        and draw near to us.

Sovereign God,
    you have broken down the barriers that keep us apart,
        sweeping away all the obstacles which separate us.
    You have provided the key to life,
        and unlocked the door to your presence.
    Merciful God, hear our thanksgiving,
        and draw near to us.

Help us to appreciate the wonder of what you have done,
        to receive the new life you offer,
        to gladly and reverently approach your throne of grace
        and know you for ourselves,
        the living God made flesh.
    Merciful God, hear our prayer,
        and draw near to us,
        in the name of Christ.
        Amen.

250

FINDING GOD EVERYWHERE

Living God,
  we praise you for the way
    we experience your presence as we come to worship,
    the way this time enables us to focus our thoughts upon you.
  Ever-present God,
    help us to find you here.

But save us from mistakenly imagining
  you are more here than anywhere else.
Teach us that you are with us wherever we may be
    and whatever we may be doing,
    and so help us consecrate not just this short time
    week by week
    but every moment of every day.
Help us to recognise you are involved
    in every aspect of our lives,
    in every part of the world and every situation,
    and grant that this brief drawing aside from the routine of life
    may equip us to go back to it
    with new conviction, vision, hope and faith.
  Ever-present God,
    help us to find you there.

Living God,
  speak to us as we worship you.
  Challenge and confront us through your word,
    meet with us in our prayers,
    respond to the worship we bring you
    and fill us with a new sense of your majesty.
  Ever-present God,
    help us to find you now.

May the affairs of daily life be illuminated
  and enriched by our being here.
And so as we return to our daily routine
  may we know you are there as much as anywhere,
  waiting to meeting us in those around us,
  unfolding your purpose in the events of life,
  demonstrating your handiwork in the wonder of creation.
Ever-present God,
  help us to find you always,
  through Jesus Christ our Lord.
  Amen.

251

LIVING FOR GOD'S SAKE

Loving God,
    you ask us whatever we do, to do it for your sake –
        to offer our whole lives,
        our every thought, word and action,
        to your service,
        for your glory.
    Help us to understand what that really means –
        to see every part of each day
        as an opportunity to work for you,
        and to approach our work and our leisure
        in such a way as to bear witness to you.
    God of love,
        for your name's sake, help us.

May everything we do be tackled with such energy,
        enthusiasm, and dedication,
        such thoroughness, determination, and cheerfulness,
        that others may recognise your hand upon us,
        your spirit with us,
        and your love in our hearts.
    God of love,
        for your name's sake, help us.

Loving God,
    we often hear the expression, 'For God's sake!'
    We may even use it ourselves:
        'For God's sake do this!'
        'For God's sake do that!'
        'For God's sake stop!'
        'For God's sake listen!'
    Yet what we really mean, if we are honest,
        is for our own sakes, not yours.
    God of love,
        for your name's sake, help us.

Loving God,
    save us from simply serving our own ends,
        from doing merely what we enjoy doing
        and leaving the rest to others.
    Save us from acting out of necessity or routine,
        but teach us instead to respond from the heart,
        dedicating all of life to you,
        remembering that Jesus died for the sake of the world.
    God of love,
        for your name's sake, help us,
        through Christ our Lord.
        Amen.

252

FREEDOM FROM FEAR

Loving God,
   in all the changes and chances of our lives,
     all the many uncertainties we face,
     we thank you that you are a God we can depend on,
     always good,
     always loving,
     always merciful and always faithful.
   God of love,
     for the knowledge that you are always with us,
     we praise you.

We thank you for the assurance
     that, whatever we may be confronted with,
     your love will go on reaching out,
     your hand go on supporting,
     and your purpose go on being fulfilled.
   God of love,
     for the knowledge that you are always with us,
     we praise you.

Help us to truly believe that,
     not just in our minds but in our hearts,
     to put our trust wholly in you,
     confident that you will never fail us.
   God of love,
     for the knowledge that you are always with us,
     we praise you.

Help us to let go of the fears and anxieties
    that weigh us down,
    that hold us back,
    that destroy our confidence and undermine our happiness,
    that alienate us from one another
    and prevent us living life to the full.
God of love,
    for the knowledge that you are always with us,
    we praise you.

Help us to receive the freedom you offer,
    the freedom that comes from knowing
    you hold all things in your hands
    and that nothing can finally separate us from your love.
God of love,
    for the knowledge that you are always with us,
    we praise you.

Give us the peace Jesus promised to all who follow him,
    the knowledge that we need neither be troubled or afraid,
    for you are with us,
    watching over us now and always.
God of love,
    for the knowledge that you are always with us,
    we praise you,
    in the name of Christ.
    Amen.

253

STRENGTH IN WEAKNESS

Transforming God,
  ever at work among the poor,
    the humble,
    the weak,
    the lowly,
    teach us to live not by our values
    but by yours.

When we feel feeble and powerless,
    incapable of meeting the challenges before us;
    when we feel our resources are too small
    and the demands put upon us too great;
    when we feel we can achieve little
    and so set limits on what you can do through us,
    teach us to live not by our values
    but by yours.

When we look around us and see no sign of your kingdom,
    when so much evil seems to triumph over so little good,
    when the problems of our world seem many
    and the answers to them few,
    when hope seems futile and despair more than justified,
    when truth and love appear overwhelmed
    by falsehood and hatred,
    teach us to live not by our values
    but by yours.

Transforming God,
  help us to recognise that you can use
      what seems small in our eyes beyond all our imagining,
      that from the smallest of beginnings
      you can bring the greatest of results.
  Teach us that you can use others,
      that you can use us,
      that you can use anyone.
  Teach us to live not by our values
      but by yours,
      to the glory of your name.
      Amen.

254

IN CHRIST, IN . . . ?

*(This prayer reminds us that faith must be earthed in our daily situation.
Insert the name of the town where you and your congregation live.)*

Living God,
we thank you for all you have done for us in Christ.
You have given a new dimension to our lives,
a hope and a purpose not of this world,
a taste of eternal life with all the fulfilment that offers,
resources to meet whatever challenges we may face.
Lord of life,
hear our prayer.

We praise you that through faith
we are able to glimpse things as yet unseen,
that we are part of the great company of your people
in heaven and on earth,
that we are pilgrims together in a journey of discovery,
that we are in Christ.
Lord of life,
hear our prayer.

But we thank you also that you have given us life in this world,
that you have called us to serve you
in a particular place and time,
that we are Christians here in . . .
Lord of life,
hear our prayer.

We thank you for all this *village/town/city* has to offer,
    for all the ways we are part of it
    and all the people who live here.
Help us to work out our faith in this place,
    offering service to the community in which we are set,
    making the Gospel real in our activities,
    our relationships, our attitudes.
Lord of life,
    hear our prayer.

Living God,
    help us to anticipate your kingdom,
        but help us also to keep our feet on the ground,
        remembering that this begins now
        and not at some distant point in the future,
        on earth and not simply in heaven,
        here in . . . as much as anywhere.
Lord of life,
    hear our prayer.

Help us truly to be in Christ, in . . .
    to the glory of your name.
    Amen.

255

LOVING

Gracious God,
> you call us to love you
> > with all our hearts and minds and soul.
>
> You challenge us to love our neighbour as ourselves.
> You tell us through Christ that the whole law
> > is summed up in one single commandment:
> > to love.
>
> It all sounds so easy, so straightforward,
> > but we know in reality it is so very difficult.

Gracious God,
> **forgive us the feebleness of our love.**

Too often we love only ourselves,
> our every thought for our own welfare,
> our own ends,
> our own esteem,
> our own pleasures.

Gracious God,
> **forgive us the feebleness of our love.**

Too often we reserve our love for the exclusive few –
> our families,
> our closest friends,
> our fellowship.

Gracious God,
> **forgive us the feebleness of our love.**

And too often we are forgetful of others,
> indifferent to them,
> even hostile.

Gracious God,
> **forgive us the feebleness of our love.**

Yet, worse than that, even when we think we love
    we are sometimes deceiving ourselves.
We are impatient of others' mistakes.
We are slow to give help when it is needed,
    especially if it means putting ourselves out.
We are envious of others' good fortune,
    more concerned with our own well-being
    than that of those around us.
Gracious God,
    forgive us the feebleness of our love.

We are careless in what we say
    and self-centred in the way we think,
    ever prone to take offence,
    bearing grievances and harbouring resentment,
    even distorting and deceiving in order to get our way,
    or to avoid facing truths we would rather ignore.
Gracious God,
    forgive us the feebleness of our love.

All too easily our love is destroyed.
Instead of holding fast through difficulties,
    we automatically find ourselves believing the worst,
    feeling ourselves betrayed,
    giving up on love instead of working to nurture it.
Gracious God,
    forgive us the feebleness of our love.

Lord of all,
    it is hard to love,
    especially when love is thrown back in our faces,
    or when those we are faced by seem unlovely,
    or when love is costly and demanding.
We confess we wonder at times
    whether love is the right way at all,
    or simply a naive illusion,
    a pleasant but foolish fantasy.
Gracious God,
    forgive us the feebleness of our love.

But you have shown us the way of love,
    made flesh in Christ –
    love that came to our world despite rejection,
    that reaches out to us in all our unloveliness,
    that was willing to pay the highest price
    and make the ultimate sacrifice.
And through that love you offer life,
    not only to us but to all people –
    a life that can one day be free from all the things
    that divide and hurt and frighten us.
Gracious God,
    forgive us the feebleness of our love.

So now, we pray, take the little love we have –
    nurture, deepen, and expand it,
    until we have learned what love really means,
    until your love flows through our hearts,
    until love is all in all.
    Amen.

256

NEEDING GOD AND BEING NEEDED BY HIM

Living God,
   unashamedly we declare our need of you.

We need your love,
      your help,
      your strength.
We need your mercy,
      your forgiveness,
      your renewing.
We need your guidance,
      your encouragement,
      your inspiration.
We need your support,
      your comfort,
      your peace.

   In so many ways we need you,
         for without you our souls are restless,
         our lives impoverished,
         our destiny hopeless.

Living God,
      we thank you that you respond to our needs,
         reaching out with immeasurable love,
         with constant compassion,
         with unfailing goodness.

   But we thank you too that, incredibly,
         you are a God who has need of us;
         a God who has chosen to make yourself
         dependent on human co-operation.

You need our faith,
    our trust,
    our commitment.
You need our hearts,
    our minds,
    our souls.
You need our hands,
    our feet,
    our actions.
You need our worship,
    our service,
    our witness.

Living God,
    we marvel that you need us as much as we need you,
        but we thank you for that great truth,
        that awesome privilege,
        that amazing responsibility.
    Help us to honour the trust you have placed in us,
        through Jesus Christ our Lord.
        Amen.

257

SEEING WITH GOD'S EYES

Living God,
  all-knowing, all-powerful, all-seeing;
    ever-active and ever-present in our world,
    help us to capture something of your wonder,
    to glimpse something of your greatness,
    to see that our small horizons are not the last word.
Living God,
  teach us to see with your eyes.

Enable us to see life from your perspective,
    with all its opportunities,
    potential,
    goodness,
    and beauty.
Living God,
  teach us to see with your eyes.

Show us that where we see no future
    your promise continues,
    where we see only obstacles
    you have planned the way through,
    where we see only our limitations
    you see opportunities,
    where we see despair
    you see hope,
    where we see division
    you work towards reconciliation,
    and where we see sorrow
    you are longing to bring joy.
Living God,
  teach us to see with your eyes.

Give us the courage to dream dreams,
>to have a vision of the future,
>for ourselves,
>our church,
>and all the world.
Living God,
>**teach us to see with your eyes.**

Give us faith to see life in a new light,
>a different way,
>and from a wider perspective.
And give us the determination not just to dream,
>but to work towards the fulfilment of our vision,
>working for your kingdom here on earth.
Living God,
>**teach us to see with your eyes,**
>**for the sake of Jesus Christ our Lord.**
>**Amen.**

258

SEND ME
(inspired by Isaiah 6:8-9)

Loving God,
 you have called us to go out into the world
   in your service,
   to proclaim the Gospel,
   to make disciples,
   to share your love,
   and to work towards the fulfilment of your purposes.
 Lord God, you are calling us now.
 Here I am – send me.

Loving God,
 forgive us that we have so often failed in that calling,
   that we are happy to come to Christ
   but unwilling to go out in his name.
 Forgive us that we are eager to receive
   but reluctant to give,
   all too easily turning faith
   into something for self and not for others.
 Lord God, you are calling us now.
 Here I am – send me.

Loving God,
 fill us now with new courage, zeal and purpose,
   new vision and resolve,
   that like the prophet Isaiah of old
   we may hear your voice,
   and, recognising your glory, gladly respond.
 Lord God, you are calling us now.
 Here I am – send me,
   in Christ's name.
   Amen.

259

WITNESSING TO CHRIST

Lord of all,
> You have called us to be witnesses to Jesus Christ,
>> to tell others what he has done for us.
>
> **Help us to do that faithfully.**

Teach us always to speak from our own experience
> rather than someone else's,
> to share what Christ means to us
> rather than what he means to others.

Help us to do that sincerely.

Teach us to be conscious of those we are talking to,
> doing all we can to ensure our words
> are relevant to their situations.

Help us to do that sensitively.

Teach us to present the message of the Gospel,
> rather than getting bogged down in thoughts and ideas
> that mean little to us and still less to others.

Help us to do that simply.

Teach us to witness
> whenever and wherever the opportunity presents itself,
> proclaiming your love to all.

Help us to do that boldly.

Lord of all,
> you have called us to make known the Good News,
>> to take it out to the ends of the earth.
>
> **Help us to do that gladly.**

And so may all people everywhere come to meet you
> and know you for themselves.

In the name of Christ we pray.
> **Amen.**

260

Telling the News

Loving God,
    you have called us to be your witnesses,
        to tell the news
        and make known what you have done for us.
    You do not simply call others,
        exempting us from responsibility,
        giving us the option of leaving it to someone else.
    You call us all, without exception,
        to go forth and tell.
    Loving God,
        we have heard and received the Good News:
        save us from keeping it to ourselves.

Forgive us for all the times we have done just that,
        all the occasions when we have missed the opportunity
        to speak out.
Forgive us that we are not as excited as we should be
        by the news we have to share,
        that we ! e become too familiar with the Gospel,
        too comfortable and complacent,
        concerned only with ourselves rather than others.
Forgive us for all those who have never heard
        because we have never told.
Loving God,
        we have heard and received the Good News:
        save us from keeping it to ourselves.

Help us to recognise afresh all we have to share,
        and make us ready to see those moments
        which cry out to us to share it.
Thrill our hearts again with the Good News of Christ.
May its message stir again our hearts
        and capture our imaginations,
        breaking through our apathy, carelessness
        and indifference.

Loving God,
we have heard and received the Good News:
save us from keeping it to ourselves,
in the name of Christ.
Amen.

261

THE EXTRA MILE
(inspired by Matthew 5:41)

Living God,
    you call us to take up our cross and deny ourselves.
    You tell us that it is only through losing our lives
        that we will truly find them.
    You challenge us through Jesus to go the extra mile,
        to do more than is asked or expected of us.
    Teach us to give
      as you have given to us in Christ.

Forgive us that we find that so hard,
      that more often than not we prefer to do
      as little as possible rather than as much,
      that we give our help, time, service and money
      grudgingly rather than cheerfully.
    Teach us to give
      as you have given to us in Christ.

Living God,
    we thank you for those people
      who are willing to go the extra mile –
      those among our family and friends,
      in our fellowship or the wider Church,
      in our society or the world as a whole
      who give freely of themselves,
      going beyond the call of duty in the service of others.
    Teach us to give
      as you have given to us in Christ.

Living God,
we praise you for Jesus Christ –
for his readiness to go not just the extra mile
but to give his all,
identifying himself with our humanity,
willingly experiencing suffering and death
so that we might discover life in its fullness.
Teach us to give
as you have given to us in Christ.

Touch our hearts through all Christ has done,
so that we may be more ready to live as his people.
Teach us in our turn to do that little bit extra,
to go beyond people's expectations,
to give and to go on giving.
And so may people glimpse in us
a little of the love we have seen in Christ.
Teach us to give
as you have given to us in Christ,
for in his name we pray.
Amen.

262

TEACH US TO PRAY
(based on Luke 11:1)

Lord God our Father,
    like the Apostles of old we ask,
        'Teach us how to pray.'

Teach us the secret of prayer –
    when to speak and when to keep silent,
    when to accept and when to keep on seeking,
    when to persevere and when to let go.
Like the Apostles of old we ask,
    'Teach us how to pray.'

Teach us the power of prayer –
    its ability to challenge,
    to encourage,
    to transform all of life.
Like the Apostles of old we ask,
    'Teach us how to pray.'

Teach us the blessing of prayer –
    its ability to teach,
    comfort,
    and strengthen.
Like the Apostles of old we ask,
    'Teach us how to pray.'

Teach us, the potential of prayer –
    its ability to help us express our worship,
    discover your will,
    and hear your voice.
Like the Apostles of old we ask,
    'Teach us how to pray.'

Teach us the joy of prayer –
   its ability to convey your forgiveness,
   to reveal more of your love,
   and open up new experiences of your presence.
Like the Apostles of old we ask,
   'Teach us how to pray.'

Lord God our Father,
   hear our prayer
      so that all we do and ask and think
      may give you the glory that is rightfully yours,
      in the name of Christ.
      Amen.

263

HEARING GOD

Loving Father,
    we thank you that you are a God
        who daily teaches us more about yourself,
        who has always more to reveal of your love.
    Speak to us now,
        and give us ears to hear!

We thank you for the many ways we hear your voice –
        through the scriptures, the world around us,
        and the people we meet;
        through prayer and reflection;
        through the experiences of life,
        and through our daily walk with you.
    Speak to us now,
        and give us ears to hear!

Loving Father,
    we thank you that day by day you speak to us.
    Help us to be open to everything you would say,
        ready to receive your instruction
        and accept your guidance.
    Speak to us now,
        and give us ears to hear!

Save us from closing our ears
        to that which we do not want to hear;
        from becoming so fixed in our ways and opinions
        that we become spiritually deaf;
        from limiting your word or denying your call
        through our unwillingness to listen.
    Speak to us now,
        and give us ears to hear,
        through Jesus Christ our Lord.
        Amen.

264

Understanding prayer

Father God,
  you have promised
    that when we pray for something
    in the name of Christ
    it will be done.
  Teach us what that really means –
    to know and love Jesus so completely
    that *our* will and *his* coincide.
  Father, we bring you this prayer
    in the name of Christ.

Forgive us when we abuse prayer,
    looking only to our ends rather than yours.
Forgive us when we pray emptily or half-heartedly,
    and then complain
    that our prayers seem to go unanswered.
Help us to recognise prayer is your gift to us,
    rather than ours to you,
    and so may we learn from it more of your purpose,
    and more about you.
Father, we bring you this prayer
    in the name of Christ.

Strengthen our faith, deepen our fellowship,
    direct our witness.
Help us to grow inwardly and outwardly,
    reaching out to you, to one another,
    and to all around us.
Father, we bring you this prayer
    in the name of Christ.

And when we cannot see any answers
    to our own needs or those of others,
    when we see only problems that seem beyond us,
    when we do not know what to pray for,
    teach us to leave all things in your hands.
Father, we bring you this prayer
    in the name of Christ.

We come then now,
    asking not for our will to be done, but yours,
    to the glory of your name.
Father, we bring you this prayer
    in the name of Christ.
    Amen.

265

WHEN GOD SEEMS SILENT

Loving God,
    we thank you for the ways you speak to us,
        through Scripture, prayer and worship,
        through the fellowship of your people
        and the daily experiences of life.
Loving God,
    open our hearts to all you would say to us.

We thank you for the ways you have spoken
    to your people across the ages,
    the ways you speak to us today,
    and the ways you will continue to speak in the days ahead.
Loving God,
    open our hearts to all you would say to us.

But today we ask for your help
    in those times when you seem to be silent,
    those days when we do not hear your voice
    no matter how we listen for it,
    those times when we feel ourselves to be alone
    and far from you.
Give us courage then to ask
    if we have closed our hearts and minds
    to what you would say,
    or if there is something in our lives
    creating a barrier between us,
    preventing us from getting close to you.
Loving God,
    open our hearts to all you would say to us.

But help us also to understand there are times
    when you expect us to get on with our discipleship
    without you always directing us,
    without your instructions being spelt out step by step.
Help us to see that your silence
    may not be a sign of our faithlessness or your displeasure,
    but rather of your love,
    offering us the opportunity
    to grow towards Christian maturity.
Loving God,
    open our hearts to all you would say to us.

And when we do not hear you speak
    help us to remember all those times
    you have spoken unmistakably,
    to us and to others,
    and let those moments sustain and direct us
    until your word comes again,
    in your own time and your own way.
Loving God,
    open our hearts to all you would say to us,
    in the name of Christ.
    Amen.

PRAYERS FOR OTHERS

266

FOR THOSE WHO HAVE LOST HOPE

Living God,
    we pray for those people who have lost hope –
        in their dreams,
        their circumstances,
        or in life itself.
    Lord of all hopefulness,
        hear our prayer.

We pray for those who have lost the hope
    of finding a partner or of raising a family,
    the hope of going to college, university, or further studies,
    the hope of finding a home
    or any permanent roof over their heads,
    the hope of securing employment or a use for their skills.
Lord of all hopefulness,
    hear our prayer.

We pray for those who despair of seeing freedom,
    justice, peace or reconciliation;
    those who despair of finding adequate food and clothing;
    those who despair of receiving help and healing.
Lord of all hopefulness,
    hear our prayer.

We pray for those who have given up on life –
    those with terminal illness
    who have lost the will to keep on fighting;
    those whose spirits have been crushed
    so that they can no longer bounce back;
    those who want to take their own lives
    because they have lost all hope;
    those so afflicted by starvation and disease
    that they cannot carry on.
Lord of all hopefulness,
    hear our prayer.

Living God,
   there is so much despair in our world,
      and for many there seems little reason to hope.
   Reach out, we pray, to all whose belief in the future
      has been destroyed,
      and grant new dreams where the old have died,
      rekindled purpose where confidence has been undermined,
      support when there seems to be nothing left to hold on to,
      and hope that one day your kingdom will come
      and your will be done.
   Lord of all hopefulness,
      hear our prayer,
      in the name of Christ.
      Amen.

267

FOR THOSE SEARCHING FOR PEACE OF MIND

Living God,
    we pray for all those who are weighed down
        by the stresses and strains of daily life –
        those who long for peace of mind,
        who crave rest for their souls,
        but cannot find it.
    Lord, in your mercy,
        hear our prayer.

We pray for those oppressed by worry,
        unable to throw off their anxieties,
        held captive by a multitude of secret fears.
    Lord, in your mercy,
        hear our prayer.

We pray for those who cannot let go,
        those who find it impossible to relax or unwind,
        always fretting over this or that.
    Lord, in your mercy,
        hear our prayer.

We pray for those who lose themselves in busyness,
        masking their true feelings
        and running from their emptiness,
        hoping that keeping active might bring them happiness.
    Lord, in your mercy,
        hear our prayer.

We pray for those who have lost time for you,
        allowing the pressures and demands of each day
        to shut you out,
        putting any thought of you off until tomorrow.
    Lord, in your mercy,
        hear our prayer.

We pray for those who have no time for you,
  no interest in anything other than their daily routine,
  no awareness of their spiritual needs.
Lord, in your mercy,
  hear our prayer.

Living God,
  speak to each one in your still small voice,
    and grant them your peace which passes understanding,
    that quiet confidence which only you can bring,
    and so may their burdens be lifted
    and their souls refreshed.
Lord, in your mercy,
  hear our prayer,
  through Jesus Christ our Lord.
  Amen.

268

FOR THOSE LACKING PEACE

Lord of all,
  we pray for all who are searching for peace in their lives –
    those burdened with anxiety,
    either about themselves or their loved ones,
    facing difficulties and problems
    to which they can see no solutions.
God of peace,
  reach out and still the storm.

We pray for those wrestling with inner fears and phobias,
  torn apart by emotional and psychological pressures.
God of peace,
  reach out and still the storm.

We pray for those living amongst change and upheaval,
  especially all who are threatened by violence and warfare.
God of peace,
  reach out and still the storm.

To all of those in chaos and turmoil,
  all who are restless and troubled,
  grant your calm,
  your tranquillity,
  your quietness,
  and your peace which passes understanding.
God of peace,
  reach out and still the storm,
  in the name of Christ.
  Amen.

269

FOR THOSE FACED BY QUESTIONS OF TRUTH

Living God,
    we pray for those wrestling
        with difficult and demanding questions –
        those facing complex matters of conscience,
        those struggling with confusing moral decisions,
        those wrestling with controversial social issues,
        those coping with challenging theological concerns.
Grant to all in such situations your wisdom,
    and help them to find the right way forward.
Lord, in your mercy,
    hear our prayer.

We pray for those who are faced
    with awkward yet important choices,
    between good and evil,
    right and wrong,
    truth and falsehood,
    love and hate;
    between the way of the world and the way of Christ,
    the way of self and the way of service.
Give to all faced with such choices
    the courage to take your way.
Lord, in your mercy,
    hear our prayer.

We pray for your Church.
Save it from naive fundamentalism,
    from judgemental attitudes,
    from dogmatically believing
    it has the answers to every situation.
Grant to your people everywhere
    the humility to recognise that asking questions
    is part of faith.
Lord, in your mercy,
    hear our prayer.

Living God,
  we pray for ourselves as day by day
    we are confronted with the need to choose.
  Sometimes the choice is clear, sometimes confusing,
    sometimes easy, sometimes hard,
    sometimes mattering little, sometimes much.
  But help us, whatever the case,
    to gladly accept the responsibility of choosing,
    recognising that it is a privilege of being human.
  Lord, in your mercy,
    hear our prayer.

Help us to decide wisely,
  seeking your will and responding to your guidance.
Help us to admit our error when we choose wrongly
  and be ready to change our decisions when necessary.
And help us to remember when we go astray
  that you are always there to help us start again.
Lord, in your mercy,
  hear our prayer,
  in the name of Christ.
  Amen.

270

FOR THOSE WHO WORK FOR JUSTICE

Loving God,
   hear our prayers for all those in our world
      who seek to further your will here on earth –
      those who work for peace,
      who campaign for justice,
      who strive to relieve poverty,
      who fight for the hungry –
      all those who struggle for the oppressed, the exploited,
      the under-privileged and all denied their proper rights.
Prosper their efforts and grant them inspiration
      so that they may challenge people everywhere
      to give of themselves in the service of others.
God of justice and mercy,
   hear our prayer.

We pray for those who serve within the judicial system –
      barristers, lawyers, judges,
      magistrates, jurors, and court officials –
      all those whose responsibility it is
      to see that justice is administered fairly, and to all.
Give them wisdom, integrity, courage and dedication,
      so that they may discharge their duties faithfully.
God of justice and mercy,
   hear our prayer.

We pray for the police and all those involved
      in the prevention or detection of crime,
      and we pray too for those who work in our prisons,
      whether as officers or governors.
Grant them your protection,
      and help them in all they do to be firm but fair.
God of justice and mercy,
   hear our prayer.

We pray for those who have strayed into a life of crime –
  prisoners on remand,
  those serving their sentences,
  and those who have been released.
Lead them to true repentance
  and give them the will and the opportunity
  to start afresh.
God of justice and mercy,
  hear our prayer.

Finally we pray for those
  who have experienced a miscarriage of justice –
  falsely accused,
  wrongfully imprisoned,
  unfairly punished.
Help them to come to terms with their experience,
  and to receive proper recompense.
God of justice and mercy,
  hear our prayer,
  through Jesus Christ our Lord.
  Amen.

271

FOR PREACHERS AND HEARERS OF THE GOSPEL

Living God,
  we pray for all those who witness for you,
    all who preach and proclaim the message of Christ,
    who challenge people with the message of the Gospel.
  Give them inspiration, courage, and sincerity,
    so that their witness may lead others
    to know Jesus for themselves.
  Lord, in your mercy,
    hear our prayer.

We pray for all those who hear,
    all who in different ways are confronted
    with the challenge to respond to Christ.
  May those who earnestly seek find faith,
    those who are undecided be convinced,
    those who glimpse a little see more clearly,
    those whose faith is shallow be led to deeper understanding,
    and those who refuse to listen be challenged to think again.
  Lord, in your mercy,
    hear our prayer,
    in the name of Christ.
    Amen.

272

FOR THOSE WHO FEEL GOD IS INACTIVE

Loving God,
  we pray for all those in our world
    who knowingly take the path of evil –
    those who follow a life of crime,
    those who cheat and deceive,
    who exploit their fellow human beings,
    who wound in body or mind,
    who kill and destroy.
  Open their eyes to the reality of your judgement,
    their minds to the damage caused by their actions,
    and their hearts to the transforming power of your grace.
  Lord, in your mercy,
    hear our prayer.

Loving God,
  we pray for those who are indifferent to you –
    those who have not heard the challenge of the Gospel,
    or who have not considered
    the claims of Christ for themselves,
    or who have a nominal faith but no real commitment.
  Open their ears to the message of Christ,
    their spirits to the reality of your presence,
    and their lives to the joy of knowing you.
  Lord, in your mercy,
    hear our prayer.

Loving God,
we pray for those who seek to serve you,
but who find faith threatened –
those who face pain and suffering,
those overwhelmed by sudden calamity,
those confused by apparent injustice,
and those whose convictions have been undermined
by the experiences of life.
Assure them of your continuing purpose,
your enduring love,
and your final triumph.
Lord, in your mercy,
hear our prayer,
through Jesus Christ our Lord.
Amen.

273

FOR THOSE UNABLE TO ATTEND CHURCH

Loving God,
    as we come together today we bring you our thanks –
        for this place where, week by week,
        we can come and share fellowship;
        for this church, dedicated to worshipping you;
        and for this time set aside from the daily tasks of life
        so that we can offer you our praise,
        reflect on your word and seek your will.
    We thank you for everything our coming here
        has meant and continues to mean.
    Lord of the Church,
        unite us through the love of Christ.

But we pray now for those who, for a variety of reasons,
    are unable to worship with us –
    those confined to their homes,
    those no longer fit enough to get out and about,
    those in hospital,
    those having to work on Sundays,
    those looking after loved ones.
Lord of the Church,
    unite us through the love of Christ.

We pray too for those who have drifted away
    from regular attendance –
    those who have lost their faith,
    or joined other churches,
    or moved to a new area among new people.
Lord of the Church,
    unite us through the love of Christ.

Loving God,
   may each of these, our friends,
      know that they are still much remembered,
      much valued,
      and much cared about.
May we find ways of expressing our concern,
      showing our support,
      and expressing our interest in their welfare.
And, whatever their situation,
      may they know you close by their side,
      joined with us and all your people
      in the fellowship which only Christ can bring.
Lord of the Church,
      unite us through the love of Christ,
      in whose name we pray.
      Amen.

274

LOVING AS JESUS LOVES US

Lord Jesus Christ,
>you gave of yourself without counting the cost,
>>offering even your own life
>>for the life of the world.

So now we pray for all those
>who seek to love you in return,
>however hesitant, partial,
>or imperfect their love might be.

Inspire them through your love.

We pray for those new in their faith,
>still learning more of you,
>still uncertain perhaps of their commitment,
>still discovering more of your love.

Keep their love always growing.

We pray for those established in their faith,
>facing the daily risk of growing complacent,
>stale, settled into a comfortable routine.

Make their love ever fresh.

We pray for those whose faith has crumbled,
>no longer holding the trust they once held,
>no longer feeling you close by their sides,
>no longer seeking to follow Christ.

Renew their love.

We pray for those who have never had faith;
>those consistently unmoved by the message of the Gospel,
>those who resist its challenge despite themselves,
>and those who wilfully go against your will.

Kindle a love for you in their hearts.

We pray for those whose faith is costly,
   those who sacrifice time, money, energy,
   security, health, and even life itself,
   in the service of others.
Reward their love.

And we pray for those who need something to put their faith in –
   the poor, the hungry, and the homeless,
   the sick, the suffering, the bereaved,
   all those broken by the tragedies and crises of life.
May they experience the fullness of your love.

Lord Jesus Christ,
   your love is for all,
      whoever they may be.
**May it reach out then into every heart in every place,
   and may we be a part of that,
      learning to love you as you love us.
      Amen.**

275

FOR YOUNG PEOPLE

Lord of all,
  we have thought of ourselves –
    now we remember others.
  And especially today we pray
    for the young people of our church,
    our country and our world;
    young people with so much to offer,
    so many gifts, so many fresh ideas,
    so much vigour and enthusiasm,
    yet faced today as never before
    by all kinds of pressures, demands and temptations.
  Lord in your mercy,
    hear our prayer.

We pray for the young people of this church.
Help us to appreciate them,
    to be open to their insights,
    to use their gifts,
    to nurture their faith,
    and to care about their welfare.
Guide them in their work and studies,
    protect them from all that may harm or lead them astray,
    encourage them in all they are doing among us,
    and show them your way for the future.
Lord in your mercy,
    hear our prayer.

We pray for the young people of our town,
    our country and the wider world,
    so often maligned on account of the few.
We pray for those in our schools and universities,
    those from broken or needy homes,
    those whose gifts lie wasted through unemployment,
    those faced by the temptation of alcohol and drug abuse,
    those burdened by the problem of debt,
    those coming to terms with the complex world
    of human relationships,
    those who are denied the resources they need
    to realise their full potential,
    and those, who because of hunger and disease,
    will almost certainly never reach adulthood.
Lord in your mercy,
    hear our prayer.

Lord of all,
    give guidance to all who work with young people –
    those in our own church,
    in youth organisations,
    in schools and colleges,
    in organisations dedicated to childcare.
Lord in your mercy,
    hear our prayer.

Loving Lord,
    we thank you for young people.
    Through our giving to and receiving from them,
    help us to make that gratitude real.
Lord in your mercy,
    hear our prayer,
    through Jesus Christ our Lord.
    Amen.

276

FOR THE WEAK AND VULNERABLE

Sovereign God,
    we pray for the weak and vulnerable in our world –
        those who feel powerless
        in the face of the massive problems that confront them.
    Help of the helpless,
        reach out to strengthen and support.

We pray for the poor,
        the hungry,
        the diseased,
        the dying.
Help of the helpless,
        reach out to strengthen and support.

We pray for the oppressed,
        the exploited,
        the abused,
        the tortured.
Help of the helpless,
        reach out to strengthen and support.

We pray for the frightened,
        the lonely,
        the hurt,
        the depressed.
Help of the helpless,
        reach out to strengthen and support.

We pray for those who live in lands racked by tension,
        those who face famine and starvation,
        those who are unemployed,
        those who are homeless.
Help of the helpless,
        reach out to strengthen and support.

Sovereign God,
you have expressed a special concern
for the bruised, the needy, and the weak of our world.
May that concern bring strength to all in such need,
and may it inspire people everywhere
to work for a more just society,
standing up for the needy,
and working for that time when there will be an end
to suffering, mourning and pain;
that time when your kingdom will come
and your will be done.
Help of the helpless,
reach out to strengthen and support,
in the name of Christ.
Amen.

277

FOR THOSE WHO FEEL UNLOVED

God of love,
    we pray for those many people in our world
        who have been deprived of love,
        who feel unloved,
        or for whom love has been painful.
Touch their hearts with the love of Christ.

We pray for those for whom love has involved pain –
    those who have faced the trauma
    of breakdown in their marriage,
    or experienced the collapse of friendships
    or romantic engagements;
    those who have come from broken homes,
    or who have become estranged from family and friends;
    those whose children have moved away
    to begin new lives of their own,
    or whose parents have become frail, confused and infirm;
    those whose loved ones have been taken from them by death,
    or those who have been forced to leave those
    they count most dear.
May the knowledge of your unending love
    be a constant source of comfort and inspiration.
Touch their hearts with the love of Christ.

We pray for those who find it hard to love –
    those whose love has been betrayed,
    those who are scarred by bitter and painful experience,
    those who have been subjected to abuse,
    those afraid of showing their true feelings,
    those oppressed by mental illness.
Touch their hearts with the love of Christ.

Loving God,
>we bring before you the complex world
>>of human relationships,
>>>capable of bringing such joy but such sorrow,
>>>so much pleasure yet also so much pain.
>We thank you for your gift of love
>>and all the love that surrounds us,
>>>but help us never to forget those who have lost love
>>>or been hurt through it.
>Restore their faith in what love can do,
>>and help them both to find love and share it.
>**Touch their hearts with the love of Christ.**

>Grant to us all the knowledge
>>that your love will never fail,
>>and never let us go.
>>**Thanks be to God, in Jesus' name.**
>>**Amen.**

278

FOR THE 'HAVE-NOTS' OF OUR WORLD

Loving God,
  We thank you for all that we have –
      our homes,
      our food,
      our clothing,
      our modern appliances,
      our public amenities,
      our opportunities for education,
      our access to healthcare,
      and so much more.
  Loving God,
      hear our prayer for the 'have-nots' of this world.

We pray for those who have no homes,
      living as refugees,
      or living rough on our streets.
  Loving God,
      hear our prayer for the 'have-nots' of this world.

We pray for those who live in inadequate housing,
      the shacks and huts of shanty towns,
      or in bed and breakfast accommodation
      because there is nowhere else for them to go.
  Loving God,
      hear our prayer for the 'have-nots' of this world.

We pray for those who have no food,
      their crops having failed,
      their economies burdened by debt,
      or their labours not fairly rewarded.
  Loving God,
      hear our prayer for the 'have-nots' of this world.

We pray for those who have no fresh water,
daily facing the threat of disease and the nightmare of drought,
and for those who have no resources,
condemned to a life of poverty with no prospect of respite,
no opportunity to help themselves.
Loving God,
hear our prayer for the 'have-nots' of this world.

We pray for those who have no access to education,
to a health service or a welfare system;
no one to turn to for help or support.
Loving God,
hear our prayer for the 'have-nots' of this world.

Loving God,
in the context of this world of ours we are the 'haves',
those who have been fortunate,
those who enjoy plenty.
Stir our hearts to respond to the 'have-nots'.
Help us to be ready to say no to ourselves
so that we may say yes to them,
to sacrifice a little that they may receive much.
Loving God,
**hear our prayer for the 'have-nots' of this world,
in the name of Christ.
Amen.**

279

BROKEN DREAMS

Loving God,
    we pray for those whose dreams have been destroyed,
        those who no longer have the heart to look forward,
        who have lost their vision for the future.
So many people, known and unknown –
        whose happiness and hopes have been dashed by tragedy,
        whose faith in loved ones has been betrayed,
        who face poverty, unemployment, homelessness,
        disease, starvation, even death –
        whose trust in you has been tested beyond the limit.
God of hope,
    light a new flame in their hearts.

We pray for all those who plod wearily through life
        with no sense of purpose –
        those who feel the future is empty, bereft of promise,
        and those who live only for today, fearful of tomorrow.
God of hope,
    light a new flame in their hearts.

Touch their hearts, we pray,
        stir their imagination,
        rekindle their faith,
        renew their hope.
And so may new dreams and new visions
        be born in the most broken of lives.
God of hope,
    light a new flame in their hearts,
    through Jesus Christ our Lord.
    Amen.

280

FOR THOSE WHO FEEL THAT LIFE HAS GONE OUT OF CONTROL

Living God,
we pray for all those who feel
they have lost control in their lives –
overwhelmed perhaps by tragedy,
or relationships having broken down;
battling against the rigours of old age,
or wrestling with terminal illness;
in pain of body,
or turmoil of mind.
Lord of all,
assure them that your purpose will finally win through.

We pray for the victims of other people's lack of control,
wounded in body or mind –
abused children,
battered wives,
broken homes,
victims of burglary, rape, or assault.
Lord of all,
assure them that your purpose will finally win through.

We pray for those who struggle
to control aspects of their character –
lust,
temper,
greed,
impatience,
envy,
intolerance.
Lord of all,
assure them that your purpose will finally win through.

Living God,
  give to all near the end of their tether
    the assurance that you are ultimately in control;
    to those who are hurt
    the comfort of your healing love;
    to those troubled in mind
    the inner peace which you alone can give;
    and to those dismayed by their repeated failings
    the gift of self-control.
  Lord of all,
    assure them that your purpose shall finally win through,
    in the name of Christ our Lord.
    Amen.

281

FOR THOSE DENIED ACCESS
TO THE THINGS WE TAKE FOR GRANTED

Loving God,
    we pray for those who are denied access
        to the things in life we take for granted –
        food and clothing,
        work,
        a basic education,
        proper housing,
        mobility,
        health,
        companionship,
        love,
        human rights,
        liberty,
        freedom of speech,
        justice,
        peace.
Lord, in your mercy,
hear our prayer.

Prosper the efforts of all who fight for their rights,
    all who labour to give them help and hope.
Lord, in your mercy,
hear our prayer.

Loving God,
    we pray for those who feel themselves denied access to you,
        separated by guilt,
        doubts,
        past mistakes,
        or lack of faith.
Lord, in your mercy,
hear our prayer.

May all who seek your presence,
  all who ask for your forgiveness,
  and all who long for your love,
  find in Jesus Christ the Way, the Truth and the Life.
Lord, in your mercy,
  hear our prayer,
  in the name of Christ.
  Amen.

282

FOR THOSE FEARFUL OF THE FUTURE

Living God,
we pray for those who face the future
with uncertainty or anxiety –
those who fear it,
who despair of it,
or who feel they have no future.

We pray for those in the troubled places of our world –
those who long for peace,
an end to conflict and a time of harmony,
but who in their hearts have given up hoping.

We pray for those who face trauma
and upheaval in their lives –
what seemed secure swept from under them,
what they had hoped for denied them,
what they had trusted in proven false.

We pray for those who doubt their ability
to cope with what life may bring –
those overwhelmed by pressures,
paralysed by fears,
crushed by sorrows.

We pray for those faced with difficult decisions –
circumstances beyond their control,
unexpected dangers,
awkward choices.

Living God,
   reach out to all for whom the future
      seems uncertain or unwelcome,
      and bring the assurance that even in the darkest moments,
      the greatest challenges,
      the most worrying times,
      you are there working out your purpose;
      able to bring light out of darkness,
      hope out of despair,
      joy out of sorrow,
      and good out of evil.

Grant the confidence that there is nothing in heaven or earth,
   in life or death,
   in the present or the future,
   that is finally able to separate us from your love.
Through Jesus Christ our Lord.
   Amen.

283

FOR THOSE IN NEED

Living God,
   you came to our world through Christ
      to help,
      to heal,
      and to save.
   So now we pray for all those in any kind of need.
   Reach out to them in your love.

We pray for the sick and suffering,
   the poor and hungry,
   the oppressed and exploited,
   the lonely and unloved,
   the aged and infirm,
   the frightened and anxious,
   the sorrowful and the bereaved,
   the helpless and the hopeless.
Reach out to them in your love.

Living God,
   there is so much need around us,
      in our neighbourhood, our town,
      our country, our world –
      so many people crying out for help.
   Reach out to them in your love.

Show us where and how we can respond.
Give us the means, the will, the commitment and the love
   to reach out in the name of Christ,
   offering something of ourselves to others,
   even as he offered his all for us.
Reach out to them in your love,
   through Jesus Christ our Lord.
   Amen.

284

FOR THOSE WHO MOURN

Loving God,
  you have promised your special blessing to those who mourn,
    your comfort to those overwhelmed by grief,
    your joy to those enduring sorrow.

So now we pray for those facing sadness,
    those burdened by misery,
    those weighed down by despair,
    those who have lost loved ones
    and who are striving to come to terms
    with the emptiness and heartbreak they feel.
  Lord, in your mercy,
    hear our prayer.

We pray for those among our families and friends
    who are facing such times,
    all those in this church and in our world.
  Lord, in your mercy,
    hear our prayer.

Loving God,
  grant to those who grieve your special blessing.
  May they know that your hand is upon them,
    your arms encircling them,
    and your heart reaching out to them.
  Lord, in your mercy,
    hear our prayer.

May all who mourn discover the comfort you have promised,
    and find strength to face tomorrow,
    until that time comes when light shall dawn again,
    and hope be born anew.
  Lord, in your mercy,
    hear our prayer,
    through Christ our Lord.
    Amen.

285

WHERE THERE SEEMS NO HOPE OF CHANGE

Loving God,
    there are times when we look at people's lives
        and find it hard to believe things can ever
        change for the better –
        we see them racked by illness,
        weighed down by anxiety,
        tormented by depression,
        crippled by debt,
        broken by alcohol,
        destroyed by drugs,
        scarred by bereavement,
        shattered through unemployment,
        and we wonder what their prospects really are,
        what hope we can realistically offer them,
        what help we can possibly give.
Transforming God,
    may your light shine where there is darkness.

We pray for such people known to us now –
    family,
    friends,
    members of our fellowship,
    colleagues at work,
    neighbours,
    acquaintances;
    as well as the countless people unknown to us,
    each struggling under their own particular burdens.
Transforming God,
    may your light shine where there is darkness.

We pray for our world –
    for those many people who face suffering,
    injustice,
    hardship,
    and death.
Transforming God,
    may your light shine where there is darkness.

Reach out to all who are in despair, we pray,
    all who long for change
    but see only hopelessness stretching before them.
Touch their lives,
    and bring help, hope, healing, and wholeness.
Transforming God,
    may your light shine where there is darkness.

Loving God,
    it is hard sometimes to believe those around us,
        still less the world around,
        can ever change for the better.
We see countries broken by war,
    people consumed by hatred,
    thousands living in fear,
    nations turned against nation,
    multitudes made homeless by disaster,
    continents facing famine,
    and again we wonder what the prospects really are,
    what hope anyone can offer,
    what help can possibly be given.
Transforming God,
    may your light shine where there is darkness.

Help us to see beneath the surface,
    recognising you are at work
    and that things can change,
Help us to see beyond appearances,
    recognising you are a God able to transform
    even the most hopeless of situations.
Give to us and to all people the assurance
    that there is no one and no situation
    unable to be transformed by your power.
Transforming God,
    may your light shine where there is darkness,
    through Jesus Christ, our Lord.
    Amen.

286

FOR THOSE FACING A DISASTER

Loving Father,
 as we think of ourselves
  so we think also of those in trouble,
  those for whom this last week
  has brought disaster and tragedy,
  those whose lives are in turmoil.
 Especially we pray for those in . . .*
  whose lives have been thrown into turmoil
  by the . . .* that has ravaged their land.
 Lord, in your mercy,
  hear our prayer.

We pray for the families of those
 who have lost their lives –
 give them comfort, support
 and the knowledge of your eternal love.
Lord, in your mercy,
 hear our prayer.

We pray for those injured or maimed;
 those who will face the rest of their days
 coming to terms with physical scars
 or deeper mental and spiritual wounds –
 grant healing and help to each one.
Lord, in your mercy,
 hear our prayer.

We pray for all those striving to give support
 amid the devastation,
 whether to body, mind or soul –
 equip them with compassion, wisdom
 and skill in all their work.
Lord, in your mercy,
 hear our prayer.

We pray for those still searching among the chaos
    as hope runs out for any last survivors –
    their homes lost,
    their *town/city* destroyed,
    their country left in shock –
    give them encouragement to persevere.
Lord, in your mercy,
    hear our prayer.

Living God,
    we believe you grieve and suffer
        wherever your people are in need.
Reach out then to these people
    in their sorrow and despair,
    and grant them help
    to rebuild their shattered lives and hopes.
Lord, in your mercy,
    hear our prayer,
    in the name of Christ.
    Amen.

* Insert details as appropriate

287

FOR THOSE WHO FEEL THEY HAVE NO ROOTS

Gracious God,
  lover of the poor, the weak,
    the vulnerable and the oppressed,
    we pray for those who feel they have no roots,
    no identity,
    no sense of belonging.
  Lord, in your mercy,
    hear our prayer.

We pray for those who live as refugees in strange lands,
    driven from their own homes and country
    by civil war,
    oppression,
    famine,
    natural disaster.
  Lord, in your mercy,
    hear our prayer.

We pray for those who have been orphaned as children;
    those who have been adopted
    and who long to discover their true parents;
    those who come from broken homes
    and are scarred by the trauma of bitter separation;
    those who have been abused;
    those who feel unloved and unwanted.
  Lord, in your mercy,
    hear our prayer.

We pray too for those who are lonely,
    deprived through age or infirmity
    of human companionship,
    or separated from others even when they are with them
    through fear,
    shyness,
    mistrust,
    or prejudice.
Lord, in your mercy,
    hear our prayer.

We pray for our society in which so much
    of the feeling of community has been lost,
    where a sense of local and national identity has long gone,
    where ties which once bound families together
    have been broken,
    where values, customs and convictions which gave stability
    have been flouted by those who live only for themselves.
Lord, in your mercy,
    hear our prayer.

We pray for churches that have become divided,
    tragically allowing the things that separate them
    to become more important than the faith which unites,
    denying through their intolerance
    the unity that Christ desires for all his people,
    and so experiencing the pain of discord and division.
Lord, in your mercy,
    hear our prayer.

Lord of our world,
    give to us all a proper sense of the worth in those around us,
        a recognition of the humanity that binds us all together,
        transcending our differences.
    Give us a sense of your love for all,
        the purpose you have for each person
        no matter what their race or culture,
        background or circumstances.
    Lord, in your mercy,
        hear our prayer.

Help your church to offer a place of acceptance,
  welcome,
  and belonging.
And help all those who feel isolated
  to find in you the true source of their being
  and the root of their lives.
Lord, in your mercy,
  hear our prayer,
  through Jesus Christ our Lord.
  Amen.

288

FOR THOSE WHO SERVE OTHERS

Lord of all,
    we pray for those who in different ways
        spend much of their lives in the service of others,
        those whose work offers us the care, the security,
        the opportunities and the support
        that we take for granted in society.
    In all their work,
        Lord, uphold them.

We think of those in hospitals or hospices,
        in the police, the armed forces or the emergency services,
        in voluntary services and charities,
        in social and community work,
        in schools, colleges and universities,
        in the Church or mission field,
        in local, national and international government.
    In all their work,
        Lord, uphold them.

Loving God,
    we thank you for all those who provide service
        in so many different ways.
    Strengthen and encourage them in their work,
        give them the support, inspiration and resources they need,
        and work through them to express your love for the world.
    In all their work,
        Lord, uphold them,
        for we ask it in the name of Christ.
        Amen.

289

FOR THOSE ELECTED TO GOVERNMENT
AND LEADERSHIP

Almighty God, ruler of the ends of the earth,
    we pray for those to whom you have entrusted
        power and responsibility.

    We think first of our own country
        and those elected to office as Members of Parliament –
        those who serve in government,
        whether in cabinet office, junior posts
        or on backbench committees;
        those in opposition with their mandate
        to challenge and debate government policies and decisions;
        and especially we pray for our Prime Minister
        and the leaders of all other parties.
Lord, in your mercy,
    hear our prayer.

Almighty God,
    grant them wisdom,
        insight,
        patience,
        dedication,
        integrity,
        open-mindedness,
        and humility,
        that each may be equipped
        to honour the trust placed in them.
Lord, in your mercy,
    hear our prayer.

We pray for those in local government,
    entrusted with representing the interests
    of local people in their communities,

taking decisions which will directly influence their lives,
wrestling with limited resources and numerous demands.
Give to them the qualities they need to serve faithfully,
staying true to their convictions
yet putting people before party.
Lord, in your mercy,
hear our prayer.

We pray for those in authority in other lands,
leaders of nations large and small,
super-powers and tiny states,
shaping the lives of millions or relatively few.
Grant them also the guidance and the gifts they need
to govern wisely,
that they may work for the good of all their people,
and strive to promote justice,
freedom of speech and opportunity,
inner harmony and international peace.
Lord, in your mercy,
hear our prayer.

Finally we pray for those nations
affected by an abuse of power,
divided by rival factions,
oppressed by military dictatorships,
exploited by corrupt regimes,
suppressed by totalitarian authorities.
Support those who suffer under such government,
and strengthen those who struggle
to bring justice to those places,
so that the time may come
when truth and justice prevail.
Lord, in your mercy,
hear our prayer,
through Jesus Christ our Lord.
Amen.

290

FOR THE SICK AND THOSE WHO CARE FOR THEM

Loving God,
    we bring before you the sick and suffering of our world,
        all those wrestling with illness in body, mind or spirit.
    Lord, in your mercy,
        hear our prayer.

We pray for those afflicted in body –
    enduring physical pain,
    overwhelmed by disabling disease,
    waiting for an operation or further treatment
    and fearful of what the future may hold,
    or living with the knowledge of a terminal illness.
Lord, in your mercy,
    hear our prayer.

We pray for those disturbed or troubled in mind –
    those whose confidence has broken down,
    those unable to cope with the pressures of daily life,
    those oppressed by false terrors of the imagination,
    those facing the dark despair of clinical depression.
Lord, in your mercy,
    hear our prayer.

We pray for those afflicted in spirit –
    those who feel their lives to be empty,
    or whose beliefs are threatened
    or who have lost their faith,
    or who worship gods of their own making
    with no power to satisfy,
    or whose hearts have become bitter and twisted,
    and their minds dark.
Lord, in your mercy,
    hear our prayer.

Living God,
    we thank you for all who work
        to bring help, wholeness and healing to the sick –
        doctors and nurses, surgeons and medical staff,
        psychiatrists, counsellors, clergy and therapists.
    Support and strengthen
        all those who share in the work of healing,
        all who strive to bring relief,
        all who minister to others.
    Lord, in your mercy,
        hear our prayer.

Grant them your wisdom and guidance,
    your care and compassion,
    your strength and support.
Equip them in all they do,
    and bring wholeness through them.
Lord, in your mercy,
    hear our prayer.

Finally we pray for your Church
    in the healing ministry you have called it to exercise,
    an inner healing of body, mind and soul
    which only you can offer.
Grant that your people everywhere
    may be so filled with your Holy Spirit,
    and so touched by the grace of Christ,
    that they may share effectively
    in the wider work of healing,
    through their life and witness
    bringing wholeness to broken people
    and a broken world.
 Lord, in your mercy,
    hear our prayer,
    in the name of Christ.
    Amen.

291

FOR THOSE RESPONSIBLE FOR MAKING JUDGEMENTS

Lord of all,
> we pray for those whose responsibility it is
>> to pass judgement and make decisions –
>> judges, magistrates and those called to jury service:
>> **grant them wisdom;**
>> those in the probation service
>> or other areas of social work:
>> **grant them wisdom;**
>> those interviewing candidates for jobs,
>> university places or other opportunities:
>> **grant them wisdom;**
>> those serving on local councils
>> or in national and international government,
>> taking decisions which will affect local communities,
>> countries and the world itself:
>> **grant them wisdom;**
>> schoolteachers and examiners assessing pupils' work:
>> **grant them wisdom;**
>> those involved in arbitration, negotiation
>> or reconciliation:
>> **grant them wisdom.**

Lord of all,
> give to all entrusted with such positions an open mind,
>> the ability to make impartial and fair decisions,
>> wisdom to discern the right way forward,
>> and strength to bear their responsibility faithfully,
>> **through Jesus Christ our Lord.**
>> **Amen.**

292

FOR THOSE WHO SEEK OR RESIST TRUTH

Lord Jesus Christ, the Way, the Truth and Life,
  we pray today for those who seek truth –
    the truth about themselves,
    about others,
    about this world we live in,
    about you.
  Lord, in your mercy,
    hear our prayer.

We pray for those who study and research
    into the workings of our universe,
    the deep mysteries of life,
    the complexities of this world,
    the mechanics of science.
  Give them insight and humility,
    patience and understanding.
  Lord, in your mercy,
    hear our prayer.

We pray for those in the mass media –
    journalists, reporters, photographers, cameramen,
    editors of news bulletins and newspapers,
    presenters and programme-makers,
    authors and script-writers –
    all those who in different ways
    have the power to shape public opinion.
  Give them honesty and integrity,
    courage and perception.
  Lord, in your mercy,
    hear our prayer.

We pray for theologians, preachers, evangelists
    and individual Christians,
        seeking to understand more about the reality of God
        and to communicate this to others,
        responsible for leading others
        to a greater knowledge of your love.
Give them vision and dedication,
    vision and open-mindedness.
Lord, in your mercy,
    hear our prayer.

We pray for those who cannot face the truth,
    who find it too challenging, too depressing,
    too frustrating or too frightening to contemplate.
Give them courage and help,
    hope and perseverance.
Lord, in your mercy,
    hear our prayer.

We pray too for those who deny the truth,
    twisting and distorting it,
    leading others astray,
    blind to right and wrong.
Give them honesty to recognise their mistakes,
    and grace to amend them.
Lord, in your mercy,
    hear our prayer.

We pray finally for those who work
    to help people come to terms with truth;
    counsellors, psychiatrists, ministers,
    writers, doctors, philosophers.
Give them compassion and sensitivity,
    understanding and inspiration.
Lord, in your mercy,
    hear our prayer,
    for in your name we ask it.
    Amen.

THE LORD'S SUPPER

293

THE LORD'S SUPPER – INVITATION 1

Once more the opportunity is before us.
Once more the table is laid, the invitation extended –
 the simplest of meals,
 the most wonderful of banquets;
 a morsel of bread and sip of wine –
 yet for us the greatest of feasts.
For Christ is here among us,
 welcoming us as his people,
 greeting us as his friends,
 offering us lasting nourishment,
 not just for our bodies
 but for our souls.

Bring then your hunger,
 your thirst,
 your emptiness,
 your barren souls,
 for you shall be filled.

Bring your weakness,
 your lack of faith,
 your fragile discipleship,
 your daily betrayal of Christ,
 for you shall find forgiveness.

Bring your fears,
 your doubts,
 your darkness,
 your despair,
 for you shall find light.

Bring your pain,
 your mortality,
 your dread of death,
 your search for some lasting meaning,
 for you shall find life.

Bring your pain,
   your hurt,
   your loneliness,
   your longing,
   for you shall find love.

The table is laid and Christ is here,
   waiting for you to join him,
   waiting for you to receive his gifts,
   waiting to bless you
   as he has blessed his people across the ages.

Come and open your heart to the one
   who alone can meet its deepest needs.
Come and rejoice in all that he has done.
Thanks be to God.
   Amen.

294

THE LORD'S SUPPER – INVITATION 2

Male or female, young or old,
 friend or stranger, weak or bold,
 sure or doubting, happy or sad,
 strong or fragile, good or bad,
 free from worry, burdened by care,
 in pleasure or pain, in hope or despair,
 come to this table where divisions are ended,
 bring all the labels that keep us apart,
 come to this place where such things are transcended,
 find a new purpose spring deep in your heart.
Offer to Jesus your love and commitment,
 offer to God your thanksgiving and praise,
 receive the gift he longs to give you –
 joy to last you all your days.
Christ is waiting here to meet us,
 ready now to lead us forward,
 give to him your heartfelt worship,
 suffering servant, risen Lord.

295

THE LORD'S SUPPER – INVITATION 3

Bring your laughter, bring your tears,
 bring your joy and bring your sorrow,
 bring your hopes, bring your fears,
 bring today and bring tomorrow.
Bring your fullness, bring your thirst,
 bring your weakness, bring your health,
 bring your best and bring your worst,
 bring your loved ones, bring yourself.
Bring your gladness, bring your cares,
 bring your faith and bring your doubt,
 bring your laughter, bring your prayers,
 bring what life is all about.
At this table Christ receives us,
 all we are and all we bring;
 come then now and meet with Jesus,
 offer to him everything.

296

THE LORD'S SUPPER – INVITATION 4

We are here to look back,
  here to look forward.
We are here to remember one who died,
  here to greet one who lives.
We are here to share bread and wine,
  here to share fellowship together.
We are here in the name of our Lord Jesus Christ
  who invites us, as he invited his first disciples,
  to take supper with him.

He shared bread and wine,
  with the one who would betray him,
  the one who would deny him,
  and those who would abandon him
  in his hour of need.
He shared bread and wine,
  with those who couldn't stay awake with him
  even for an hour,
  those who for all their enthusiasm couldn't understand,
  those who were puzzled and confused,
  full of doubt and fear.

He invites us to share bread and wine,
  you and I who are weak and sinful,
  who daily fail him,
  who prefer our way to his,
  who have barely begun to understand
  the true meaning of discipleship.
Though your faith is frail,
  and your faults are many,
  though you have many questions,
  and much to learn,
  come now and share bread and wine,
  come and find life for your souls.
  Amen.

297

EUCHARISTIC PRAYER OF THANKSGIVING 1

Loving God,
>we thank you that you have called us together –
>>as your people,
>>your Church,
>>your family united in Christ.
>**In his name we praise you.**

>We thank you for your love and acceptance
>>shown through him –
>>for his willingness to eat
>>with those rejected by society,
>>his readiness to mix
>>with anyone prepared to receive him,
>>his openness to others
>>that crossed all barriers.
>**In his name we praise you.**

>We thank you that Jesus has called us his friends –
>>that as we meet together in his name
>>so he is here among us,
>>as we eat together around this table
>>he is by our side,
>>and as we share with him we share with you,
>>tasting life in all its fullness.
>**In his name we praise you.**

Loving God,
>we thank you for this Last Supper,
>>instituted by Christ himself –
>>a memorial to his death
>>but also a celebration of his continuing life;
>>a reminder to his disciples then
>>and his followers always
>>of your love for all.
>**In his name we praise you.**
>**Amen.**

298

EUCHARISTIC PRAYER OF THANKSGIVING 2

Gracious God,
  reminded at this table of how much you love us,
    how far you were prepared to go on our behalf,
    how total a sacrifice you made in Christ,
    we come to celebrate your going the whole way
    in taking on human flesh,
    how you went the whole way
    in surrendering your only Son,
    enduring death and agony on the cross.

Gracious God,
  remind us once more
    through the bread and the wine we shall share,
    the words we shall hear,
    and the prayers we shall offer,
    of all you have done and all you have given,
    and so help us in return to give our all to you,
    in the name of Christ.
    Amen.

Prayers of Dismissal

299

Lord Jesus Christ,
  we have remembered your death.
  We have celebrated your resurrection.
  We have rejoiced in the wonder of your love.
  Send us out now to proclaim the good news,
    so that others will know you died for them,
    and in turn celebrate the new life you offer,
    and the love you so freely give.
  Amen.

300

Lord Jesus Christ,
  we thank you that you have satisfied
    our hunger and our thirst
    with living bread and new wine.
  Go with us now,
    and help us to share what we have received,
    so that those we meet
    may glimpse a little of your love,
    and through coming to know you
    find nourishment for their souls.
  Amen.

301

Lord Jesus Christ,
    you commanded us to break bread and share wine
        until you come.
    Send us out then,
        to prepare your way,
        to work for your kingdom,
        and to do all we can
        to bring that day of your coming nearer.
    Amen.

302

The bread has been broken,
    the wine poured out.
    The supper is over,
        and the world still waits.
Go then,
    and offer your service,
    your faith and your love,
    until the world rejoices,
    and the kingdom is come.
And may God go with you
    this day and always.
    Amen.

BLESSINGS

BLESSINGS

303

Go now,
    with laughter in your eyes,
        a smile on your lips,
        a song in your heart,
        and merriment in your soul,
        and share the joy that Christ has given you.
        Amen.

304

To God who has given us every moment
    to celebrate,
        to savour
        and satisfy,
        be heartfelt praise
        and joyful thanksgiving,
        now and always.
        Amen.

305

As you have come to worship,
    so go now to serve,
        showing the truth in your lives
        of what you have declared with your lips,
        in the name of Christ.
        Amen.

306

Go now and proclaim the Gospel,
  not just through words but deeds –
    through what you say,
    what you do,
    and who you are.
May others, as they meet with you,
    meet with Christ,
    and know his living presence for themselves.
    Amen.

307

God, go with us on our journey of faith –
  revive us when we grow weary,
    direct us when we go astray,
    inspire us when we lose heart,
    reprove us when we turn back.
Keep us travelling ever-onwards,
    a pilgrim people,
    looking to Jesus Christ
    who has run the race before us,
    and who waits to welcome us home.
    Amen.

308

Living God,
  we have come to you,
    to seek your help,
    offer our worship,
    and declare our faith.
  Now we go for you,
    to work for your kingdom,
    proclaim your love,
    and make known the Gospel of Jesus Christ.
  Go with us and grant us grace to serve you,
    even as through him you have served us.
    Amen.

309

  Loving God,
    lead us out into the world,
      renewed in vigour,
      in hope,
      in faith,
      and in purpose.
    Send us back to live and work for you,
      sharing your love
      and living your life.
    Through Jesus Christ our Lord.
    Amen.

310

Our worship has not ended –
  it has only just begun –
    for God is with us every moment of every day!
  Go then, and offer the worship he desires –
    to do justice,
    to love kindness,
    and to walk humbly with him,
    every step along our way.
    Amen.

311

To God who is always forgiving,
  always loving,
  always offering a new beginning,
  be honour and glory,
  praise and thanksgiving,
  this day and for ever.
  Amen.

312

God of life,
  may the promise of the sunrise
    be echoed in our minds.
  May the warmth of the midday sun
    flow through our hearts.
  May the peace of the sunset
    touch our souls.
  And when life seems dark
    teach us to remember even then you are with us,
    and that we will again see your light.
  In the name of Christ.
  Amen.

313

To the one whose goodness is without equal,
   whose love is beyond comparison,
      whose mercy is beyond understanding,
      and whose power is beyond words,
      be praise and glory,
      worship and thanksgiving,
      now and always.
      Amen.

314

May the world continue to surprise us,
   love continue to astonish us,
      life continue to captivate us,
      faith continue to sustain us,
      and may God go with us always,
      now and for evermore.
      Amen.

315

The grace of God thrill your hearts,
   the mercy of God transform your minds,
      the peace of God flood your souls,
      and the love of God flow through your lives,
      to the honour of his name.
      Amen.

316

Let the love of the Father
course through our veins.
Let the goodness of Christ
pulse through our bodies.
Let the power of the Spirit
flow through our souls.
Let the wonder of God
resonate through our minds.
Glory be to God,
Father, Son and Holy Spirit,
now and for all eternity.
Amen.

317

Gracious God,
send us back to the world
with your eyes rather than ours.
Help us to see not only the bad but the good,
not simply the ugly but the beautiful,
not just the worst but the best.
Help us to see around us the seeds of your kingdom,
and to nurture them lovingly
until that day comes when your will is done
and you are all in all.
Amen.

318

Gracious God,
    take this moment,
        this minute
        this hour,
        this day.
    Take our lives,
        and use them for your kingdom,
        in the name of Christ.
        Amen.

319

Go back to the daily round of life,
    and may what you have shared here
        transform all you do and experience there.
    In the name of Christ.
    Amen.

320

Go out into the world rejoicing,
    for God is waiting to meet you
        and surprise you with the beauty of his presence.
    In the song of a blackbird, the hooting of an owl,
        the cry of a fox;
        in the opening of a bud, the fragrance of a flower,
        the falling of a leaf;
        in the murmur of the breeze, the rushing of the wind,
        the howling of the gale;
        in the babbling of the brook, the rippling of the stream,
        the crashing of the waves;
        in the peace of the meadows, the freedom of the hills,
        the grandeur of the mountains;
        in the cry of a baby, the laughter of children,
        the hum of conversation;
        in the pat on the shoulder, the handshake of welcome,
        the embrace of a loved one;
        in the noise of the factory, the routine of the office,
        the bustle of the shop –
        God is here,
        God is there,
        God is everywhere.
    Go then,
        and walk with him,
        in the light of his love,
        and the fullness of life.
        Amen.

INDEX

INDEX

References are to prayer rather than page numbers. Major references to a theme are highlighted in bold type where they are a part of a list.